The Eater Reader

OTHER TITLES IN THE LONGMAN TOPICS READER SERIES

A Longman Topics Reader

The Eater Reader

JAMES MILLER
University of Wisconsin-Whitewater

Longman
Boston Columbus Indianapolis New York San Francisco Upper Saddle River
Amsterdam Cape Town Dubai London Madrid Milan Munich
Paris Montreal Toronto Delhi Mexico City Sao Paulo Sydney Hong Kong
Seoul Singapore Taipei Tokyo

Editorial Director: Joe Opiela
Senior Acquisitions Editor: Brad Pottfhoff
Marketing Manager: Sandra McGuire
Editorial Assistant: Nancy C. Lee
Associate Managing Editor: Bayani Mendoza de Leon
Production Manager: Kathleen Sleys
Design Director: Jayne Conte
Cover Designer: Karen Salzbach
Cover Image: Photos.com, a division of Getty Images
Project Coordination, Text Design, and Electronic Page Makeup: Jogender
    Taneja/Aptara®, Inc.
Printer/Binder: Edwards Brothers
Cover Printer: Lehigh-Phoenix

Library of Congress Cataloging-in-Publication Data
Miller, James S.,
    The eater reader / James Miller.
      p. cm.
    ISBN-13: 978-0-205-77805-8
    ISBN-10: 0-205-77805-4
1. Food habits.   2. Food preferences.   3. Nutrition.   4. Diet.   I. Title.
    GT2850.M55 2011
    394.1'2—dc22   2010037862

2 3 4 5 6 7 8 9 10—EB—13 12 11
Longman
is an imprint of

www.pearsonhighered.com ISBN 10:   0-205-77805-4
ISBN 13: 978-0-205-77805-8

For Henry, Eliza, and Hope

CONTENTS

The last several years have witnessed an explosion of popular interest in all things eating related. Across the pop culture landscape, it seems, food is suddenly everywhere. From best-selling books like *Fast Food Nation* and *The Omnivore's Dilemma* to movies like *Supersize Me* and *Ratatouille*, from the rise of celebrity chefs like Rachel Ray to the growing popularity of the Food network, from the annual broadcast of the Nathan's Hot-Dog-Eating contest to the enduring appeal of the South Beach or Atkins diet, *how, what,* and *why* we eat has become one of the most absorbing topics of our time.

Despite this, however, no effort has yet been made to gather this diverse and wide-ranging material together in one place. Even though it stands as one of the signature preoccupations of our era, no one has yet attempted to examine what our pervasive fascination with food tells us about the state of our contemporary culture—that is, until now. Introducing *The Eater Reader,* the first volume to take a critical and comprehensive look at the place that eating and eating-related issues occupy in modern life. Bringing together a broad and representative sampling of the most contemporary writing about food—from academic essays about food culture to Web sites about health and nutrition, journalistic exposés of industrial food production to reviews of reality cooking shows—*The Eater Reader* taps into the current cultural zeitgeist around food, inviting students to explore the countless and complex ways this subject informs how we think about ourselves, each other, and the world around us.

Starting from the assumption that eating is about a whole lot more than food, *The Eater Reader* presents students with an overview of the many issues, questions, and controversies to which this activity is connected: from standards of health nutrition to messages about body image, from debates over environmentalism or consumerism to issues of gender, racial, and class difference. Using food as a lens for looking at and thinking about our larger culture, this book organizes each of its chapters around a focus on a different aspect of public life: e.g., health/nutrition, technology, ethics, or work. Seeking to acquaint readers with sheer scope and variety of eating-related issues in our world, the book uses this chapter organization to pose a number of key questions. Among them:

- "How are healthy people supposed to eat?"
- "Can good food be invented?"
- "Does eating—or not eating—make us beautiful?"
- "Where does our food come from?"
- "Is taste something that can be sold?"
- "Is eating an environmental act?"
- "What are the costs of eating well?"
- "Can food be a status symbol?"
- "Can food be Other?"
- "What are the different ways eating can become a job?"

The author wishes to thank the reviewers for their helpful evaluations and suggestions during the development of *The Eater Reader*: Carla Bell, Henry Ford Community College; Peggy Davis, UCLA; Aeron Haynie, University of Wisconsin–Green Bay; Jennifer Hurley, Ohlone College; Katherine Harris, San Jose State University; Gloria Larrieu, Kalamazoo Valley Community College; Dana Hood Morgan, Santa Monica College; and Susan Slavicz, Florida Community College at Jacksonville.

James Miller

The Eater Reader

INTRODUCTION

PERSONAL TASTE

What did you have for breakfast this morning? Fruit and granola? A bagel with cream cheese? A piece of leftover pizza? Whatever the case—whether you took the time to whip up a full plate of bacon and eggs or just downed a quick cup of coffee as you headed out the door—chances are you didn't spend a whole lot of time agonizing over *why* you made this particular choice. Indeed there are few things in life that feel as basic, as simple, as self-evident as eating. We do it so routinely, and for reasons that seem so obvious, it's hard at first to believe there's really anything all that complicated about it. You're hungry, you eat. End of story, right?

Well, not exactly. On the surface, of course, a question like "what do I want to eat?" couldn't sound more ordinary or innocuous. But notice how many other considerations underlie this simple query. For example: How nutritious is it? Is it good or bad for my health? How many calories, carbohydrates, or grams of fat does it contain? What kinds of chemicals or preservatives are in it? Will this make me feel better or worse about how I look? How much does it cost? Where did this food come from? Do I know where it was grown or how it was manufactured? We could go on, but even a short list like this is long enough to prove the point. Our daily decisions about how and what to eat may well begin with a simple sounding "what am I in the mood for?" or "does this taste good?"; but as a general rule they don't end there. No, more often than not when we ask ourselves this kind of question, we are asking ourselves a number of other questions as well.

This, in fact, may well be the central irony of modern American eating. To be sure, we have grown highly accustomed to regarding eating as more or less a personal concern. But it is equally true that there are few activities which connect us more immediately and directly to the broader world around us. Eating may feel like a private act, but it is one that carries very public ramifications. It is intimately tied to the ways we think about health and nutrition; it plays a key role in shaping our responses to technology, industrialization, and the environment; it lies at the heart of the ways we are taught to view, at times even judge, our own bodies; it is a central aspect of our relationship to the larger commercial marketplace, helping to define the role we play as consumers; it raises pointed questions about money and social class, poverty and privilege; and, in its own way, it even influences the boundaries that get drawn around gender and racial difference. In our world, in other words, eating is about a good deal more than just food.

To illustrate this point, let's return briefly to our breakfast example. As we've already begun to see, deciding what to eat in the morning is an endeavor that rests upon multiple calculations—from questions of taste ("what do I feel like eating?"), to concerns over nutrition ("is this good for me?"), to issues of convenience ("what do I have time for?"). When we tally up these various considerations, one thing becomes abundantly clear: our breakfast choices say more about us than simply what we like to eat. In a very real sense, they are also statements about who we are and what we value: a way of drawing distinctions between the things that matter to us and the things that don't. To opt for a breakfast bar on the bus rather than scrambled eggs and juice at home, for example, is to say something about the importance (or perhaps necessity) of efficiency versus the rewards of leisure. To forgo chocolate chip pancakes in favor of a protein drink is to rank concerns over nutrition or calorie counting higher on our scale of priorities than the pleasures of taste. To choose an organic cereal over one laced with processed sugar and preservatives is to register a degree of sympathy with those environmental critiques of industrialized food. More than mere expressions of personal taste, our eating choices are also an index of the views and values we use to make our way through daily life.

If the stakes involved in our day-to-day eating decisions really are this high, then it would seem we have some important questions to address. Foremost among them: where exactly do these views and values come from? When it comes to standards of taste, how do we learn to distinguish the delicious from the disgusting? On the topic of health and nutrition, who teaches us where to draw the line between what is good for us and what is bad? When thinking about our bodies or our physical appearance, what sources do we consult to figure out how much is okay to eat and how much is too much? Certainly when we confine our focus to something straightforward, like "what do I want to eat?," it's easy to see that ours is a world which confronts us with a dizzying array of options: meat or vegetarian? Homemade or take-out? Organic or processed? Fresh from a wok or out of a microwave oven? And on, and on. These options have come to feel so familiar, however, that they sometimes cause us to overlook an equally important corollary: namely, that the decisions we make around food have to do not only with how we *act* but with how we *think* as well. Connected as they are to some of our era's most topical and pressing issues, our eating choices play a key role in framing how we see and make sense of the world around us—with consequences that extend far beyond the kitchen counter, the restaurant booth, or the dinner table. Given this, the question with which we began this discussion would seem to be one especially worth answering. When it comes to the countless food-related decisions confronting us every day, how exactly *do* we make up our minds?

FOOD, FOOD EVERYWHERE: EATING AS A CULTURAL LENS

The short answer is we don't—or at least not all on our own. We get a lot of help. Whether it's diet books or FDA guidelines, fast food commercials or gourmet magazines, our daily lives are filled with instructions, images, and information, all of which aim in some way to teach us our "proper" relationship to food. The last several years in particular have witnessed an explosion of popular interest in all things eating-related. Across the media landscape, it seems, food is suddenly everywhere. From best-selling books like *Fast Food Nation* and *The Omnivore's Dilemma* to movies like *Food Inc.* and *Ratatouille*, from the rise of celebrity chefs like Rachel Ray to the growing popularity of The Food Network, from ESPN's annual broadcast of Nathan's Hot-Dog-Eating Contest to the enduring appeal of the South Beach or Atkins diet, *how*, *what*, and *why* we eat has become one of the most absorbing topics of our time.

It is precisely this cultural trend that *The Eater Reader* takes as its starting point. What, it asks, does the pervasive public fascination with food—one of the signature preoccupations of our era—tell us about the place that eating and eating-related issues have come to occupy in modern life? Bringing together a broad and representative sampling of the most contemporary writing on this subject—from academic essays about food culture to discussions of health and nutrition, journalistic exposés of industrial food production to reviews of reality cooking shows, personal memoirs about eating to social critiques of diet fads—this book taps into the current cultural zeitgeist around food, inviting us to explore the countless and complex ways this subject informs how we act and think. Proceeding from the assumption that eating is a profoundly cultural act, *The Eater Reader* uses food as a lens for examining the issues and debates that define modern public life—from health and nutrition to the modern beauty industry, globalization and environmentalism to advertising and consumerism, science and technology to social justice and modern ethics. When we consider the merits of buying pesticide-free produce, we ask, to what extent are we also participating in larger debates over industrial farming, the organic food movement, or environmentalism in general? When we reheat a frozen dinner in the microwave, in what ways are we confronting questions about the role of science and technology in our eating lives? When we catch the latest diet infomercial on late-night TV, how might we be working through our culture's dominant messages regarding beauty or our bodies?

13 WAYS OF LOOKING AT A BIG MAC

Clearly, undertaking a project like this requires that we adopt a more complex attitude toward food—that we attempt to understand it not only as a tangible or edible object but as a cultural touchstone as well. All very intriguing, you may be thinking; but what does this sort of perspective actually look like? What kind of work does it involve? What forms of analysis? In order to answer these questions, it might be helpful to look at an example of a food that clearly straddles the divide between the tangible and the cultural. For instance, the Big Mac. Whatever our personal feelings, few of us would dispute that the Big Mac is a food which has achieved an almost legendary status in our culture. Enormously popular and universally recognized, this iconic hamburger has come to be viewed by many as the classic or quintessential national snack—a resonant symbol not only of American eating habits, but of America itself. Given this, the Big Mac would seem an ideal example through which to model the different types of analysis *The Eater Reader* invites you to undertake. Included below is a quick overview of the questions and considerations each of these different approaches might involve:

- Appraising the Big Mac as actual food, as edible object: what does a Big Mac taste like? Which ingredients, which aspects of its preparation, account for its huge popularity?

- Examining the Big Mac as an example of American nutritional habits: what are the key health risks posed by this type of fast food? In what ways can the Big Mac be said to contribute to such health crises as: diabetes, heart disease, obesity, etc.? To what extent, in effect, does the Big Mac exemplify or crystallize prevailing public attitudes regarding eating and health?

- Analyzing the Big Mac as a cultural symbol: how has this particular food come to stand as a symbol for certain quintessentially American ideals, values, or stereotypes? What does the Big Mac's enduring appeal tell us about the state of American culture?

- Assessing the Big Mac as a commercial brand: how has this sandwich come to stand as a symbol not just of American culture more broadly but of the McDonalds corporation more specifically? How has the Big Mac been constructed as a commercial image? And how has this image been promoted in order to advance a particular vision of what the McDonalds corporation itself is like?

- Approaching the Big Mac as an emblem of industrialization; that is, reading the Big Mac as a blueprint of all industrial, technological, and economic changes that define modern "fast food": to what extent is the Big Mac representative of the ways all sorts of different foods—from frozen TV dinners to Wonder Bread—now get manufactured?

- Big Mac as social/class marker: how does the Big Mac connect to the issue of economics and class? Given its relative affordability compared to other foods, what does the Big Mac have to say about the relationship between income and eating habits?

As we can see, each of these approaches asks us to conduct a different form of analysis: to pose different questions, focus on different contexts, draw different connections. Assessing the Big Mac as a cultural object, for example, might lead us into an historical investigation, in which we track the different values it has symbolized over the years—from comfort and convenience to efficiency and speed. Paying particular attention to the "big" in its title, we might then supplement such historical work by analyzing the Big Mac as a symbol of our own times: an example of the cultural logic that defines "bigger" as automatically "better." If on the other hand we wanted to connect the Big Mac to questions of health, we might undertake a more detailed assessment of this food's nutritional content, reading such information in the context of current medical or scientific research on the subject. How, we might ask, does such research encourage us to rethink the image of the Big Mac promoted by McDonalds itself? This type of inquiry could easily segue next into a more extensive examination of the Big Mac as a media image or commercial brand. How does our impression of a typical Big Mac ad change when placed alongside, say, the cover photo of a fitness magazine? To what extent does this kind of juxtaposition recast the Big Mac as a threat to or violation of our culture's prevailing messages around body image?

FOOD AND CULTURE/FOOD AS CULTURE

Whichever direction these various approaches might lead, the larger point they illustrate remains the same: food is one of the most complex, multifaceted, and encompassing subjects in modern life. It stands at the center of our most fundamental personal choices and touches upon our most current and topical public debates. It indexes our most deeply held values and instigates our most deeply held anxieties. This is the complexity which *The Eater Reader,* in the final analysis, aims to comprehend. Because eating is connected to so many different aspects of public life, each chapter focuses on a discrete cultural domain. Here is a list of some of the key issues and questions that underlie this organization:

- Nutrition/Health ("How are healthy people supposed to eat?")
- Science/Technology ("Can good food be invented?")
- Body Image ("Does eating—or not eating—make us beautiful?")
- Ethics ("What does it mean to eat well?")
- Consumerism ("Is taste something that can be sold?")
- Work ("What are the different ways eating can become a job?")
- Environmentalism ("Is eating an environmental act?")
- Economics ("What are the costs of eating well?")
- Social Class ("Can food be a status symbol?")
- Gender ("What does it mean to eat like a man? Like a woman?")
- Race/Ethnicity ("Can food be Other?")

Not surprisingly, exploring a set of themes as rich and various as this requires that we hone an equally broad range of critical thinking, reading, and writing skills. Among them: critical close reading of written and visual texts; comparing and contrasting different food-related artifacts or issues; situating a food-related question, idea, or problem within a broader cultural context; finding and analyzing the connections that link different food-related activities and concerns across the larger culture. And most important of all: connecting all this cultural analysis to our own experience as individual eaters. As we have already noted, eating offers such a fruitful topic for inquiry in part because it straddles the boundary conventionally believed to separate the private from the public. Eating resides at the intersection where the personal meets the cultural: where our individual choices and actions reveal themselves to have, at least partly, social origins. To investigate the place food occupies in our lives, in other words, is always to investigate our own cultural place as well. Indeed this insight may well constitute the ultimate objective *The Eater Reader* sets out to accomplish: to view eating not simply as one of countless actions we undertake within culture, but as a powerful vehicle through which we participate in, make sense of, and perhaps even *create* culture.

CHAPTER 1

Nutrition

GOOD AND GOOD FOR YOU: TASTE AND THE RISE OF NUTRITION

Of all the standards for figuring out what we should and should not eat, none seems in greater vogue these days than nutrition. To be sure, restaurant reviews and gourmet cookbooks still wax lyrical over the subtle pleasures or complex flavors of their favorite dishes; supermarkets continue to plaster their windows with ads proclaiming "price buster" bargains for meat or produce; commercials extolling the ease and convenience of fast food remain a staple of our television airwaves; and bookstore shelves still overflow with diet manuals promoting the cosmetic benefits of low-calorie snacks. In terms of sheer influence, however, none of these methods for measuring the value of food outstrips our current preoccupation with physical health. Across the entire food spectrum—from Whole Foods to KFC—it has become second nature for purveyors to tout the nutritional benefits of their products ("0 grams trans fat!"; "100% daily allowance of vitamin C!") just as routinely as flavor, convenience, or cost. So much so, in fact, that for many consumers it has now become a kind of commonplace to regard eating itself as little more than a nutrition delivery service: a mechanism for accessing our requisite daily allotments of vitamins, minerals, and irons.

The key question, of course, is whether or not this shift in eating attitudes is a good thing. In the wake of this new nutritional paradigm, are we truly better off than we were before? At first glimpse, it is tempting to respond with a resounding "yes." It would be difficult if not outright perverse, after all, to argue that we should be *denied* greater information about what we eat. Armed with reams of nutritional data, we would seem to be in an undeniably better position than previous generations to make savvy, well informed decisions about food.

And yet we still might want to pause before embracing this development as unequivocal proof of our social and scientific progress. Most immediately, of course, there is the question of what all this specialized information—the facts and statistics, descriptions and terminology—actually tells us. As food shoppers, are we truly in a position to distinguish between information that is accurate or reliable and information that is misleading or bogus? Do these nutritional inventories supply us with tools we can actually use? Or are they included more as a marketing gimmick, designed simply to stamp these products with the generic imprimatur of "science"? We might also wonder about how a heightened preoccupation with nutrition affects the way we approach eating itself. Do we run the risk of diminishing a meal's pleasure or appeal when we reduce the food on our plate to an assemblage of calories, vitamins, and minerals? Beyond this are questions about how a preoccupation with food's nutritional content affects our attitudes toward and assumptions about physical health. Does a tendency to make food the linchpin of our physical well-being encourage us to overlook or downplay other, equally meaningful, priorities essential to our physical health? Is it possible, in other words, we have become too reliant on nutrition for our own good?

One way to answer this question is to look more closely at the goals this emphasis on nutrition seems designed to achieve. As most of us know from firsthand experience, there is hardly a food item these days that doesn't come attached with a synopsis of its core ingredients. Whether it be the fat content on a package of hamburger, the amount of vitamin C in a container of orange juice, the quotient of antioxidants in a bunch of bananas, virtually every edible item we encounter carries with it some kind of nutritional catalogue, intended it would seem, to assure customers of the health benefits it provides. Even if we don't always know exactly what these terms mean—what is "xanthan gum" anyway? Is "high fructose corn syrup" good or bad for us?—we have nonetheless come to expect and rely upon them a good deal. Indeed we have grown so accustomed to perusing these authoritative-sounding catalogues that it's difficult to imagine making a food-related decision without them. On first inspection, these lists appear to serve a function that is purely informational. Cast in the opaque and abstract terminology of food science, they present themselves as objective descriptions, neutral catalogues. Standing in marked contrast to the overheated language of commercial promotion found elsewhere, the information included here seems to advocate no position, to take no side—aiming instead to serve merely as an educational guide for the health-conscious food shopper.

When we look beyond what these lists explicitly *say* to what they *imply*, however, we discover a number of unspoken assumptions at work which belie this stance of objectivity. Assumptions like: health trumps taste when it comes to deciding what to eat; making valid choices about food requires a degree of technical, scientific expertise; nutritionists and food scientists know as much about what is right for us to eat as we do ourselves; we learn more about food by breaking it down to its individual components than by assessing it in its whole or finished form. Viewed from this vantage, in fact, these lists of ingredients start to look less like an objective litany of facts and more like an encoded set of instructions: lessons designed to teach consumers the specific things they need to consider and the specific authorities they need to consult when making decisions about what to eat.

To test out the validity of these assumptions, imagine for a moment what an alternative food label might look like. Instead of the usual collection of facts and figures, consider how it would feel to come across a food label that showcased, say, anecdotes and testimonials from individual eaters. No technical terminology, no scientific evaluation, no itemized list of health benefits. Just a randomly assembled set of stories and impressions from other consumers. "I loved this dish!" "The perfect food to enjoy with family." "I ate it every day for six straight weeks!" This kind of marketing ploy would no doubt strike us as a good deal more informal and idiosyncratic. But does this mean it would also strike us automatically as less valid? Read in light of our current mania for nutrition, of course, basing our eating choices on the personal experiences of our fellow eaters would seem absurd. It seems so, however, only because this approach encourages us to adopt a different set of assumptions when deciding how and what to eat—assumptions that run counter to the tenets of our dominant nutritional paradigm. Rather than foreground the putative health effects of a given food, our hypothetical counterexample posits the pleasures of taste or the social rewards of eating with friends and family as the basis for evaluation. The point here is not that we have to choose between these respective rubrics. The point rather is to remind us that no rubric is so familiar, influential, or pervasive that it cannot be subject to scrutiny or reevaluation.

Taking this insight as its starting point, this chapter looks at the role food has come to play in shaping contemporary ideas about and definitions of physical health. To what extent, it asks, has the emergence of nutrition as a cornerstone concern succeeded in transforming food into a barometer of our society's attitudes and anxieties regarding health? In order to address this question, the chapter assembles a set of readings, each of which examines the implications—physical or medical, social or ethical—of adhering to our culture's prevailing norms concerning what is and is not "healthy" or "good" to eat.

"Nutritionism," from *In Defense of Food* (2008)
MICHAEL POLLAN

When is a food not a food? According to Pollan, when we become so obsessed with nutrition that concerns over our physical health become our sole motivation for eating. Challenging the increasing dominance of what he calls "nutritionism," Pollan makes an elegant and convincing case for thinking beyond the parameters of our current food-related norms.

---------------- ✦ ----------------

"If you spent any time at all in a supermarket in the 1980's, you might have noticed something peculiar going on. The food was gradually disappearing from the shelves . . . Where once the names of familiar comestibles—things like eggs or breakfast cereals or snack foods—claimed pride of place on the brightly colored packages crowding the aisles, now new scientific-sounding terms like 'cholesterol' and 'fiber' and 'saturated fat' began rising to large-type prominence."

FROM FOODS TO NUTRIENTS

If you spent any time at all in a supermarket in the 1980s, you might have noticed something peculiar going on. The food was gradually disappearing from the shelves. Not literally vanishing—I'm not talking about Soviet-style shortages. No, the shelves and refrigerated cases still groaned with packages and boxes and bags of various edibles, more of them landing every year in fact, but a great many of the traditional supermarket foods were steadily being replaced by "nutrients," which are not the same thing. Where once the familiar names of recognizable comestibles—things like eggs or breakfast cereals or snack foods—claimed pride of place on the brightly colored packages crowding the aisles, now new, scientific-sounding terms like "cholesterol" and "fiber" and "saturated fat" began rising to large-type prominence. More important than mere foods, the presence or absence of these invisible substances was now generally believed to confer health benefits on their eaters. The implicit message was that foods, by comparison, were coarse, old-fashioned, and decidedly unscientific things—who could say *what* was in them really? But nutrients—those chemical compounds and minerals in foods that scientists have identified as important to our health—gleamed with the promise of scientific certainty. Eat more of the right ones, fewer of the wrong, and you would live longer, avoid chronic diseases, and lose weight.

BEYOND THE PLEASURE PRINCIPLE

We eaters, alas, don't reap nearly as much benefit from nutritionism as food producers. Beyond providing a license to eat more of the latest approved foodlike substance, which we surely do appreciate, nutritionism tends to foster a great deal of anxiety around the experience of shopping for food and eating it. To do it right, you've got to be up on the latest scientific research, study ever-longer and more confusing ingredients labels,* sift through increasingly dubious health claims, and then attempt to enjoy foods that have been engineered with many other objectives in

---

*Geoffrey Cannon points out that nutrition labels, which have become the single most ubiquitous medium of chemical information in our lives, "are advertisements for the chemical principle of nutrition."

view than simply tasting good. To think of some of the most delicious components of food as toxins, as nutritionism has taught
us to do in the case of fat, does little for our happiness as eaters.
Americans have embraced a "nutritional philosophy," to borrow
Jane Brody's words, that, regardless of whether that philosophy
does anything for our health, surely takes much of the pleasure
out of eating.

But why do we even need a nutritional philosophy in the first
place? Perhaps because we Americans have always had a problem taking pleasure in eating. We certainly have gone to unusual
lengths to avoid it. Harvey Levenstein, who has written two illu-
minating histories of American food culture, suggests that the
sheer abundance of food in America has bred "a vague indiffer-
ence to food, manifested in a tendency to eat and run, rather than
to dine and savor." To savor food, to conceive of a meal as an aesthetic experience, has been regarded as evidence of effeteness, a
form of foreign foppery. (Few things have been more likely to get
an American political candidate in hot water than a taste for fine
food, as Martin Van Buren discovered during his failed 1840 re-
election campaign. Van Buren had brought a French chef to the
White House, a blunder seized on by his opponent, William
Henry Harrison, who made much of the fact that *he* subsisted on
"raw beef and salt." George H. W. Bush's predilection for pork
rinds and Bill Clinton's for Big Macs were politically astute tastes
to show off.)

It could well be that, as Levenstein contends, the sheer abundance of food in America has fostered a culture of careless, per-
functory eating. But our Puritan roots also impeded a sensual or
aesthetic enjoyment of food. Like sex, the need to eat links us to
the animals, and historically a great deal of Protestant energy has
gone into helping us keep all such animal appetites under strict
control. To the Christian social reformers of the nineteenth century,
"The naked act of eating was little more than unavoidable . . .
and was not to be considered a pleasure except with great discre-
tion." I'm quoting from Laura Shapiro's Perfection Salad, which
recounts the campaign of these domestic reformers to convince
Americans, in the words of one, "that eating is something more than
animal indulgence, and that cooking has a nobler purpose than
the gratification of appetite and the sense of taste." And what
might that nobler purpose be? Sound nutrition and good sanitation. By elevating those scientific principles and "disdaining the
proof of the palate," Shapiro writes, "they made it possible for

American cooking to accept a flood of damaging innovations for years to come"—low-fat processed food products prominent among them.

So scientific eating is an old and venerable tradition in America. Here's how Harvey Levenstein sums up the quasiscientific beliefs that have shaped American attitudes toward food for more than a century: "that taste is not a true guide to what should be eaten; that one should not simply eat what one enjoys; that the important components of foods cannot be seen or tasted, but are discernible only in scientific laboratories; and mat experimental science has produced rules of nutrition which will prevent illness and encourage longevity." Levenstein could be describing the main tenets of nutritionism.

Perhaps the most notorious flowering of pseudoscientific eating (and protonutritionism) came in the early years of the twentieth century when John Harvey Kellogg and Horace Fletcher persuaded thousands of Americans to trade all pleasure in eating for health-promoting dietary regimens of truly breathtaking rigor and perversity. The two diet gurus were united in their contempt for animal protein, the consumption of which Dr. Kellogg, a Seventh-Day Adventist who bore a striking resemblance to KFC's Colonel Sanders, firmly believed promoted both masturbation and the proliferation of toxic bacteria in the colon. During this, the first golden age of American food faddism, protein performed much the same role that fat would perform during the next. At Kellogg's Battle Creek sanitarium, patients (who included John D. Rockefeller and Theodore Roosevelt) paid a small fortune to be subjected to such "scientific" practices as hourly yogurt enemas (to undo the damage that protein supposedly wreaked on the colon); electrical stimulation and "massive vibration" of the abdomen; diets consisting of nothing but grapes (ten to fourteen pounds of them a day); and at every meal, "Fletcherizing," the practice of chewing each bite of food approximately one hundred times. (Often to the rousing accompaniment of special chewing songs.) The theory was that thorough mastication would reduce protein intake (this seems certain) and thereby improve "subjective and objective well-being." Horace Fletcher (aka "the great masticator") had no scientific credentials whatsoever, but the example of his own extraordinary fitness—at fifty he could bound up and down the Washington Monument's 898 steps without pausing to catch his breath—while existing on a daily regimen of only 45 well-chewed grams of protein was all the proof his adherents needed.* The brothers Henry and William James both became enthusiastic "chewers."†

Whatever their biological efficacy, all these dietary exertions had the effect of removing eating from social life and pleasure from eating; compulsive chewing (much less hourly enema breaks) is not exactly conducive to the pleasures of the table. Also, Fletcherizing would have forcibly drained food of the very last glimmer of flavor long before the hundredth contraction of the jaw had been counted. Kellogg himself was outspoken in his hostility to the pleasures of eating: "The decline of a nation commences when gourmandizing begins."

If that is so, America had little reason to worry.

America's early attraction to various forms of scientific eating may also have reflected discomfort about the way other people eat: the weird, messy, smelly, and mixed-up eating habits of immigrants. ‡How a people eats is one of the most powerful ways they have to express, and preserve, their cultural identity, which is exactly what you don't want in a society dedicated to the ideal of "Americanization." To make food choices more scientific is to empty them of their ethnic content and history; in theory, at least, nutritionism proposes a neutral, modernist, forward-looking, and potentially unifying answer to the question of what it might mean to eat like an American. It is also a way to moralize about

---

*According to Levenstein, scientists seeking the secret of Fletcher's exemplary health scrupulously monitored his ingestions and excretions, "noting with regard to the latter, as all observers did, the remarkable absence of odor" (Levenstein, Revolution of the Table, p. 89).

†William James wrote of Fletcher that "if his observations on diet, confirmed already on a limited scale, should prove true on a universal scale, it is impossible to overestimate their revolutionary import." Fletcher returned the favor, assuring the philosopher that Fletcherism was "advancing the same cause as Pragmatism" (Levenstein, Revolution of the Table, p. 92).

‡Americans were particularly disturbed by the way many immigrant groups mixed their foods in stews and such, in contrast to the Anglo-American practice of keeping foods separate on the plate, the culinary format anthropologist Mary Douglas calls " 1A plus 2B"—one chunk of animal protein plus two vegetables or starches. Perhaps the disdain for mixing foods reflected anxieties about other kinds of mixing.

other people's choices without seeming to. In this, nutritionism is a little like the institution of the American front lawn, an unobjectionable, if bland, way to pave over our differences and Americanize the landscape. Of course in both cases unity comes at the price of aesthetic diversity and sensory pleasure. Which may be precisely the point.

Discussion/Writing Prompts

- The key opposition Pollan establishes in this essay is between "nutrients" and "food." According to Pollan, there is a fundamental difference between measuring an edible item in terms of its "nutritional content" and viewing it as "food." Do you agree? How do you understand the relationship between these terms?
- The term Pollan coins to capture our current preoccupation with the nutritional content of food is: "nutritionism." Why do you think he describes this food standard as if it were a political doctrine or belief system? What larger point about this standard does Pollan seem to be trying to make? Next, write a one-page essay in which you offer your own definition of "nutritionism." What understanding of food—and our relationship to it as eaters—does this definition reflect? What values or priorities does it emphasize? And to what extent does it differ from Pollan's?
- In its own way, Ettlinger's examination of the Twinkie can be read as a commentary on our contemporary nutrition standards. Based on his critique of "nutritionism," how do you think Pollan would respond to Ettlinger's essay?

"Where Does Polysorbate 60 Come From, Daddy?" in *Twinkie, Deconstructed* (2008)
STEVE ETTLINGER

While we all know what it's like to scan the ingredient list on the back of a food package, this doesn't necessarily mean we always know what these lists mean. Confronting his own ignorance about food head on, Ettlinger attempts to unearth the story of where the Twinkie comes from—an effort that yields some surprising answers about the ingredients at the heart of this all-American snack food.

◆

"I'd always wondered what those strange-sounding ingredients were as I read labels purely out of habit, going through the motions without ever understanding or even gaining any knowledge. Then and there, I decided to put an end to the mystery and find out. I had to find the polysorbate . . . tree or whatever it came from."

It all came to a head as I was sitting at a picnic table near the beach in Connecticut one fine August day, feeding my two little kids ice cream bars and, out of habit, casually reading the ingredient label.

"Whatcha reading, Daddy?" my six-year-old girl asked. "Uh, the ingredient label, honey. It tells us what's inside your ice cream bar." Oops. Slippery slope. Glancing back down at it, I realized it was totally incomprehensible and most terms only barely pronounceable.

"So what's in it, Dad?" asked my son, a big sixth grader, who started reading his own label aloud. "Oooooh—high fructose corn syrup! What's that? And what's pol-y-sor-bate six-tee?"

I started to sweat.

And then my sweet little girl (who at that age still thought Daddy knew everything) pitched the zinger: "Where does pol-y-sor-bate six-tee come from, Daddy?"

It was a moment of truth that every parent recognizes. When you must admit your fallibility to your worshipful children.

"Uhh . . . umm . . . I uh . . . don't have a clue, honey," was the rather disappointing—but honest—answer I mustered. Some father I was! I could speak with a fair amount of authority about Greek olives, Spanish clementines, and tuna fish. But when faced with high fructose corn syrup, I was lost.

Being a curious, food-loving guy, I actually began to think about the question more seriously. I'd always wondered what those strange-sounding ingredients were as I read labels purely out of habit, going through the motions without ever understanding or even gaining any knowledge. Then and there, I decided to put an end to the mystery and find out. I had to find the polysorbate . . . tree or wherever it came from.

While the drive to make better food goes back to the dawn of humanity, the drive to create Twinkies started during the Great Depression, near Chicago. Back in 1930, James Dewar, a vice president at Continental Bakeries, bakers of Wonder® Bread and a variety of cakes, came up with a way to use the idle baking pans for Hostess's Little Shortbread Fingers, a summer strawberry treat, during their off-season. His idea, sponge cake with a creamy filling, was inexpensive enough that two cakes could sell for a nickel. Inspired by a billboard advertising "Twinkle-Toe" shoes that he passed en route to a meeting to promote his new idea, Dewar dubbed the snack cake "Twinkies." "The best darn-tootin' idea I ever had!" he is oft quoted as saying (he was widely interviewed for the cake's fiftieth anniversary in 1980). But he would soon learn that even the best darn-tootin' ideas can be fundamentally flawed.

The shelf life of the original Twinkie—two, possibly three days—posed a huge problem, a fact that dogged Dewar, according to his family. In order to maintain freshness, he had his sales reps remove unsold cakes every few days, but this was costly and inefficient. His ingredient options were also quite limited: the cake was similar to the homemade kind, as far as I can tell (no written history exists), using whole eggs for emulsifiers and lard for shortening (plus flour, water, and salt). Still, Twinkies were instantly and hugely popular, and Dewar credited this focus on freshness to his product's success. The challenge was to find a way to keep the product on the shelves longer while reducing the number of trips the salesmen (and they were all men back then) had to make to each store. With consumer products like these, shelf life is almost always a primary consideration. Even today, food scientists generally agree that aside from the overriding need to keep costs to a minimum, shelf life (cake or bread staling) is the first problem to solve. (The rather unpalatable problem of leaking moisture and fat run a close second.)

Modern food technology was Twinkies' salvation. The chemical industry worldwide exploded with innovation just after World War II, driven in part by the war itself. Simultaneously, American demand for convenience foods (and higher profits) blossomed along with the maturing of our highway system for efficient distribution. In the 1950s, Twinkies' shelf life extended along with its ingredient list.

The result today is a cake known for its secret recipe and long shelf life. Its taste is so appealing that Hostess claims it sells 500 million a year, yet most of us don't have a clue how the Twinkie's major, basic food ingredients (wheat, sugar, soybeans, and eggs) are processed, let alone how its more unfamiliar ingredients are made—or even what they are.

Understanding the ingredients in the greater context of food industry rather than simply understanding the recipe for this particular snack cake became my goal. Investigating ingredients such as sodium stearoyl lactylate or enriched, bleached flour—with ingredients coming from various states and/or foreign countries—makes you wonder why we work so hard to make any food, especially a nonnutritive snack food. After all, most of these ingredients are in the thousands of other familiar processed foods we eat, including salad dressings, sports drinks, bread, and ice cream. Examine these and you are examining much of our modern food supply.

Some ingredients, like most of those at the top of the Twinkies ingredient list, retain aspects of their agricultural origins, while others, like most of those at the bottom of the list, are either minerals or are so highly processed that they really do qualify as chemicals rather than foods. While exploring complex industrial or chemical processes, I became eager to learn how we came to know how to do this, often finding the answer rooted in history. Phosphoric acid may be an important ingredient in Coca-Cola®, but how did we come to use it in baking powder? Why did we start using chlorine for bleaching flour? What did we use in cakes before, say, polysorbate 60 or sweet dairy whey? Are any of the chemically named items extracted from vegetables or fruit? (I thought for sure something must be extracted from cranberries or tree bark, and wanted to find out.) And perhaps the most important question of all: if you can make a cake at home with just flour, sugar, butter, eggs, and water (OK, and a little flavoring, plus cream for a filling, and baking powder if you insist), how is it that thirty-nine ingredients are needed to make a Twinkie? Why do they use so many unfoodlike ingredients at all?

And then there were the intriguing, inspiring tidbits that made me want to dig even deeper, like a dictionary definition of phosphates (part of baking powder) that says, "Obtained from phosphate rock . . . Phosphorus was formerly used to treat rickets and degenerative disorders and is now used as a mineral supplement for foods; also in incendiary bombs and tracer bullets." Sure makes you wonder about what's in those cakes. Since when—and why—do we grind up rocks for food? Or, for that matter, since when do we find it necessary to reduce naturally occurring resources like corn, soybeans, and petroleum into a brown goo that is so strong in its pure form it will blow out your taste buds, yet apparently is fine to consume in cake form? How are noxious-sounding substances transformed into innocuous processed food ingredients? How is calcium sulfate (the food additive) different from calcium sulfate (the soil amendment), or from its most common form, plaster?

If you are what you eat, then it behooves you to know exactly what you are eating. Especially if you eat a lot of polysorbate 60, cellulose gum, and Red No. 40.

Finding out where, at the lowest level, these subingredients come from, tracing every finished product back down the processing chain (doing what scientists call a root tracer) is a way to give a sense of place to each ingredient. And there are some surprising stories about how each ingredient came to be made and used. Every chemical in the Twinkie comes from somewhere, and is made from things that come from somewhere else—usually from the ground. (That leads to "Aren't they all natural if they come from the earth?"—a question that dogs me still.) Organic Twinkies, not. What they are, how they are made, and how or why they are used and interact with the other ingredients are the bigger, guiding issues.

It became evident that the Twinkie is a dynamic, complex food system, where the proteins (flour, caseinates, whey, and egg) build structure and the fat and sugar (oils, emulsifiers, and sweeteners of many kinds) fight with that structure, in order to provide moisture and tenderness. Everything else on the list serves to balance out these two tendencies, some siding with moisture preservation (think "Shelf life! Shelf life!") and some helping the batter to stand up to the rigors of the commercial baking process (and to reduce overall cost). And then there's the difference between the foods at the top of the list and the chemicals at the bottom—what's that all about? Why don't I need those ingredients (calcium sulfate, sorbic acid, coloring, etc.) in my homemade cakes? Sometimes it became difficult to relate the massive industrial and technical activities involved to making the ingredients for a simple baked good. There is, in fact, quite a disconnect.

As I watched mountains being moved to get at a mineral or visited mile-long factories to see things being refined, brewed, reacted, crushed, or dried, when I began to consider the awesome number of truck, ship, and trainloads involved, when I became aware of all the cooking and slicing and dicing of molecules, I began to question how we managed to engage serious science in the pursuit of creating something that isn't even necessary to our existence. I tried to find out how we came to make food additives on a global scale, and I had to wonder why we make such an enormous industrial effort to create artificial replacements for relatively unprocessed things like sugar. I wondered where this industry fit in with the major industries of the world.

And, from the start, I wanted to know: when can I go see where they come from?

Discussion/Writing Prompts

- As Ettlinger reminds us, there are a number of "myths" that have attached them-selves to the Twinkie. Among them: they are so chemical-filled they will last for twenty-five years; they were all baked decades ago; they will last seven years if left on the roof of a house. In a one-page essay, describe the stereotypes and preconceptions you have learned to associate with this particular snack food. What key words or images come to mind? Next, offer a quick discussion of whether or not Ettlinger's essay helps challenge or dispel these associations.
- In tracing a Twinkie's key ingredients back to their origins, Ettlinger discovers that a number of these core components "are made from things that come from the ground." Does this fact, in your view, make any difference? Does this connection to a source we are conditioned to regard as "natural" alter or af-fect your understanding of the Twinkie's overall nutritional content? Does a snack food need to carry a nutritional benefit in order to be worth eating?
- In a sense, Ettlinger's attempt to decipher the lengthy, almost impenetrable list of Twinkie ingredients represents the flip side of Pollan's discussion of nu-tritionism. While Pollan chronicles the public fascination with food ingredi-ents that are supposedly good for us, Ettlinger focuses on the opposite: ingredients so artificial and highly processed as to have no apparent health benefit whatsoever. In another sense, however, these essays are related, in-sofar as each offers a commentary on the eating practices and norms of the modern American public. Write a one-page essay in which you outline the parallels that connect these two pieces. To what extent do they invite read-ers to draw similar conclusions about the state of our modern food culture?

The French Paradox, from *Salon* (Feb. 4, 2000)

Laura Fraser

We have long been accustomed to thinking of cholesterol and fat as the twin enemies lurking within the modern diet. But if this is so, asks Fraser, how do we explain the statistics that consistently rank

France, a country widely known for its high-caloric cuisine, at the top of the world health pyramid? Attempting to make sense of what has come to be called "the French paradox," Fraser outlines the features of a dietary model that seems not only to contradict but also to challenge many of our own most deeply held food orthodoxies.

———————— ✦ ————————

"Nutritionally speaking, the French have been getting away with murder. They eat all the butter, cream, foie gras, pastry, and cheese their hearts desire, and yet their rates of heart disease and obesity are lower than ours."

AMERICANS STILL DON'T UNDERSTAND HOW THE FRENCH EAT WHATEVER THEY WANT AND LIVE TO TELL ABOUT IT.

For much of the past decade, American and British scientists have been annoyed by the phenomenon known as the French Paradox. Nutritionally speaking, the French have been getting away with murder: They eat all the butter, cream, foie gras, pastry and cheese that their hearts desire, and yet their rates of obesity and heart disease are much lower than ours. The French eat three times as much saturated animal fat as Americans do, and only a third as many die of heart attacks. It's maddening.

Baffled, scientists struggled to come up with a few hypotheses: Maybe it was something in the red wine, they said. But while winemakers worldwide celebrated that news, more sober research has suggested that any alcohol—whether Lafite Rothschild, a banana daiquiri or a cold Bud—pretty much has the same nice, relaxing effect. So while a little wine is apt to do you good, the French aren't so special in having a drink now and then (though the fact that they drink wine moderately and slowly with meals, instead of downing shots at the bar, could make a difference).

After the wine argument, scientists ventured that it must be the olive oil that keeps the French healthy. But this doesn't explain the butter or brie. Then, voilà, French scientist Serge Renaud (made famous on "60 Minutes" as an expert on the French Paradox) said it's the foie gras that melts away cholesterol. This, too, is dicey: While people in Toulouse—the fattened force-fed duck-liver-eating area of France—do indeed have one of the lowest rates of heart disease in the developed world, they actually only eat the delicacy about six times a year. And they're a lot more likely to die of stroke than we are anyway.

Other researchers, perhaps sponsored by the garlic and onion industry, suggested that the French Paradox effect is due to garlic and onions. Claude Fischler, a nutritional sociologist at INSERM, the French equivalent of America's National Institutes of Health, says all these single hypotheses are more wishful thinking than science.

"The government loves the French Paradox because it sells red wine—Bordeaux wine in particular—it sells French lifestyle and a number of other French products," he tells me over dinner at an outdoor Paris bistro. "It's something in the cheese! Something from the fat from ducks! It's butter! Really, we're a long way from science here."

More than anything, Fischler thinks the French Paradox is a kind of cultural Rorschach test. "Americans think it's unfair, and Francophiles think it's wonderful."

Last May, researchers writing in the British Medical Journal came up with the least cheerful hypothesis of all. They argued that it's just a matter of time before the French—who are in fact eating more hamburgers and french fries these days—catch up with Americans, and begin suffering the same high rates of cardiovascular disease.

These researchers, Malcolm Law and Nicholas Wald (who must have thought up their hypothesis over dry kidney pie, while dreaming of the kind of duck in red wine and honey sauce I had with Claude Fischler), call this the "time lag explanation" for the French Paradox. As far as they are concerned, the McDonaldization (this is a French catch-all term for the importation of fast food and other American cultural horrors) of France will continue at a frantic pace, and it is as inevitable that French men will start keeling over of heart attacks as it is that French women will eventually wear jean shorts and marshmallow tennis shoes on the streets of Paris.

Nutritionists on this side of the Atlantic are just as dour in their predictions. Marion Nestle, chair of New York University's department of nutrition, says that the wonderful food she found on every street corner in Paris when she lived there in 1983 has changed. "Then you could go into some local bar, and you would be given a little tart, a little salad and a little quiche that would knock your socks off," she says wistfully. But now, she says, the quality of ingredients, the concern about flavor and the freshness of the food has declined. "Last time I was in Paris, everything seemed bigger, softer and more commercially prepared. If you wanted really high quality food, you had to pay for it." When she looked at food data in France, she saw that indeed the amount of fat has risen, and the French are snacking more, eating fewer long meals and visiting McDonald's more often on the sly. She, like Law and Wald, says, "Just wait."

The French, however, disagree about this time lag hypothesis. Nor do they believe that Parisian women will start wearing Nikes with skirts to work anytime soon. "It's hilarious!" says Fischler, finishing a fresh ricotta-stuffed tortellini appetizer. "The American attitude is always to look for a silver bullet—it's the wine, the cheese—or else it has to be nothing, we'll get worse, we haven't had time to get the terrible consequences of modern eating." Instead, says Fischler, the deeply rooted French traditions of eating not only explain the French Paradox, but will insure that it continues, even if it decreases somewhat.

Americans, he says, are always painting the picture in extremes. The French, he continues over a piece of grilled fish, pouring me another glass of that medicinal red wine, have a long-evolved culture of eating that emphasizes pleasure—and order. The French eat comme il faut, "the way it should be done." They may eat whatever they want, but they eat by strict rules: no snacking, no seconds, no skipping meals, no bolting down food, no heading straight for dessert before first filling up on vegetables, salad and meat. They savor their food and eat smaller portions than Americans do.

They also eat a greater diversity of food, which could have something to do with their health, too. And while traditions are loosening in France—more women are working, and so people are more apt to grab a sandwich at lunch—a recent survey Fischler took showed that while more people will skip the cheese course or the first course once or twice a week, they still don't skip meals. The French sit down at the table for well-prepared meals, with high-quality foods, and between times they don't eat. Period.

"In France, we eat in a socially controlled and regulated way, but it's pleasant," says Fischler. "Structure is something that constrains you but also supports you." Fischler and a food-loving

University of Pennsylvania psychologist, Paul Rozin, say the fact that the French have lower rates of coronary artery disease and are skinnier than Americans doesn't have so much to do with what they eat, but how they eat—especially their positive attitudes about food. Talk to a French woman about whether she ever feels guilty about what she eats and she will tell you, as one impossibly young-looking 46-year-old dancer told me, "Absolutely not—I eat exactly what I please."

Then try to find a woman in the U.S. who will answer the same way. There's no magic ingredient that keeps French arteries clear, but instead a whole system of eating that allows them to indulge without overdoing it, and without feeling guilty. Fischler and Rozin say that the biggest predictor of health may not be the content of someone's diet, but how stressed out they are about food, and how relaxed they are about eating. In other words, the more pleasurable it is to eat, the healthier it is for you.

In a study published in the October issue of the journal Appetite, Fischler and Rozin surveyed 1,281 French, American, Japanese and Flemish people about their attitudes toward food. Participants were asked how much they worried about food and the healthiness of their diet, whether they bought low-fat and other diet foods and how much importance they placed on food as a positive force in life. Americans, it turned out, were much more likely than the French to worry about what they eat, buy diet foods and still think of themselves as unhealthy eaters. The French and Belgians were at the other extreme, thinking about food as mainly a great pleasure, and feeling fine about how healthy their diet was. In word association tests, given "chocolate cake," the French would say "celebration," and Americans, "guilt." Given "heavy cream," the French said "whipped," while the Americans responded "unhealthy." Says Rozin, "The French are more inclined to think of food as something you eat and experience, and the Americans are thinking about some sort of chemicals that are getting into your body."

Americans have the worst of both worlds, Rozin says—they have greater concerns about their diets, and they are much more dissatisfied with what they eat. And that sort of stress, he says, can result in a lot of poor eating habits for Americans—extreme dieting, bingeing, overeating and constantly obsessing about food—which are ultimately unhealthy. The real paradox, Rozin says, isn't that the French enjoy food and remain thin and heart disease-free. It's that Americans worry so much about food, do so much more to control their weight and end up so much more dissatisfied with their meals.

American researchers are tentative about Fischler and Rozin's pleasure hypothesis. Eric Rimm, a nutritional epidemiologist at Harvard, says a pleasurable way of eating may be part of the puzzle. "There is something to eating patterns that makes a difference to overall health," he says. "It can't just be the total calories you get at the end of the day."

Eating slowly, he points out, may make a difference. And then there are psychosocial effects. "In France they eat with large families and social networks, which may be important to peace of mind, which has been linked to coronary disease." He hesitates. "Maybe there are psychological effects to the way they eat in France, too."

As the French would say, with just a hint of derision, "Mais oui—but of course." And then, like Claude Fischler and me, they would finish off a long, perfect meal with a couple little spoonfuls of intensely rich chocolate souffli.

Discussion/Writing Prompts

- One of the key differences between the American and French dietary models, Fraser writes, revolves around the gustatory pleasures of eating. While Americans seem entirely comfortable choosing food on the basis of its healthfulness, the French are much more likely to base the value of a given meal on how satisfying it tastes. How accurate do you find this distinction to be? In your view, do Americans have a cultural predisposition against using taste as a dietary guide? And if so, is this a good or bad thing?
- In trying to explain why statistics show the French to be so much healthier than Americans, Fraser considers the possibility that we have come to link definitions of physical health too narrowly to how and what we eat. Do you agree? Do we rely too much on diet in our assessments of how to be healthy? In a one-page essay, offer a description of a program for physical health that extends beyond the single issue of diet. What other behavior or activities would you proscribe? To what extent does this model resemble the one Fraser uses to evaluate the French?
- While Fraser and Ettlinger both focus on eating practices that appear, at least on the surface, to be unhealthy, the ultimate conclusions they draw are not exactly the same. In a one-page essay, offer an analysis of how well you think the Twinkie would fit into the French dietary model Fraser outlines. In your view, is this all-American snack food an eligible candidate for the "French paradox"? How or how not?

"The Queen of Mold", in *Tender at the Bone* (1998)
RUTH REICHL

It's one thing to be casual about how our food tastes, but is it acceptable to extend this same cavalier attitude to questions of health? Recounting her experiences growing up in the shadow of her mother's unorthodox cooking style, food critic Reichl offers a tongue-in-cheek memoir that manages at the same time to raise serious questions about how we define a worthwhile meal.

———————— ✦ ————————

"My parents entertained a great deal, and before I was ten I had appointed myself guardian of the guests. My mission was to keep Mom from killing anybody who came to dinner."

This is a true story.
Imagine a New York City apartment at six in the morning. It is a modest apartment in Greenwich Village. Coffee is bubbling in an electric percolator. On the table is a basket of rye bread, an entire coffee cake, a few cheeses, a platter of cold cuts. My mother has been making breakfast—a major meal in our house, one where we sit down to fresh orange juice every morning, clink our glasses as if they held wine, and toast each other with "Cheerio. Have a nice day."

Right now she is the only one awake, but she is getting impatient for the day to begin and she cranks WQXR up a little louder on the radio, hoping that the noise will rouse everyone else. But Dad and I are good sleepers, and when the sounds of martial music have no effect she barges into the bedroom and shakes my father awake.

"Darling," she says, "I need you. Get up and come into the kitchen."

My father, a sweet and accommodating person, shuffles sleepily down the hall. He is wearing loose pajamas, and the strand of hair he combs over his bald spot stands straight up. He leans against the sink, holding on to it a little, and obediently opens his mouth when my mother says, "Try this."

Later, when he told the story, he attempted to convey the awful-
ness of what she had given him. The first time he said that it tasted
like cat toes and rotted barley, but over the years the description got
better. Two years later it had turned into pigs' snouts and mud and
five years later he had refined the flavor into a mixture of antique
anchovies and moldy chocolate.

Whatever it tasted like, he said it was the worst thing he had
ever had in his mouth, so terrible that it was impossible to swal-
low, so terrible that he leaned over and spit it into the sink and then
grabbed the coffeepot, put the spout into his mouth, and tried to
eradicate the flavor.

My mother stood there watching all this. When my father
finally put the coffeepot down she smiled and said, "Just as I
thought. Spoiled!"

And then she threw the mess into the garbage can and sat
down to drink her orange juice.

For the longest time I thought I had made this story up. But
my brother insists that my father told it often, and with a certain
amount of pride. As far as I know, my mother was never embarrassed by the telling, never even knew that she should have been.
It was just the way she was.

Which was taste-blind and unafraid of rot. "Oh, it's just a little
mold," I can remember her saying on the many occasions she
scraped the fuzzy blue stuff off some concoction before serving
what was left for dinner. She had an iron stomach and was inca-
pable of understanding that other people did not.

This taught me many things. The first was that food could be
dangerous, especially to those who loved it. I took this very seriously. My parents entertained a great deal, and before I was ten I
had appointed myself guardian of the guests. My mission was to
keep Mom from killing anybody who came to dinner.

Her friends seemed surprisingly unaware that they took their
lives in their hands each time they ate with us. They chalked their
ailments up to the weather, the flu, or one of my mother's more unusual dishes. "No more sea urchins for me," I imagined Burt
Langner saying to his wife, Ruth, after a dinner at our house, "they
just don't agree with me." Little did he know that it was not the sea
urchins that had made him ill, but that bargain beef my mother
had found so irresistible.

"I can make a meal out of anything," Mom told her friends
proudly. She liked to brag about "Everything Stew," a dish

invented while she was concocting a casserole out of a two-week-old turkey carcass. (The very fact that my mother confessed to cooking with two-week-old turkey says a lot about her.) She put the turkey and a half can of mushroom soup into the pot. Then she began rummaging around in the refrigerator. She found some leftover broccoli and added that. A few carrots went in, and then a half carton of sour cream. In a hurry, as usual, she added green beans and cranberry sauce. And then, somehow, half an apple pie slipped into the dish. Mom looked momentarily horrified. Then she shrugged and said, "Who knows? Maybe it will be good." And she began throwing everything in the refrigerator in along with it—leftover pâté, some cheese ends, a few squishy tomatoes.

That night I set up camp in the dining room. I was particularly worried about the big eaters, and I stared at my favorite people as they approached the buffet, willing them away from the casserole. I actually stood directly in front of Burt Langner so he couldn't reach the turkey disaster. I loved him, and I knew that he loved food.

Unknowingly I had started sorting people by their tastes. Like a hearing child born to deaf parents, I was shaped by my mother's handicap, discovering that food could be a way of making sense of the world.

At first I paid attention only to taste, storing away the knowledge that my father preferred salt to sugar and my mother had a sweet tooth. Later I also began to note how people ate, and where. My brother liked fancy food in fine surroundings, my father only cared about the company, and Mom would eat anything so long as the location was exotic. I was slowly discovering that if you watched people as they ate, you could find out who they were.

Then I began listening to the way people talked about food, looking for clues to their personalities. "What is she really saying?" I asked myself when Mom bragged about the invention of her famous corned beef ham.

"I was giving a party," she'd begin, "and as usual I left everything for the last minute." Here she'd look at her audience, laughing softly at herself. "I asked Ernst to do the shopping, but you know how absentminded he is! Instead of picking up a ham he brought me corned beef." She'd look pointedly at Dad, who would look properly sheepish.

"What could I do?" Mom asked. "I had people coming in a couple of hours. I had no choice. I simply pretended it was a ham." With that Dad would look admiringly at my mother, pick up his carving knife, and start serving the masterpiece.

Miriam Reichi's Corned Beef Ham

4 pounds whole corned beef	¼ cup brown sugar
5 bay leaves	Whole cloves
1 onion, chopped	1 can (1 pound 15 ounces)
1 tablespoon prepared	spiced peaches
mustard	

Cover corned beef with water in a large pot. Add bay leaves and onion. Cook over medium heat about 3 hours, until meat is very tender.

While meat is cooking, mix mustard and brown sugar.

Preheat oven to 325°.

Take meat from water and remove all visible fat. Insert cloves into meat as if it were ham. Cover the meat with the mustard mixture and bake 1 hour, basting frequently with the peach syrup.

Surround meat with spiced peaches and serve.

Serves 6.

Discussion/Writing Prompts

- Take a moment to reflect upon the title of this essay. Why does she choose to designate her mother the "queen of mold"? What larger message about cooking, food, and motherhood does this title seem designed to convey? What vision of Reichl's mother as a chef does this title evoke?

- In many ways, the portrait of her mother Reichl draws here runs counter to the dominant gender stereotypes historically promoted in our culture— particularly those related to women and "the home." In a one-page essay, offer an analysis of the ways you see this essay challenging or rewriting these stereotypes. What aspects of Reichl's portrait do not fit the mold of the traditional "housewife"? And in your view, is this alternative portrait more legitimate or compelling? Why?

- In contrast to what Fraser says about the French, Reichl's mother seems to have almost no interest in the gustatory pleasures of food—that is, in how food tastes. Based on Fraser's essay, what do you imagine the typical French reaction would be to a meal prepared by Reichl's mother? How would this hypothetical French eater react to and evaluate this food? How do you think Reichl's mother would react? How might she defend or justify her meal in response?

Tying It All Together: Assignments for Writing and Research

1. RHETORICAL ANALYSIS: "GOOD AND GOOD FOR YOU"

As we have already noted, our modern food culture abounds with different facts, statistics, and guidelines—all of which serve in one way or another to set the standard for what is and is not healthy. Choose a food product that displays this kind of nutritional information. Then write a two- to three-page essay in which you identify and describe the particular messages or advice about being healthy you think this information aims to convey. Based on the ingredients it lists and the benefits it promises, what standard of health would you say this product is attempting to sell? After you've completed this analysis, present your own evaluation of these messages. Do the standards and definition being promoted here reflect your own? What are the key similarities? The key differences?

2. PERSONAL REFLECTION: "COUNTING CALORIES"

Look up the FDA Food Pyramid online. First write a one-page description of the general guidelines and advice concerning eating that you think this chart promotes. Based on the food categories and food distinctions it presents, how would you say the FDA Food Pyramid defines the ideal diet? Next, keep a journal of the different foods you eat for a week. When you're done, write another one-page essay assessing how your own eating choices for the week compare with the advice modeled in the Food Pyramid. How closely do your own eating practices adhere to the standards being modeled? Does this comparison give you any ideas for how your own eating might be changed? How or how not?

3. COMPARE AND CONTRAST: "TASTE VS. NUTRITION"

As we all know from personal experience, it is just as easy to find a food that falls short of our current nutritional standards as it is to find one that fulfills them. Indeed may of the foods that are supposedly "bad" for us are precisely the ones we take the greatest pleasures in eating. Choose two foods, one which fits our culture's prevailing definition of nutritious and one which does not. Then write a two- to three-page essay in which you compare the relative benefits and/or pleasures of eating each. Ultimately, how do you weigh the appeal of taste against the benefits of nutrition? How, in your own experience, do you decide which of these considerations matters more?

4. VISUAL ANALYSIS: "I'M NOT A DOCTOR BUT I PLAY ONE ON TV"

As we have also seen, our culture's messages about nutrition rely upon the authority of science. We are far more inclined to be swayed by the nutritional claims made for a given food if they are backed by the sanction of the scientific or medical establishment. Choose a food advertisement (e.g., TV commercial, magazine ad, billboard, Web site) that, in your view, invokes the authority of science to market its product. Then write a two- to three-page essay in which you analyze the specific ways this ad uses the idea or image of science to enhance the appeal of the food presented. Does this strategy have its intended effect upon you? How or how not?

5. ARGUMENT-BASED/PERSUASIVE WRITING: "AGAINST NUTRITION"

It is an article of faith in today's society that we should care a great deal about the nutritional content of what we put into our bodies. But what about the downside? Are there any disadvantages, any hidden problems or costs, to the emphasis we currently place upon eating healthy? In a two- to three-page essay, make an argument about the downside to our current cultural obsession with nutrition. What aspects of the eating experience does this standard leave out? And why should we not overlook them?

CHAPTER 2

Consumerism

WHERE THE SUPERMARKET MEETS THE MASS MARKET: THE COMMERCIALIZATION OF EATING

What does it mean to be a food consumer in the 21st century? Amidst the welter of competing claims and come-ons—from FDA guidelines to reality cooking shows, diet books to fast food commercials—how do we tell what the right eating choices are? What happens, in other words, when we stop thinking of eating as a solely personal decision, and start thinking of it as a *commercial* act? Taking up these questions, this chapter presents a closer look at the prominent and contested role the commercial marketplace plays in shaping how and what we eat. Surveying our pop culture landscape—the images and messages, instruction and advice about food that proliferate in our media every day—it invites readers to think more deeply about the ways it shapes not only our behavior as eaters, but our underlying attitudes, assumptions, and values as well.

Put differently: this chapter asks us to explore those places in our lives where food and commercialism intersect, where the supermarket meets the mass market. Assembling an inventory of some of the most representative ways food gets presented, promoted, and marketed in our culture, it poses hard questions about what it means to live in a world where eating has become a thoroughly and irrevocably commercialized activity. What happens when food is transformed from a raw material or edible object into a commodity, a product, a brand? When are we taught to approach and appraise food as much for its symbolic as for its physical qualities?

While admittedly less tangible, the symbolism of what we eat (e.g., the way different products come to be associated with different images and ideals, values and lifestyles) exerts an enormous influence over our actions when it comes to food. Every time we purchase an apple harvested in Argentina or an orange grown in South Africa at our local supermarket, every time we exit the highway to pull into a McDonalds or Burger King drive-thru, every time we pop a frozen TV dinner into our microwave, we bear witness to the market's power to influence, bracket, or otherwise manage our eating behavior. And of course, beyond the question of how we act is the additional (and trickier) question of how we *think*. No doubt we can all cite examples of ads—whether for organic fruit or a Big Mac—in which a given food comes to serve as the vehicle for promoting (or perhaps more accurately, selling) a range of other ideas as well. As we all know from first-hand experience, every attempt to market food as a commodity involves a concomitant effort to connect this product to particular images, ideas, and/or rewards—each one calculated to enhance this product's overall appeal.

Advertising images and media messages in particular have long shown themselves to be formative factors in framing both how we act and how we think. From an advertiser's point of view, food sells best when it can be convincingly conscripted as a stand-in or substitute for other things the buying public is presumed to find desirable: wealth, popularity, status, happiness, etc. This in fact may explain why so many of the icons and images used to sell food have so little immediate or direct connection to food at all. Ads for beer feature not the beverage itself, but scantily clad twenty-somethings frolicking at the beach; fast food commercials showcase their product not with pictures of hamburgers or milkshakes, but with footage of sports celebrities competing on the court or field; billboards for chewing gum feature vistas of snow-capped mountains. Directing our attention elsewhere, such visual iconography encourages us to focus less on eating per se than on the putative pleasures and pay-offs eating will supposedly yield. Food itself, in these cases, seems to take a back seat.

When viewed from this perspective, the modern marketing of food could be said to concern itself less with what we eat than with how we *feel about* what we eat: the pleasures or pay-offs we are told will follow if we buy what these ads are selling. Another way to state this is to say that, as customers targeted by advertisers, what we are encouraged to consume is less the food itself than the ideas, values, and images that advertisers connect to food. To come across a Wheaties box adorned with the latest Olympic gold medalist is not simply to be sold a particular cereal. It is also to be encouraged to buy into the set of values (e.g., athleticism, success, competition) this product is simultaneously using to sell this cereal—values celebrated as desirable, right, and utterly worthwhile. To be sure, it is a cliché to note that what gets sold to the general public (from toys to clothing, home furnishings to automobiles) is often less the product itself than the image or aura advertisers labor to attach to it. And yet because food strikes so many of us as less artificial, less manufactured than other commercial products, this remains a truism often overlooked when it comes to how we eat. On a daily basis we encounter undeniable proof that food, like everything else in the commercial marketplace, is a commodity. And yet intuitively we still sometimes harbor feelings that food might nonetheless prove the exception to the rule.

In order to dispel such conceits, let's consider a concrete example—for instance, the Starbucks latte. Measured solely in physical terms, it is not hard to offer a description of what is being sold. Two shots espresso, a cup of steamed milk, a pinch of sugar, a dash of cinnamon, all vigorously mixed together in a green and white paper cup. How difficult is that? But notice what happens when we assess this beverage not in physical but in commercial terms: not as a drink per se, but as a brand, a product designed to evoke certain associations, to symbolize particular values or ideas. Whether we are a die-hard patron of Starbucks or not, chances are we can still recite the list of cultural stereotypes that have come to be associated with buying and drinking this particular drink. Fairly or unfairly, the Starbucks latte has lodged itself in the public imagination as an especially succinct shorthand for a specific type of lifestyle: urban and urbane, upwardly mobile and self-consciously hip. And whether we regard this lifestyle as a model to be emulated or a cliché to be mocked, the larger point remains irrefutable: this is a food product that speaks as much to our social aspirations and emotional needs as to our physical taste. Beyond the pleasing commingling of milk and coffee flavors or the energizing buzz of caffeine, the Starbucks latte also beckons us with a different sort of reward: the prospect of embellishing or enhancing who and what we are.

The million-dollar question, of course, is: when a food product beckons us in this way, should we accept? When it comes to the countless marketing strategies used to sell food, how do we disentangle the truth from the lies? What is bogus or overblown from what is legitimate? To pose such questions is to do more than challenge the veracity of a given advertising campaign. It is, more fundamentally, to mount an inquiry into the role that mass marketing in general plays in dictating, shaping, or otherwise influencing how we see ourselves. When we survey the range of logos, brands, and images that advertisers use to sell food, we are on another level taking inventory of the language the commercial marketplace wants us to use to define who and what we are. From a variety of perspectives, the selections assembled below assay the consequences—baleful and beneficent, deleterious and delightful—of approaching eating in precisely these terms. Showcasing a range of ways food gets mass-marketed in our culture, they invite us to consider more critically exactly what vision, view, values we implicitly endorse when we choose to buy.

"Do You Want Lies With That?" in *Don't Eat This Book* (2005)
MORGAN SPURLOCK

The forces of commercialism have so thoroughly infiltrated our eating lives, says filmmaker and author Spurlock, that we have lost our capacity to distinguish advertisers' "lies" about food from the truth. Wondering about where this situation might be leading us, he offers readers a pointed warning about the consequences—for our health, our economic security, our overall happiness—of taking the commercial claims about food at face value.

———————————— ✦ ————————————

> *"Every waking moment of our lives, we swim in an ocean of advertising, all of it telling us the same thing: Consume. Consume. And then, consume some more."*

ONE: DO YOU WANT LIES WITH THAT?

Don't do it. Please. I know this book looks delicious, with its light-weight pages sliced thin as prosciutto and swiss, stacked in a way that would make Dagwood salivate. The scent of freshly baked words wafting up with every turn of the page. *Mmmm*, page. But don't do it. Not yet. Don't eat this book.

We turn just about everything you can imagine into food. You can eat coins, toys, cigars, cigarettes, rings, necklaces, lips, cars, babies, teeth, cameras, film, even underwear (which come in a variety of scents, sizes, styles and flavors). Why not a book?

In fact, we put so many things in our mouths, we constantly have to be reminded what *not* to eat. Look at that little package of silicon gel that's inside your new pair of sneakers. It says DO NOT EAT for a reason. Somewhere, sometime, some genius bought a pair of sneakers and said, "Ooooh, look. They give you free mints with the shoes!"—soon followed, no doubt, by the lawsuit charging the manufacturer with negligence, something along the lines of, "Well, it didn't say *not* to eat those things."

And thus was born the "warning label." To avoid getting sued, corporate America now labels everything. Thank the genius who first decided to take a bath and blow-dry her hair at the same time. The Rhodes scholar who first reached down into a running garbage disposal. That one-armed guy down the street who felt around under his power mower while it was running.

Yes, thanks to them, blow-dryers now come with the label DO NOT SUBMERGE IN WATER WHILE PLUGGED IN. Power mowers warn KEEP HANDS AND FEET AWAY FROM MOVING BLADES. And curling irons bear tags that read FOR EXTERNAL USE ONLY.

And that's why I warn you—please!—do not eat this book. This book is FOR EXTERNAL USE ONLY. Except maybe as food for thought.

We live in a ridiculously litigious society. Opportunists know that a wet floor or a hot cup of coffee can put them on easy street. Like most of you, I find many of these lawsuits pointless and frivolous. No wonder the big corporations and the politicians they own have been pushing so hard for tort reform.

Fifty years ago it was a different story. Fifty years ago, adult human beings were presumed to have enough sense not to stick their fingers in whirring blades of steel. And if they did, that was their own fault.

Take smoking. For most of us, the idea that "smoking kills" is a given. My mom and dad know smoking is bad, but they don't stop. My grandfather smoked all the way up until his death at a grand old age, and my folks are just following in his footsteps—despite the terrifying warning on every pack.

They're not alone, of course. It's estimated that over a billion people in the world are smokers. Worldwide, roughly 5 million people died from smoking in 2000. Smoking kills 440,000 Americans every year. All despite that surgeon general's warning on every single pack.

What is going on here? It's too easy to write off all billion-plus smokers as idiots with a death wish. My parents aren't idiots. I don't think they want to die. (When I was younger, there were times when I wanted to kill them, but that's different.) We all know that tobacco is extremely addictive. And that the tobacco companies used to add chemicals to make cigarettes even more addictive, until they got nailed for it. And that for several generations—again, until they got busted for it—the big tobacco companies aimed their marketing and advertising at kids and young people. Big Tobacco spent billions of dollars to get people hooked as early as they could, and to keep them as "brand-loyal" slaves for the rest of their unnaturally shortened lives. Cigarettes were cool, cigarettes were hip, cigarettes were sexy. Smoking made you look like a cowboy or a movie starlet.

And it worked. When my parents were young, everybody smoked. Doctors smoked. Athletes smoked. Pregnant women smoked. Their kids came out of the womb looking around the delivery room for an ashtray to ash their Lucky Strikes. Everyone smoked.

The change began in 1964, when the first surgeon general's warning about smoking and cancer scared the bejesus out of everybody. In 1971, cigarette ads were banned from TV, and much later they disappeared from billboards. Little by little, smoking was restricted in airplanes and airports, in public and private workplaces, in restaurants and bars. Tobacco sponsorship of sporting events decreased. Tighter controls were placed on selling cigarettes to minors. Everyone didn't quit overnight, but overall rates of smoking began to decrease—from 42 percent of adults in 1965 to 23 percent in 2000, and from 36 percent of high school kids in 1997 to 29 percent in 2001. The number of adults who have never smoked more than doubled from 1965 to 2000.

Big tobacco companies knew it was a war they couldn't win, but they didn't give up without a fight. They threw billions and billions of more dollars into making smoking look cool, hip, sexy—and safe.

They targeted new markets, like women, who increased their rate of smoking 400 percent *after* the surgeon general's report. Yeah, you've come a long way, baby—all the way from the kitchen to the cancer ward. They expanded their markets in the Third World and undeveloped nations, getting hundreds of millions of people hooked; it's estimated that more than four out of five current smokers are in developing countries. As if people without a regular source of drinking water didn't have enough to worry about already. Big Tobacco denied the health risks of smoking, lied about what they were putting into cigarettes and lobbied like hell against every government agency or legislative act aimed at curbing their deadly impact.

Which brings me back to those "frivolous" lawsuits. Back when people were first suing the tobacco companies for giving them cancer, a lot of folks scoffed. (And coughed. But they still scoffed.) Smokers knew the dangers of smoking, everyone said. If they decided to keep smoking for thirty, forty years and then got lung cancer, they couldn't blame the tobacco companies.

Then a funny thing happened. As the lawsuits progressed, it became more and more apparent that smokers did *not* know all the dangers of smoking. They couldn't know, because Big Tobacco was hiding the truth from them—lying to them about the health risks, and lying about the additives they were putting in cigarettes to make them more addictive. Marketing cigarettes to children, to get them hooked early and keep them puffing away almost literally from the cradle to the early grave, among other nefarious dealings.

In the mid-1990s, shouldering the crushing burden of soaring Medicare costs due to smoking-related illnesses, individual states began to imitate those "ambulance-chasers," bringing their own class-action lawsuits against Big Tobacco. In 1998, without ever explicitly admitting to any wrongdoing, the big tobacco companies agreed to a massive $246 billion settlement, to be paid to forty-fix states and five territories over twenty-five years. (The other four states had already settled in individual cases.)

Two hundred and forty-six billion dollars is a whole lot of frivolous, man.

What these lawsuits drove home was the relationship between personal responsibility and corporate responsibility. Suddenly it was apparent that sticking a cigarette in your mouth was not *quite* the same thing as sticking those sneaker mints in your mouth. No one spent billions and billions of dollars in marketing, advertising and promotions telling that guy those sneaker mints would make him cool, hip and sexy. Big Tobacco did exactly that to smokers.

Still, a lot of people were skeptical about those lawsuits. Are the big bad corporations with all their big bad money and big bad mind-altering advertising really so powerful that we as individuals cannot think for ourselves anymore? Are we really so easily swayed by the simplest of pleasant images that we'll jump at the chance to share in some of that glorious, spring-scented, new and improved, because-you-deserve-it goodness, without a thought about what's best for us anymore?

You tell me. Every waking moment of our lives, we swim in an ocean of advertising, all of it telling us the same thing: Consume. Consume. And then consume some more.

In 2003, the auto industry spent $18.2 billion telling us we needed a new car, more cars, bigger cars. Over the last twenty-five years, the number of household vehicles in the United States has doubled. The rate of increase in the number of cars, vans and SUVs for personal travel has been six times the rate of population increase. In fact, according to the Department of Transportation, there are now, for the first time in history, *more cars than drivers* in America. That's ridiculous!

Did we suddenly *need* so many more vehicles? Or were we sold the idea?

We drive everywhere now. Almost nine-tenths of our daily travel takes place in a personal vehicle. Walking, actually using the legs and feet God gave us, accounts for appallingly little of our day-to-day getting around. Even on trips of under one mile, according to the Department of Transportation, we walked only 24 percent of the time in 2001 (and rode a bike under 2 percent). Walking declined by almost half in the two decades between 1980 and 2000. In Los Angeles, you can get arrested for walking. The cops figure if you're not in a car you can't be up to any good. If you're not in a car, you're a vagrant. Same goes for the suburbs, where so many of us now live.

And what do you put inside that SUV, minivan or pickup truck you're driving everywhere, other than your kids? Well, lots of *stuff*, that's what. In 2002, the retail industry in this country spent $13.5 billion telling us what to buy, and we must have been listening, because in 2003 we spent nearly $8 *trillion* on all kinds of crap. That's right, trillion. How insane is that? We are the biggest consuming culture on the planet. We buy almost twice as much crap as our nearest competitor, Japan. We spend more on ourselves than the entire gross national product of any nation in the world.

And all that shopping—whew, has it made us hungry. Every year, the food industry spends around $33 billion convincing us that we're famished. So we all climb back into our giant vehicle filled with all our stuff from Wal-Mart, and we cruise to the nearest fast-food joint. If not McDonald's or Burger King or Taco Bell, then a "fast casual" restaurant like Outback Steakhouse or TGI Friday's or the Olive Garden, where they serve us portions larger than our smallest kid, with the calories to match.

What does all that consumption do for us? Does it make us happy? You tell me. If we were all so happy, would we be on so many drugs? Antidepressant use in the U.S. nearly *tripled* in the past decade. We've got drugs in America we can take for anything: if we're feeling too bad, too good, too skinny, too fat, too sleepy, too wide awake, too unmanly. We've got drugs to counteract the disastrous health effects of all our overconsumption—diet drugs, heart drugs, liver drugs, drugs to make our hair grow back and our willies stiff. In 2003, we Americans spent $227 billion on medications. That's a whole lot of drugs!

This is the power of advertising at work, of billions of hooks that've been cast into our heads in the last thirty years, billions of messages telling us what we want, what we need and what we should do to feel happy. We all buy into it to some degree, because none of us is as young as we'd like to be, or as thin, or as strong.

Yet none of the stuff we consume—no matter how much bigger our SUV is than our neighbor's, no matter how many Whoppers we wolf down, no matter how many DVDs we own or how much Zoloft we take—makes us feel full, or satisfied or happy.

So we consume some more.

And the line between personal responsibility and corporate responsibility gets finer and more blurred. Yes, you're still responsible for your own life, your own health, your own happiness. But your *desires*, the things you *want*, the things you think you *need*— that's all manipulated by corporate advertising and marketing that now whisper and shout and wink at you from every corner of your life—at home, at work, at school, at play.

Consume. Consume. Still not happy? Then you obviously haven't consumed enough.

Like this book, the epidemic of overconsumption that's plaguing the nation begins with the things we put in our mouths. Since the 1960s, everyone has known that smoking kills, but it's only been in the last few years that we've become hip to a new killer, one that now rivals smoking as the leading cause of preventable deaths in America and, if current trends continue, will soon be the leading cause: overeating.

Americans are eating themselves to death.

Discussion/Writing Prompts

- Spurlock sees a number of parallels between the way food gets marketed in our culture and the way other products (e.g., tobacco, automobiles, lawn mowers, prescription drugs) are sold. Do you think this comparison is valid? In your view, are there more similarities or differences in how these respective commodities get promoted? Is there something about food that makes it a different, even unique, sort of commodity?

- As the title of this piece suggests, Spurlock views the mass marketing of food as an extended attempt to manipulate, deceive, and/or dupe us. Choose a particular product that in your opinion is representative of the ways food gets marketed in our culture more generally. Then write a one-page essay in which you use this product as a case study for testing Spurlock's argument. Based on how this product gets promoted, does it support or refute Spurlock's contention that the eating public is being largely lied to? How or how not?

- When it comes to the mass marketing of food, Spurlock poses a very simple question: "What does all that consumption do for us? Does it make us happy?" Choose another one of the authors included among these selections, the one whose own essay, in your view, offers the most direct response to Spurlock's query. In a one-page essay, outline the ways that this writer's portrait of commercialized eating addresses the fundamental issue of individual happiness that Spurlock raises.

"Escalated Dining: Is Mall Food Becoming Classy?," *Slate* (May 21, 2004)

SARA DICKERMAN

Is it possible to enjoy a "fine dining" experience at the mall? Or is there something simply so incompatible about the prospect of a gourmet restaurant next to a Footlocker as to make such an experience feel next to impossible? Examining some of the ways we've been taught to define "haute cuisine," Dickerman offers us a different perspective on the role food plays as a status symbol in our culture.

——————— ✦ ———————

"My gut told me that people would feel odd about showing off for clients or proposing to a girlfriend at a mall. And it seems my gut was right."

When I first moved to Seattle from Los Angeles, I was offered a job at the about-to-open branch of Stars, the renowned San Francisco restaurant. The job paid well, the kitchen was gorgeous, and I liked the chef, but I turned it down. In order to get to the restaurant, a diner had to ascend to the fourth floor of the Pacific Place mall—a glamorous, late-1990s mall, but a mall just the same. My gut told me that people would feel odd about showing off for clients or proposing to a girlfriend over dinner at a mall. And it seems my gut was right. About a year later, employees found themselves locked out of the kitchen without jobs, and the dream of a fine mall restaurant was quashed. The space has since been refilled by a much more mall-appropriate, all-you-can-eat sushi buffet. Business seems to be booming.

Are fine dining and mall culture at odds? In the popular imagination, at least, fancy restaurants are the ultimate independent business, helmed by culinary mavericks who wouldn't dream of setting up shop next to the Footlocker. Malls, by contrast, are thought to be characterized by uniformity and tackiness and crass commercialism. And let's be honest, the conflict can be boiled down to a single question: Who wants to ascend an escalator to a fancy dinner?

But that prejudice may be diminishing. No end of press has been devoted to the new Time Warner Center shopping center, where some of the best-known names from the world of highbrow cuisine—Jean-Georges Vongerichten (of the eponymous Jean Georges and countless others), Charlie Trotter (of Charlie Trotter's), Gary Kunz (formerly of Lespinasse), Thomas Keller (of French Laundry and Bouchon), Masa Takayama (formerly of Ginza Sushiko)—have elected to open restaurants. Despite its classy name, The Shops at Columbus Circle is a mall, and together the restaurants make up a food court the likes of which the world has never seen. Several other mall-like entities—New York's Chelsea Market, for example, and San Francisco's Ferry Building

Marketplace—also showcase fine food and restaurants, but without the retail stores of the Columbus Circle development. (Of course nothing compares to the star wattage assembled at Time Warner.)

New York is, of course, a place of singular, and often hidden, restaurant gems—from the posh white-linen restaurants where New York's high society noshes on slightly old-fashioned Euro-food, to the downtown Ukrainian diners that keep struggling writers and artists nourished by hunters' stew and coffee, to obscure street food vendors (like this one) fervently catalogued on posting boards like Chowhound. Indeed, the very idea that one building could be home to multiple restaurants seems like an affront to the city's unique restaurant culture. Is the Time Warner experiment just another exception in an exceptional city, or is the world now ready for the ultimate oxymoron—classy dining in a mall?

To answer that question, we should first consider the history of mall food and what it means in the culture's imagination. The first enclosed malls in America, like those built by Victor Gruen (recently profiled by Malcolm Gladwell in *The New Yorker*), had large courtyards in their centers, where cafes were located. Not yet full-blown food courts, these spaces were modeled on something like a European city square; they were intended as a humanizing element within the impersonal, commercial realm of the mall. But locating restaurants at the heart of a mall is problematic, Gladwell told me in a recent conversation. Restaurants aren't always busy during key shopping hours, causing potential dead spots in the mall that in turn might lead a wayward shopper to (gasp) turn around instead of walking and seeing what new retail opportunities are to be found around the bend. For that reason, mall planners tend to put the restaurants on the higher floors of malls, above and away from the shops (and often near the multiplexes, which create a similar dead zone when people are inside watching movies). This is even true of The Shops at Columbus Circle: The restaurants are located on the third and fourth floors, out of sight of mall standards like Crabtree and Evelyn, Benetton, and J. Crew. (Non-shopping diners, in turn, can avoid feeling tainted by the mallness of the center by accessing the restaurants with slightly difficult-to-find elevators that go directly from the street to the dining level.)

Sequestered on those upper floors, mall restaurants often took an abbreviated form—as various takeout counters with shared seating at the center of the common space. And so evolved the

"food court" as we know it. Although particular brands come and
go, the typical high-fat, high-sugar quasi-international lineup has
not changed much over the decades: It will often include some in-
ferior Chinese food, a taco booth, a pizza-by-the-slice stand, a
"healthy" smoothie option (often as not an Orange Julius), and a
Cinnabon responsible for the vanilla and cinnamon odors wafting
throughout the mall. The food court has also strongly influenced
food service beyond the mall, especially corporate and college
cafeterias where multiple food stations appeal to a short culinary
attention span.

In recent years, some upscale, casual dining restaurant
chains—the Cheesecake Factories, the PF Chang's China Bistros,
the Rainforest Grills—have been setting up shop in malls. Often
these restaurants are not isolated on the top floors of malls but
have their own entrances on the street level, both providing
street-level advertising and establishing a psychological difference
between the mall and the restaurant. While in the past these establishments—which are not fine dining, but aren't cheap either—
might have preferred to be located in a free-standing building, the
tough economy has increased competition for well-trafficked
mall space.

But it's not only the economy that has driven restaurants to
malls. There's another factor that has gone mostly unrecognized:
the influence of Las Vegas. The city has done more to legitimize
mall food than any other city in the country: In recent years, Vegas
has become its own hermetically sealed world, and casinos have
become like an extended mall. In the '90s, developers began to attract famous chefs to expand restaurants within these sprawling
casino/hotel/mall microcosms. Wolfgang Puck was a pioneer; others, including Charlie Palmer, Jean-Georges and Todd English,
and Julian Serrano soon followed. (The main draw was surely economic: While tourists are caught in the city's fantastic grip, they
are willing to spend money in ways they would normally never
consider, on fine food and even finer wine. Las Vegas wine lists are
full of blingy selections, like four- and five-figure cult bottles.) By
this time, the mall/casino taboo has been entirely obliterated: Before the end of 2005, Vegas will also boast restaurants from Keller,
Alain Ducasse, Hubert Keller, Rick Bayless, and Joel Robuchon.
The mall at Columbus Circle is an obvious sign that top-dollar
chefs, taking a cue from Vegas, are willing to toss themselves into
unconventional restaurant situations. (It is also a sign that great
chefs no longer fear a public backlash for turning their name into

a luxury brand.) Maybe what happens in Vegas doesn't stay in Vegas after all.

In truth, though, I think the present and future of mall food is not to be found in the vast enclosed shopping centers of the Columbus Circle variety, but in the strip mall. Five years in Los Angeles—the capital of strip malls—taught me that independent restaurants can thrive in those one- or two-story commercial developments. Strip malls are often home to surprising, niche-market restaurants: a stellar Oaxacan restaurant, a dosa/idli-centric South Indian joint, a Salvadoran bakery or a Muslim Chinese restaurant. (One of the most famous examples is Sushi Nozawa in the San Fernando Valley, which has an almost cultlike following.) In the strip mall, the specialized restaurant can live and breathe with neither the exorbitant overhead of a free-standing, independent restaurant nor the crushing uniformity demanded by most multitiered malls. And so, community planning be damned, I say viva la strip mall.

Discussion/Writing Prompts

- In Dickerman's estimation, there is something incongruous, even contradictory, about locating a "high end" or "fine dining" restaurant within a mall. Do you agree? What are some of the specific ideas or images we have been taught to associate with the mall? To what extent do they conflict with those we have learned to associate with the concept of "fine dining"? And finally, does Dickerman's essay offer us a way to reconcile these contrasting associations?

- Dickerman summarizes the tension between "fine dining" and "mall culture" in this way: "In the popular imagination . . . fancy restaurants are the ultimate independent business, helmed by culinary mavericks who wouldn't dream of setting up shop next to the Footlocker. Malls, by contrast, are thought to be characterized by uniformity, tackiness, and crass commercialism." Write a one-page response in which you assess the validity of this distinction. In your view, is it true the "fancy restaurant" stands in the public imagination as a site free from the influence or taint of "commercialism"? If so, how does this view help enhance the appeal or the status of such restaurants?

- One of the questions underlying Dickerman's essay concerns the ways that food can stand in our culture as its own kind of status symbol. Can you think of a particular food or meal that performs this sort of role—that enhances the stature, prestige, or rank of the person buying and/or eating it? Next, write a quick (one-page) description of how this view of food compares with the argument advanced by Spurlock? Based on his essay, what sorts of conclusions do you think he would draw about the way food functions as a status symbol?

"Open for Business: Eating Out as Group Therapy in Post-Katrina New Orleans," *The Atlantic* (March 2006)

CORBY KUMMER

As many of the selections included in this chapter attest, it is easy to point out the problems which the modern commercialization of food seems to raise. So easy, in fact, that we can sometimes overlook its advantages and benefits. Relating the story of his first visit to post-Katrina New Orleans, noted food writer Kummer redresses this imbalance, chronicling the power of "eating out" to redeem and heal a community traumatized by disaster.

--------------- ◆ ---------------

"Loyalty and the tug of home were what made most restaurants reopen, as families—both biological and collegial—reunited.

A post-Katrina visit to the restaurants of New Orleans, where eating out has become essential group therapy

by Corby Kummer

In December I had dinner with friends at Lilette, a French bistro with exceptionally polished food on Magazine Street, in New Orleans. The friends, the menu, and the well-heeled, old-line crowd were identical to those at a dinner I'd had at the same restaurant in late July. If anything, the room had a brighter gleam, and the food was even better than before—more focused, as if the cooks were taking a special, private pleasure in doing what they know how to do. The only visible differences from my visit five months earlier were the view through the plate-glass windows of lined-up branches, disembodied kitchen cabinets, and mattresses heaped on the sidewalk, and a bright-pink sign from the Office of Public Health taped to the front door: APPROVED FOR RE-OPENING FOLLOWING HURRICANE KATRINA.

Of course, much was very different. Our young waiter had run several city magazines that vanished with the storm; he came back because he didn't want to leave the city. Other friends at a table I later joined talked of how many times they had moved in the past three months, the gas and hot water that were still some-time things, and whether their jobs would continue and they could keep paying the rent, which rose after the storm. The bon-homie at our long table both masked and was fueled by their hav-ing no idea how long they could afford to live in the place they loved most.

This was how it went over several days of dining in New Orleans restaurants that had reopened as soon as they could: im-maculate food prepared and consumed with joy, need, and uncer-tainty. At August, a tony restaurant with what may be the most ambitious and original food in the city, Tywon Morgan, a host, prac-tically danced up and down the stairs between the kitchen and the banquet room. He explained when he stopped by our table. "Our first private party!" he said. "Sixty people! Business is coming back!"

He was reflecting the anxious optimism I had heard expressed by restaurant owners in recent days. They were hoping for cus-tomers in three waves of increasing magnitude: families and busi-ness people who would return for the opening of schools in January—the first test of how many residents would actually come back; revelers for Mardi Gras, which, everyone hoped, would kick-start the crucial tourist trade; and conventioneers, the biggest question mark of all, who would trickle back as early as spring.

John Besh, the chef and co-owner of August, cooked as if he were unconcerned. True, the city's wine supply had been badly de-pleted. "Definitely a post-K list," said Brett Anderson, the restau-rant critic of *TheTimes-Picayune* and my friend and guide, as he opened August's leather-bound wine menu. Lolis Eric Elie, a columnist for the paper and, like Anderson, a passionate, witty chronicler of city life since the storm, reminded him of the many wine cellars that had been lost completely, notably the 5,000 bot-tles at Susan Spicer's Bayona.

But the food was even better than what I had tasted in July. A plate of chilled seafood was startlingly fresh, with little cres-cents of Louisiana shrimp and beautifully sweet crabmeat in rav-igote sauce, the Tabasco-spiked mayonnaise that is a New

Orleans hallmark. Besh, who cooked at the elegant Windsor Court Hotel, across the street, made his name with nouvelle cuisine–influenced dishes based on solid French technique and using many local ingredients. I had, for instance, pumpkin soup drizzled with pumpkin-seed oil and garnished with crab flakes, and pheasant breaded with panko crumbs, sautéed and in a sweetish sauce reminiscent of Chinese food. But since the storm Besh had begun to include the dishes of his bayou youth and the city's heritage, such as that ravigote sauce and gumbo at Friday lunch, the Sunday supper of New Orleans.

Besh clearly saw a void that needed filling. He had made August an elegant and innovative alternative to Antoine's and Galatoire's, but neither of them had yet been able to reopen. Antoine's, the 800-seat landmark that claims to have invented crabmeat ravigote, lost its maître d', Clifton Lachney, who drowned with his son; the restaurant also suffered damage to a brick wall that would take months to repair. Galatoire's, which claims to be the home of shrimp remoulade, went ahead with long-contemplated plans to open a branch in Baton Rouge, promising to reopen its Bourbon Street flagship early in the new year.

This was outright treason in a city that had already suffered unexpected indignities: Emeril Lagasse, New Orleans's best-known chef, kept a low profile after the storm; the corporate owners of Ruth's Chris Steak House immediately pulled up stakes and moved their headquarters to Orlando, claiming that Ruth Fertel, the tireless and much-loved founder of the chain, would have pragmatically done the same. "It just isn't so," her son, Randy Fertel, said solemnly and angrily at an October conference of the Southern Foodways Alliance, in Oxford, Mississippi. The news from Galatoire's was particularly galling. "First the storm, then the floods," Anderson wrote when announcing the Baton Rouge defection. "Now hell is apparently freezing over."

Loyalty and the tug of home were what made most restaurants reopen, as families—both biological and collegial—reunited. In mid-September, JoAnn Clevenger, proprietor of the Garden District restaurant Upperline and a defender and champion of her city and its food, called her husband back from England, where he works half the year, and her son from St. Louis, where he teaches philosophy, to help with the cooking and to serve customers. Alex Patout, a well-known local chef, cooked on the line to help out. Tacked to the front of the airy, bright, tearoom-like restaurant were three shirt cardboards inscribed with "We're glad you're here!" The menu was simplified, but offered the kind of food I most want to eat, each dish speaking of local ingredients and local cuisine: fried green tomatoes with shrimp remoulade; duck and andouille gumbo; Cane River country shrimp with mushroom, bacon, and garlic served over crispy grits.

At the Southern Foodways Alliance conference, Clevenger had described the impossibility of finding people to work because housing was so rare, and recounted how neighborhood spirit helped people get up and running; she cheered on neighbors like Clancy's, an uptown hangout and the place Anderson went for his last meal before evacuating the city. Clancy's became one of the first restaurants to reopen, on October 17. Although it is owned by a native Iowan, Brad Hollingsworth, it has become practically a club for the multigeneration Garden District families who rely on its unfussy Creole food.

When I stopped by Clancy's, it was just past eleven, almost three hours before the city's curfew, but dinner service had ended, and the cooks and managers were having a nightcap at the bar. The place felt like a jazz club after hours, when the players swap stories and wind down. Everyone smoked. Nash Laurent, the maître d', put Armand Jonté, the guest chef, in a headlock to wish him good night. Jonté, whose Mississippi gulf house was swept to pilings, was working in the kitchen with Steve Manning, an old friend of his. The group talked fondly of the school-less high school teacher and the wine salesman who had both come in to wash dishes after the reopening. After a few laughs about regulars like the "vodka ladies," Michael Laurent, who had come back to help his father, brought the conversation around to where every conversation ended up or started. "Okay, who's living at their own house?" he asked. He and his family were living at his in-laws'. Only three hands went up.

Informal and formal networks are working to bring back the small eating places most at risk—the po' boy shops and gumbo dives that have always given the city its character. (I saw markedly more white faces in December than on any of my previous visits to the city over two decades.) The Southern Foodways Alliance in November announced a series of "volunteer vacation" weekends to help rebuild Willie Mae's Scotch House, a modest but legendary restaurant serving what many consider the city's finest fried chicken, made by the eighty-nine-year-old Willie Mae Seaton. "No experience is necessary!" the alliance promised, throwing in the incentive of dinners with Elie, the

Times-Picayune columnist, and the writer Pableaux Johnson
(whose recent *Eating New Orleans,* published last summer, is
now as much testament as guide).

The Brennans, the first family of New Orleans restaurateurs,
began trying to find jobs and housing for displaced workers immediately after the storm, operating a job Web site (at "www.
cirajobs.com) out of a family member's restaurant, Brennan's of
Houston. Dickie Brennan, owner of three French Quarter
restaurants, kept 400 workers on his payroll for five weeks after
the storm, while two employees worked full-time on the phone
to find out where people had landed and whether they would
come back, giving out all available information on how to file
FEMA and insurance claims.

When I visited Bourbon House, the first of Dickie Brennan's
three businesses to reopen, the ornate two-level restaurant was
bright and crowded, like something out of the Diamond Jim Brady
era; most of the customers were reconstruction workers and locals
who had come back, but I did notice a very few obvious tourists.
Bourbon House was the first in the French Quarter to serve fresh
Louisiana oysters again, and an owner of a well-established
seafood distributor stood behind the shucking bar for four nights
to reassure diners about safety. "People weren't concerned," Steve
Pettus, a managing partner, told me with surprise. "They were like,
'Gimme oysters.'" Pettus spoke of how good the fish was: "The guy
who catches catfish for us called up right away and said, 'I'm here,
I'm still fishing.'" Several chefs told me that the very lack of restaurants competing for the best ingredients helped them find even
better fish and seafood than usual. Local produce would be another matter; Brennan had already held a benefit for farmers
around Baton Rouge who had long supplied local restaurants. At-
tracting diners was no problem, he said. "You go outside the
restaurant and it's gloom and doom, it's hard work, it's a bad day
I'm having. You get inside and people see each other, hug each
other. Eating out is therapeutic."

On my last morning I began, as I had each previous day, with
biscuits from Mother's, a home-style Creole cafeteria near Canal
and Tchoupitoulas, and chicory-laced coffee from Café Du Monde,
a ten-minute walk away on Decatur Street, along the waterfront. I
noticed a landmark that hadn't been open before: Central Grocery,
an Italian-American emporium with imported pasta, cheeses, and
the city's premier muffulettas—cold-cut-stuffed hero sandwiches
on fat baguettes soaked with Central's famous olive salad. The

bread, the salad, and the sandwiches had been back for only three hours, I was told by Larry Tusa, one of the three owners. He and his family had been determined to reopen, he said, in time to celebrate the store's hundredth anniversary, on February 28.

Tusa used to live in the Lakeview neighborhood, very near the 17th Street Canal break. His house was ruined. A neighbor and friend since grade school had seen his wife drown; Tusa had counseled another friend against suicide. He would never go back to Lakeview, he said. Neither would his father, Charles, in his eighties, who plans to move to a condo on higher ground. "He worked all his life for this and this city," Tusa said, gesturing at the long, old-fashioned deli counter and the workers behind it—four of the original ten. "If I didn't have this business, I'd be in Houston with my daughter." But stay he would. "New Orleans is one of the gateways to the United States, and I don't think they should forget us. Don't give anybody false hopes. Commit to whatever it takes to rebuild."

On my way back to the hotel to pack, I stopped, distracted, at Aunt Sally's Praline Shop, one of the few souvenir shops to have reopened on the very touristy riverfront strip. The manager was on the phone; she covered the mouthpiece to call out to me, "Sir, is Central Grocery open?" I'd bought a jar of olive salad, and was carrying a bag showing the store's big green logo. Yes, I said, as of three hours ago. "Central's open!" she said excitedly into the phone. "You'll have lunch today."

Discussion/Writing Prompts

- At the heart of Kummer's portrait is a view of the public restaurant as both an eating venue and a kind of home: a gathering place for people to reconnect with each other. How do you react to this depiction? In your own experience, is it often the case that a restaurant can fulfill such a communal purpose? What is it about the typical restaurant that, in your view, works against this goal?

- Another one of Kummer's key claims here has to do with the power of food to serve as a social bond. In Kummer's view, sharing a meal, even with strangers at a restaurant, can foster a greater sense of connection and community. In a one-page essay, offer an evaluation of this claim. Is there a particular kind of eating experience that, in your view, confirms Kummer's argument? How closely does it resemble the portrait of restaurant life sketched in this essay?

- Kummer's depiction of the post-Katrina restaurant scene in New Orleans shares one thing in common with Dickerman's examination of mall culture: both writers focus on the phenomenon of "fine dining." It is here, however, that the similarity ends. In a one-page essay, offer an assessment of how these two portraits use this focus to differing ends. How does Dickerman use "fine dining" as a pretext for drawing particular conclusions about "commercialism" and "status"? And how does this approach differ from Kummer's description of "fine dining" and "community"? Which approach do you find more compelling? Why?

"The Deadly Little Secret: Candy Cigarettes," *The Big Fat Marketing Blog* (July 20, 2009) www.bigfatmarketingblog.com
PATTY ODELL

To many of us, candy cigarettes—those chocolate sticks crafted to look exactly like a pack of Lucky Strikes—are a thing of the past. As Odell reminds us, however, for some this iconic and problematic snack food is alive and well. Pondering what their enduring popularity says about the state of our current food culture, she presents the candy cigarette as an object lesson in the need for greater oversight and regulation of food marketing.

———————— ✦ ————————

> *"I was walking down the street in my hometown the other day and I saw a child walk out of a candy shop with a cigarette hanging from his mouth."*

I was walking down the street in my hometown the other day and I saw a child walk out of a candy shop with a cigarette hanging out of his mouth.

That would be a "Victory" cigarette, a look-alike candy version of the real deadly tobacco kind. If the brand name Victory sounds familiar, it should, its toxic similarity to Viceroy cigarettes made by Brown & Williamson can't be missed.

Where are those lawmakers stamping down on tobacco marketers, implementing tough legislation that gives the Food and Drug Administration sweeping control over how marketers package, manufacturer and market tobacco products?

The manufacturer of the candy the boy had, World Confections in Brooklyn, NY, markets the candies in packages that look just like packs of cigarettes with many of them named after tobacco products. Here's another example. Candy cigarettes called Lucky Lights sure sound like and look a lot like Lucky Strikes.

I stopped into the store to see how the owner was marketing them. There were none on any of the shelves. The packs were all hidden away behind the counter. So moms had to ask for them, signaling to kids that something wasn't exactly right, but whatever it was it was tantalizing, exciting, even daring.

The tobacco legislation is important. Ads for cigarettes and chew should be kept far away from young eyes and ears and if tobacco marketers can't do it on their own, there should be regulation and enforcement. But what about the marketers and manufacturers of candy cigarettes? They need to be regulated too.

As for that young boy on the street? He moved on, blowing imaginary smoke rings as he went.

Discussion/Writing Prompts

- In this day and age, it's easy to identify what is dangerous, even unethical, about marketing candy cigarettes to children. But what about the appeal this sort of product holds? According to Odell, the candy cigarette still carries a cache that makes it seem "tantalizing, exciting, even daring." How do you respond to this claim? In your view, does Odell's analysis adequately account for the enduring popularity of the candy cigarette? How or how not?

- Odell focuses much of her critique on those responsible for marketing and selling this product. Put yourself in the position of an advertiser tasked with creating an effective campaign for the candy cigarette. Then write a one-page essay in which you outline the particular strategy you would use to "sell" a buying public on the appeal of your product. Next, imagine yourself in the position of a public health official. In another one-page essay, present a description of the critique you think such an official would level against such an ad campaign.

- From a very different perspective, Odell's blog shares with Spurlock's essay an interest in exploring the ways advertising elicits and manipulates desire.

How do their respective treatments of this question compare? In what ways (if any) does Odell's indictment of candy cigarette marketing relate to Spurlock's critique of corporate advertising?

Tying It All Together: Assignments for Writing and Research

1. RHETORICAL ANALYSIS: "FOOD AS A CULTURAL SYMBOL"

Choose an advertisement designed to promote a particular food. This can be a print ad, TV commercial, billboard, Web site, even a brand or logo affixed to the product itself. Then write a three- to five-page essay in which you analyze the particular ways this food is presented as a stand-in or symbol for other ideas or values. First, identify the specific aspects of this ad—from its visual elements to the written text it includes—that, in your view, serve to turn this food into an image or metaphor. Next, speculate about why an advertiser might want to present its product in this particular way. Does this strategy enhance this product's appeal? If so, how? To whom? And finally, offer your own personal assessment of how effective this marketing strategy is. Do you find yourself convinced or compelled? How or how not?

2. PERSONAL REFLECTION: "KEEPING A SHOPPING LIST"

When we look at the countless tactics advertisers use to sell us food, how do we learn to distinguish the true messages from the false? For one week, keep a written record of all the food purchases you make: what you bought and where, how much you spent, etc. After each entry, present a quick description of how and where you have seen this particular product advertised. On television? In your favorite magazine? As a pop-up ad on a Web site? At the end of the week, spend some time looking over the list and descriptions you've put together. Then write a two- to three-page essay in which you reflect upon the role that advertising played in the selections you made. Based on this written record, what kind of influence over your shopping decisions would you say advertising exerted? And are you comfortable with this degree of influence? How or how not?

3. COMPARE AND CONTRAST: "CONSUMING FOOD/CONSUMER CULTURE"

Each of the readings assembled here invites us to think about the ways our personal eating choices are shaped, framed, or otherwise influenced by our larger commercial culture. Choose two readings from this chapter that, in your view, offer contrasting views on this phenomenon. Then write a three- to five-page essay in which you outline the key differences between them. What larger attitude toward or conclusion about commercial culture does each essay present? And what specific claims does each make to support its particular view? Finally, present a brief explanation of which critique you find most effective or convincing, and why.

4. VISUAL ANALYSIS: "FOOD AND DESIRE"

A number of the selections above examine the ways our commercial culture attempts to foster and channel consumer "desire." Choose a commercial image of food from our current media. Then in a two- to three-page essay identify and analyze the specific ways this image seems designed to spur "desire" on the part of its viewers. What specific attitudes toward or feelings about this particular food does this image attempt to foster in its audience? And what particular aspects of the image seem designed to achieve this goal? And finally, how does this intended goal compare to your own reaction? Does this image succeed in fostering your desire for this product? How or how not?

5. ARGUMENT-BASED/PERSUASIVE WRITING: "CRITIQUING COMMERCIALISM"

One of the unspoken questions underlying this chapter is whether there exists any viable alternative to our current commercialized approach to eating. If the mass production and mass marketing of food poses such stark problems, should we spend more time developing an alternative relationship to what we eat? Write a three- to five-page essay in which you argue either for or against this proposition. In your estimation, is our current commercialized food system so problematic, even harmful, that it needs to be changed? If so, why? And what alternative model would you promote in its stead? If not, what aspects or features of the current system make it worth preserving? And why?

CHAPTER 3

Body Image

OUR BODIES/OURSELVES

It is a commonplace that eating, as the activity perhaps most closely related to issues of health and nutrition, focuses our attention on the internal dynamics of our bodies. In ways no less consequential, however, eating also orients us in the opposite direction, toward those external concerns that often get gathered under the heading of "body image." Taking up this focus, this chapter explores the complex role that eating and food play in shaping how we look at and think about, work on and worry over, our physical appearance. What, we ask, are the specific expectations and standards that in our culture define how we are and are not supposed to look. How do these norms influence the way others see us? The way we see ourselves? And to what extent, finally, does eating, in particular, offer us a vehicle for navigating this tricky terrain?

Few assumptions are more ingrained these days than the idea that we need to be vigilant observers of our own bodies. Whether it be the thin body or the fit body, the youthful body or the healthy body, our culture is replete with different "looks" that get promoted as an ideal to which we are expected to aspire. But where exactly do these definitions and standards come from? And by what process do we learn to regard the particular body types they proscribe as so admirable, so desirable, so right for ourselves? In answering such questions, we might begin by stating the obvious: the rules in place dictating how our bodies are supposed to look are not ones we have come up with all on our own. From fitness magazines to diet fads, fashion catalogues to FDA guidelines, our media landscape is littered with different (cultural, social, scientific) messages, each of which functions as a kind of tutorial in the "proper" body image it is supposedly our duty to adopt as our own. To the extent that we do, we respond to these sorts of instructions because embedded within them is a powerful, if often unspoken, promise: namely, that conforming our appearance to their proscriptions will bring clear and tangible pay-offs. Whether it be an increased sense of our own attractiveness, the greater admiration of our peers, or the prospect of a longer life, living up to our culture's body image ideals is, we are told, *good* for us—a decision that not only enhances how we look but also enriches who and what we are.

WATCHING WHAT WE EAT: BODY TYPE, BODY IMAGE AND THE CULTURAL FUNCTION OF FOOD

It doesn't take a lot of effort to see how intimately connected all of this is to how and what we eat. Indeed the choices we make around food could well be said to lie at the very heart of our culture's current obsession with body image. We are all familiar with the cliché "you are what you eat." But when we consider this nostrum in the context of our cultural obsession with "looks," we begin to see that it contains more than a grain of truth. For starters, there is the obvious physiological link between eating and appearance. Whether we choose to limit our sugar intake or go "carb free," commit to a vegan diet or opt for a steady intake of red meat, the decisions we make regarding food have a direct and tangible impact on the shape our bodies assume. Beyond this, however, are the myriad social and psychological consequences our food-related choices carry. As we have already seen, eating is more than a physical act, designed simply to satisfy the objective demands of our body or the subjective stimuli of our personal taste. It is also a profoundly cultural undertaking, one that, like it or not, brings us directly into contact with the ways we have been taught to define, appraise, and rank different body types—and by extension each other. To adhere to an eating regimen that results, for example, in a leaner physique is to find ourselves subject to a very different set of assumptions (about our character as well as our attractiveness, our social as well as our physical merits) than to follow, say, a diet loaded with sugars and fats. Regardless of how misguided or unfair it may be, we live in a world where physical appearance and self-worth have become deeply entwined, if not outright synonymous, where being deemed to have an acceptable or attractive body has become the necessary precursor to being seen as (socially or physically, medically or morally) "better." Whether we accept this formula or fight against it, the conjunction between outward appearance and personal value it establishes has long since cemented itself as an indisputable fact of our daily lives: a culturally mandated expectation we may decry but must nonetheless negotiate.

This is not to say that, every time we sit down at a restaurant or at the kitchen counter, concerns about our physical appearance are automatically uppermost in our mind. Chances are we don't approach the question "what's for dinner?" as if it were merely an occasion for calculating the particular body image we want to display. But by the same token, neither is it true that our eating choices remain blissfully unaffected by such concerns. It would be naïve in the extreme to claim that our attitudes about and approach to food bear no relation at all to the countless messages we encounter telling us the "right" and "wrong" ways we are supposed to look. Willingly or not, as eaters we are all part of our culture's larger visual economy—so much a part in fact that disentangling our personal tastes from larger societal standards about appearance can often be a very difficult business. When we forgo a second helping of pasta or take pains to consume the requisite daily amount of leafy green vegetables, where exactly does the consideration about being healthy end and the desire for looking trim begin? Likewise when we opt for the double-chocolate milkshake after work or say yes to the slice of cake at a birthday party. While clearly choices that express our own individual food preferences, they are also decisions that put us square up against the prevailing ideals in our world decreeing what our proper weight or appropriate physique should be. For better or worse, it would seem, eating invariably performs this kind of double duty.

THE PICTURE OF HEALTH: EATING, DIET, AND BODY IMAGE

To illustrate, let's turn to a specific example. Consider the following hypothetical scenario. After consulting with your doctor, let's say you are considering embarking on a new diet designed to lower your overall cholesterol level. As you are mulling over this decision, you find yourself in a number of conversations with friends and family members, each of whom offers her or his own testimonial to the benefits of following a low-fat, high-fiber eating regimen. These conversations, furthermore, follow on the heels of a new exercise book you've just finished reading, one that itemizes advantages of combining a regular exercise routine with a comprehensive low-fat diet. And to top it off, just yesterday you caught the tail end a news report on the radio detailing the latest scientific findings about diet, fat, and long-term life expectancy. Taken together, the combined message of all this feedback couldn't be clearer: changing your eating habits in this way is well worth doing because it will be such an obvious boon to your health.

But consider what could easily happen next. Using your doctor's suggestions and the recipes included in your exercise book as a guide, you start your new diet. Following its instructions to the letter, you reduce your consumption of processed foods and red meat, and increase your daily intake of leafy greens and high-fiber foods. And sure enough, after several weeks you begin to feel an undeniable boost in your physical well-being: you have more energy, you sleep more soundly, your overall mood improves. And perhaps most importantly, on your return visit your doctor reports a measurable decrease in your overall cholesterol levels. Your diet, in short, seems to be working exactly as planned. Little by little, however, you begin to notice that the improvements wrought by this diet register themselves not only in how you *feel* but also in how you are *seen*. Indeed by the end of the first month, acquaintances of all stripes have taken to commenting regularly on your "new and improved" appearance: your svelte physique, reduced waist size, increased muscle tone. Prompted by such gratifying response, you start to take a more conscious, active interest in your public image. You now linger a moment or two in front of the mirror in the morning and catch glimpses of your reflection as you pass by a store window. At the same time, it also begins to dawn on you how often some version of this self-same body type gets showcased—on magazine covers at the grocery line checkout, on billboards promoting the newest blockbuster movie, on Web sites detailing the "real-life" escapades of cavorting celebrities—as an emblem of attractiveness, glamour, and success. By the end of the second month, in fact, the pleasure of hearing your newfound physical appearance praised by friends and seeing it promoted as a media ideal has grown so familiar that maintaining this image has come to overshadow your original health concerns as the primary motivation for continuing the diet altogether. Gradually but undeniably, you've stopped consulting doctors' advice and nutrition manuals for guidance about what to eat, and started basing your food decisions on their potential for maintaining your new look. Somewhere along the line, eating itself has morphed from a strategy for ensuring your bodily well-being into a tactic for constructing and exhibiting your body image.

To be sure, the foregoing example is only speculation. No doubt every one of us can cite a moment from our own experience that makes the opposite point: a moment where we successfully resisted the lure of our culture's siren song about appearance, beauty, and body image. Speculative or not, however, this hypothetical scenario does underscore how complex our choices about eating and food can become when they are made in a world where health and looks are so thoroughly intermingled. Indeed this very complexity confronts us with a crucial question. Does it make more sense to think of our eating choices as an empowering tool, a way of "talking back" to a larger culture bent on shaping our public appearance to its own preconceptions? Or are these choices better understood as an act of conformity, evidence of how fully we have internalized our culture's edicts and expectations about our bodies? Is eating an instrument for exercising our right to self-expression, or an ingrained set of habits through which we slot ourselves into predetermined or "pre-digested" stereotypes? What makes this question so vexing, of course, is that in either case, the answer could easily be "yes." Whether we are aware of it or not, when we choose a particular food based on its taste or health benefits, we are also making a decision that carries concrete consequences for how we are viewed and judged by those around us. Given this unavoidable fact, it would seem to be of more than minor importance to understand how much ownership over our body image eating actually gives us: to know whether our food-related choices help us to become the owners and authors of our own public image or whether they instead simply script us according to the models created by forces beyond our control.

COSTS AND CONSEQUENCES: LIVING INSIDE OUR CULTURE'S BODY IDEALS

This, of course, is more than merely a rhetorical question. In many respects, the stakes involved in whether we emulate or evade, embrace or spurn our culture's proscribed body types couldn't be higher. As we've already noted, the benefits we are told will flow from cultivating one of our culture's ideal looks are legion. Some are emotional or psychological: the boost in self-esteem, the heightened self-image that, we are led to believe, will effortlessly follow from being viewed as attractive, fit, or beautiful. Other advantages are more social in nature, having to do with boosts in stature or prestige, popularity or rank that such looks are presumed to yield. Still other benefits play themselves out in professional or economic terms. There is no shortage of studies, for example, that document the effects of image-specific biases upon different workplace pecking orders. Across the spectrum, employees regarded as more conventionally attractive, we have learned, are more likely to be hired, are often promoted more quickly, and even enjoy higher rates of compensation than their counterparts.

Ranged against such putative pay-offs are the tolls these standards can exact. At the most fundamental level, for instance, we could easily question the beneficence of a world in which so prominent a part of who we are is predicated on how we look. What gets lost in a system that teaches us to focus so intently and exclusively on our external appearance? What other ways of measuring our self-worth, of defining our identity, does such a formula encourage us to overlook? In addition, we could also pose some hard questions about the essential fairness of this arrangement. On what basis (if any) is it possible to defend a set of standards that apportion the benefits of different body images in such patently unjust and arbitrary ways? Beyond basic considerations over equity, furthermore, we might also extend our inquiry into the more particular kinds of harm these standards also inflict. To put it mildly, not all of the emotional, physical, or social consequences of navigating our culture's body ideals are benign. From social stigmatization to clinical depression, the consequences for both those who pursue or reject our culture's prevailing body image ideals can be extreme and debilitating. Witness our current societal epidemic of eating disorders, a crisis which is at least partly the result of our relentless celebration of thinness as a physical and a social ideal. Indeed when viewed through the lens of diseases such as these, the cultural standards around body image could well be said to look like their own kind of malady: a symptom of how "disordered" our dominant ideas about appearance and image truly are.

While they span a range of issues and limn a variety of contexts, the readings assembled below can be read as an extended attempt to make sense of precisely these consequences: to sort through the benefits and the costs, the promise and the pitfalls of our culture's overdetermined connection between eating and appearance. Culled from an array of sources—journalism pieces to scholarly studies, personal memoirs to Web ads—each invites us to consider the ways eating serves as an instrument for shaping our public image. Taking a closer look at the specific topics and issues each of these selections raises, this chapter organizes our investigation around three discrete, interrelated questions. First, the relationship between what/how we eat and how we look (i.e., between our actual eating practices and the particular body type they help produce). Second, the relationship between our own individual body type and the body image ideals that get promoted within our larger culture (i.e., how our respective physical appearance gets appraised and ranked in relation to our society's prevailing standards). And third, the effect these body image ideals have on the ways we view ourselves (i.e., how these cultural standards influence or inform our own sense of who and what we are).

Along the way, we will also uncover the range of other issues (social, cultural, political, economic, psychological, ethical) to which our eating and body image norms are connected. Whatever its individual purview, each of the selections below is motivated by an awareness that in our world the question of "how we look" is always more than purely personal. Cultural mandates around our physical appearance lie at the heart of some of the most fundamental aesthetic, social, and moral distinctions we are taught to make: between beauty and ugliness, health and sickness, virtue and vice. They underwrite some of our most urgent contemporary debates—over celebrity and commercialism, exercise and fitness, technology and medicine—and shape our fundamental assumptions about power and privilege, money and social rank.

"How to Address Obesity in a Fat-Phobic Society," *AlterNet.org* (Oct. 17, 2007)
COURTNEY E. MARTIN

Taking a closer look at our current cultural obsession with obesity, Martin argues that our understanding of this "health crisis" derives as much from media messages and social stereotypes as from sound medical evidence. Looking squarely at the cultural biases that feed into the public fear of "fatness," she argues for a more measured and scientifically informed approach to resolving this social and medical problem.

———————— ✦ ————————

"It's time to stop treating obesity as the problem of a lazy individual."

A friend of mine—I'll call her Ellen—recently went to her regular medical clinic after realizing that she was newly suffering from an old family problem: acid reflux. Her doctor was out on maternity leave, so she met with a replacement. Without asking Ellen any questions about her relationship to her weight (she is overweight and well aware of it), he launched into a robotic exposition about dieting.

Ellen explained to him that she worked out regularly and also did her best to eat healthy, but had a philosophical problem with turning food into the enemy. He simply retorted: "The only way you're going to lose weight is to cut the carbs. So . . . cut the carbs."

"When he brought up my weight I wanted to have a real conversation with him, but instead he gave me his version of my 'problem'," Ellen said. "It made me really angry."

My friend's experience is not an anomaly. In fact, it is representative of a still unchanged attitude among too many medical doctors and nutritionists that fat people are problems to be solved; if they can just come up with the perfect equation, they figure, BMIs can be lowered and the supposed obesity epidemic eradicated.

This attitude shows up in doctor's offices where overweight and obese patients are often subjected to inquisition-like questioning. Yet they are rarely asked other, arguably more important questions: *What's your experience of your body? How is your quality of life? How do you feel about your weight?*

It also shows up in obesity intervention programs throughout the country, where a person's culture, class, education, or even genetics, are overlooked in the dogged pursuit to motivate what too many clinicians see as "lazy Americans" to lose pounds.

It's not as if we don't have the evidence that these factors—culture, class, education, genetics—matter. Yet another *study* just came out by University of Washington researchers who found gaping disparities in obesity rates among ZIP codes in the Seattle area. Every $100,000 in median home value for a ZIP code corresponded with a 2 percent drop in obesity.

Adam Drewnowski, director of the UW Center for Obesity Research, told the Seattle Post-Intelligencer, "If you have this mind-set that obesity has to do with the individual alone, then ZIP codes or areas really should not come into this. But they do, big-time."

This is not to say that individual behavior doesn't play a vital role in our country's obesity rate, but we too often neglect to think about the cultural and institutional influences on a person's behavior when it comes to eating and exercise.

You would never look at a working class, single mother driving a jalopy with three kids crawling around in the back and say, "Gees, what's her problem? Why can't she drive the Lexus hybrid like me?" You understand that she doesn't have the means, and furthermore, probably doesn't have the peer influence that would make it seem like a viable option.

Our judgmental, fat-phobic society seems even more ridiculous when you consider that there is a strong genetic component to weight. We now have ample scientific evidence suggesting that we are each born with a set point within which our metabolism will automatically adjust no matter how many calories we consume. It's like our working class mom could be dedicatedly saving up for that hybrid, but the money just keeps disappearing from her bank account.

Instead of vilifying fat people, this country needs to look long and hard at the roots of our obesity epidemic. While we can't change someone's genetics, we can work to change the institutional disparities that make maintaining a healthy weight difficult for people with less money. Encouraging supermarkets to open up in poor neighborhoods by adjusting zoning laws and creating tax-incentive programs is a start. More funding for public schools in low-income areas would translate into better quality food in the cafeterias and more nutrition and physical education.

In addition to addressing these classist systems, we need to do some soul searching about our own attitudes about fat. Until those of us who care about public health can truly separate the potential health risks of being overweight from our own internalized stigmas about fat, we won't be effective. We have to learn to distinguish between those who are satisfied with their current body size and those who wants to lose weight, and then, learn to provide complex guidance that takes societal and genetic factors into account.

Those in the field of public health need to remember how motivation really works (hint: not by coercion or humiliation) and rethink how quality of life is measured when it comes to overweight patients. It is not the clinician's—often prejudiced, frequently rushed—point of view that matters most, but the individual's.

Dr. Janell Mensinger, the Director of the Clinical Research Unit at The Reading Hospital & Medical Center, also recommends shifting the goals of obesity intervention programs: "Focusing on health indicators such as blood pressure, cholesterol, blood sugar would serve to de-stigmatize obese individuals and help them engage in better eating habits and physical activity for the purpose of healthier living as opposed to simply being thinner. Although I see some programs shifting in this direction, I don't think they have gone far enough."

Mensinger adds, "We have to avoid promoting the dieting mentality! Encourage acceptance of all shapes and sizes while promoting the importance of physical activity and eating well for the purpose of living and feeling better, mentally and physically. The people that most successfully achieve this goal are those with an expertise in eating disorders as well as obesity. They know best what can happen if the message is misconstrued."

Whether you are a primary care provider, a nurse practitioner, a nutritionist, or a community health advocate, I urge you to treat your next patient like a living, breathing human being with complicated feelings, economic concerns, and cultural affiliations. Weight loss isn't the ultimate goal; economic equality, cultural diversity, wellness and happiness are.

Discussion/Writing Prompts

- Martin begins her essay by recounting her friend's experience at the doctor's office. Why do you think she chooses to begin this way? Does this focus on medical professionals and medical settings preview the larger argument Martin is making about our cultural attitudes toward obesity?
- How do you respond to Martin's characterization of our society as "fat-phobic"? What does this term mean to you? And, in your view, does it accurately capture prevailing public attitudes concerning bodies, weight, and body image? How or how not?
- Even though it addresses our culture's obsession with weight from the opposite end of the spectrum, Hornbacher's essay makes its own points about the ways we are taught to think about "being fat." How does Hornbacher's argument compare to Martin's? In your view, do they offer a similar or contrasting critique of our attitudes toward being overweight?

"Childhood," in *Wasted:* *A Memoir of Anorexia and Bulimia* (2006)

MARYA HORNBACHER

In this harrowing account of her childhood struggles with anorexia and bulimia, Hornbacher details the small, at times even imperceptible, ways that an obsession with being "thin" can take over one's life. Recounting the personal, familial, and social pressures that gave rise to these diseases, Hornbacher offers her own childhood experiences as a cautionary tale about the ways our culture more generally can foster "disordered" relationships to food and eating.

———————— ✦ ————————

"I remember my body from the outside in. It makes me sad when I think about it, to hate that body so much."

"Well, it's no use your talking about waking him," said Tweedledum, "when you're only one of the things in his dream. You know very well you're not real."

"I am real!" said Alice, and began to cry.

"You won't make yourself a bit realer by crying," Tweedledee remarked: "there's nothing to cry about."

"If I wasn't real," Alice said—half laughing through her tears, it all seemed so ridiculous— "I shouldn't be able to cry."

"I hope you don't think those are real tears?" Tweedledee interrupted in a tone of great contempt.
—Lewis Carroll, *Alice's Adventures in Wonderland*

It was that simple: One minute I was your average nine-year-old, shorts and a T-shirt and long brown braids, sitting in the yellow kitchen, watching *Brady Bunch* reruns, munching on a bag of Fritos, scratching the dog with my foot. The next minute I was walking, in a surreal haze I would later compare to the hum induced by speed, out of the kitchen, down the stairs, into the bathroom, shutting the door, putting the toilet seat up, pulling my braids back with one hand, sticking my first two fingers down my throat, and throwing up until I spat blood.

Flushing the toilet, washing my hands and face, smoothing my hair, walking back up the stairs of the sunny, empty house, sitting down in front of the television, picking up my bag of Fritos, scratching the dog with my foot.

How did your eating disorder start? the therapists ask years later, watching me pick at my nails, curled up in a ball in an endless series of leather chairs. I shrug. Hell if I know, I say.

I just wanted to see what would happen. Curiosity, of course, killed the cat.

It wouldn't hit me, what I'd done, until the next day in school. I would be in the lunchroom of Concord Elementary, Edina, Minnesota, sitting among my prepubescent, gangly friends, hunched over painful nubs of breasts and staring at my lunch tray. I would realize that, having done it once, I'd have to keep doing it. I would panic. My head would throb, my heart do a little arrhythmic dance, my newly imbalanced chemistry making it seem as though the walls were tilting, the floor undulating beneath my penny-loafered feet. I'd push my tray away. Not hungry, I'd say. I did not say: I'd rather starve than spit blood.

And so I went through the looking glass, stepped into the netherworld, where up is down and food is greed, where convex mirrors cover the walls, where death is honor and flesh is weak. It is ever so easy to go. Harder to find your way back.

I look back on my life the way one watches a badly scripted action flick, sitting at the edge of the seat, bursting out, "No, no, don't open that door! The bad guy is in there and he'll grab you and put his hand over your mouth and tie you up and then you'll miss the train and everything will fall apart!" Except there is no bad guy in this tale. The person who jumped through the door and grabbed me and tied me up was, unfortunately, me. My double image, the evil skinny chick who hisses, *Don't eat. I'm not going to let you eat. I'll let you go as soon as you're thin, I swear I will. Everything will be okay when you're thin.*

Liar. She never let me go. And I've never quite been able to wriggle my way free.

CALIFORNIA

Five years old. Gina Lucarelli and I are standing in my parents' kitchen, heads level with the countertops, searching for something to eat. Gina says, You guys don't have any normal food. I say apologetically, I know. My parents are weird about food. She asks, Do you have any chips? No. Cookies? No. We stand together, staring into the refrigerator. I announce, We have peanut butter. She pulls it out, sticks a grimy finger into it, licks it off. It's weird, she says. I know, I say. It's unsalted. She makes a face, says, Ick. I agree. We stare into the abyss of food that falls into two categories: Healthy Things and Things We Are Too Short to Cook—carrots, eggs, bread, nasty peanut butter, alfalfa sprouts, cucumbers, a six-pack of Diet Lipton Iced Tea in blue cans with a little yellow lemon above the word *Tea*. Tab in the pink can. I offer, We could have toast. She peers at the bread and declares, It's brown. We put the bread back. I say, inspired, We have cereal! We go to the cupboard, the one by the floor. We stare at the cereal. She says, It's weird. I say, I know. I pull out a box, look at the nutritional information, run my finger down the side and authoritatively note, It only has five grams of sugar in it. I stick my chin up and brag, We don't eat sugar cereals. They make you *fat*. Gina, competitive, says, I wouldn't even eat that. I wouldn't eat anything with more than *two* grams of sugar. I say, Me neither, put the cereal back, as if it's contaminated. I bounce up from the floor, stick my tongue out at Gina. *I'm* on a *diet*, I say. Me too, she says, face screwing up in a scowl. Nuh-uh, I say. Uh-huh, she retorts. I turn my back and say, Well, I wasn't hungry *anyway*. Me neither, she says. I go to the fridge, make a show of taking out a Diet Lipton Iced Tea with Little Yellow Lemon, pop it open, sip loudly, *tttthhhppptt*. It tastes like sawdust, dries out my mouth. See? I say, pointing to *Diet*, I'm gonna be as thin as my mom when I grow up.

I think of Gina's mom, who I know for a *fact* buys sugar cereal. I know because every time I sleep over there we have Froot Loops for breakfast, the artificial colors turning the milk red. Gina and I suck it up with straws, seeing who can be louder.

Your mom, I say out of pure spite, *is fat*.

Gina says, At least my mom knows how to *cook*.

At least my mom has *a job*, I shout.

At least my mom is *nice*, she sneers.

I clock her. She cries. Baby, I say. I flounce out onto the deck, climb onto the picnic table, pull on my blue plastic Mickey Mouse sunglasses, imagining mat I am the sophisticated bathing suit lady in the Diet Lipton Iced Tea commercials, tan and long and thin. I lean back casually, lift the can to my mouth. I begin to take a bitter sip and spill it all over my shirt.

That night, while my father is cooking dinner, I lean against his knees and announce, I'm not hungry. I'm on a diet. My father laughs. Feet dangling from my chair at the table, I stare at the food, push it around, glance surreptitiously at my mother's plate, her nervous little bites. The way she leans back in her chair, setting down her fork to gesture rapidly with her hands as she speaks. My father, bent over his plate, eating in huge bites. My mother shoves her dinner away, precisely half eaten. My father tells her she wastes food, that he hates the way she always wastes food. My mother snaps back defensively, I'm full, *dear.* Glares. I push my plate away, say loudly, I'm full.

And all eyes turn to me. Come on, Piglet, says my mother. A few more bites.Two more, she says.

Three, says my father. They glare at each other.

I eat a pea.

I was never normal about food, even as a baby. My mother was unable to breast-feed me because it made her feel as if she were being devoured. I was allergic to cow's milk, soy milk, rice milk. My parents had to feed me a vile concoction of ground lamb and goat's milk that made them both positively ill. Apparently I guzzled it up. Later they gave me orange juice in a bottle, which rotted my teeth. I suspect that I may not even have been normal about food in utero; my mother's eating habits verge on the bizarre. As a child, I had endless food allergies. Sugar, food coloring, and preservatives sent me into hyperactive orbit, sleepless and wild for days. My parents were usually good about making sure that we had dinner together, that I ate three meals a day, that I didn't eat too much junk food and ate my vegetables. They were also given to sudden fits of paranoid "healthy eating," or fast-food eating, or impulsive decisions to dine out at 11 P.M. (as I slid under the table, asleep).

I have had moments of appearing normal: eating pizza at girl-hood slumber parties, a cream puff on Valentine's Day when I was nine, a grilled cheese sandwich as I hung upside down off the big black chair in the living room when I was four. It is only now, in context, that these things seem strange—the fact that I remember, in detail, the pepperoni pizza, the way we all ostentatiously blotted the grease with our paper napkins, and how many slices I ate (two), and how many slices every other girl ate (two, except for Leah, who ate one, and Joy, who ate four), and the frantic fear that followed, that my rear end had somehow expanded and now was busting out of my shortie pajamas. I remember begging my mother to make cream puffs. I remember that before the cream puffs we had steak and peas. I also recall my mother making grilled cheese sandwiches or scrambled eggs for me on Saturday afternoons when everything was quiet and calm. They were special because *she* made them, and so I have always associated grilled cheese sandwiches and scrambled eggs with quiet and my mother and calm. Some people who are obsessed with food become gourmet chefs. Others get eating disorders.

I have never been normal about my body. It has always seemed to me a strange and foreign entity. I don't know that there was ever a time when I was not conscious of it. As far back as I can think, I was aware of my corporeality, my physical imposition on space.

My first memory is of running away from home for no particular reason when I was three. I remember walking along Walnut Boulevard, in Walnut Creek, California, picking roses from other peoples' front yards. My father, furious and worried, caught me. I remember being carted home by the arm and spanked, for the first and last time in my life. I hollered like hell that he was mean and rotten, and then hid in the clothes hamper in my mother's closet. I remember being delighted that I was precisely the right *size* to fit in the clothes hamper so I could stay there forever and ever. I sat there in the dark like a mole, giggling. I remember the whole thing as if I were *watching* myself: I see me being spanked from across the room, I see me hiding in the hamper from above. It's as if a part of my brain had split off and was keeping an eye on me, making sure I knew how I looked at all times.

I feel as if a small camera was planted on my body, recording for posterity a child bent over a scraped knee, a child pushing her food around her plate, a child with her foot on the floor while her half-brother tied her shoe, a child leaning over her mother's chair as her mother did magic things with cotton and lace. Dresses, like angels, appeared and fluttered from a hanger on the door. A child in the bathtub, looking down at her body submerged in the water as if it were a separate thing inexplicably attached to her head.

My memory of early life veers back and forth from the sensate to the disembodied, from specific recall of the smell of my grandmother's perfume to one of slapping my own face because I thought it was fat and ugly, seeing the red print of my hand but not feeling the pain. I do not remember very many things from the inside out. I do not remember what it felt like to touch things, or how bathwater traveled over my skin. I did not like to be touched, but it was a strange dislike. I did not like to be touched because I craved it too much. I wanted to be held very tight so I would not break. Even now, when people lean down to touch me, or hug me, or put a hand on my shoulder, I hold my breath. I turn my face. I want to cry.

I remember the body from the outside in. It makes me sad when I think about it, to hate that body so much. It was just a typical little girl body, round and healthy, given to climbing, nakedness, the hungers of the flesh. I remember wanting. And I remember being at once afraid and ashamed that I wanted. I felt like yearning was specific to me, and the guilt that it brought was mine alone.

Somehow, I learned before I could articulate it that the body—my body—was dangerous. The body was dark and possibly dank, and maybe dirty. And silent, the body was silent, not to be spoken of. I did not trust it. It seemed treacherous. I watched it with a wary eye.

I will learn, later, that this is called "objectification consciousness." There will be copious research on the habit of women with eating disorders perceiving themselves through other eyes, as if there were some Great Observer looking over their shoulder. Looking, in particular, at their bodies and finding, more and more often as they get older, countless flaws.

I remember my entire life as a progression of mirrors. My world, as a child, was defined by mirrors, storefront windows, hoods of cars. My face always peered back at me, anxious, checking for a hair out of place, searching for anything that was different, shorts hiked up or shirt untucked, butt too round or thighs too soft, belly sucked in hard. I started holding my breath to keep my stomach concave when I was five, and at times, even now, I catch myself doing it. My mother, as I scuttled along sideways beside her like a crab, staring into every reflective surface, would sniff and say, Oh, Marya. You're so vain.

That, I think, was inaccurate. I was not seeking my image in the mirror out of vain pride. On the contrary, my vigilance was something else—both a need to see that I appeared, on the surface at least, acceptable, and a need for reassurance that I was still *there.*

I was about four when I first fell into the mirror. I sat in front of my mother's bathroom mirror singing and playing dress up by myself, digging through my mother's huge magical box of stage makeup that sighed a musty perfumed breath when you opened its brass latch. I painted my face with elaborate greens and blues on the eyes, bright streaks of red on the cheeks, garish orange lipstick, and then I stared at myself in the mirror for a long time. I suddenly felt a split in my brain: I didn't recognize her. I divided into two: the self in my head and the girl in the mirror. It was a strange, not unpleasant feeling of disorientation, dissociation. I began to return to the mirror often, to see if I could get that feeling back. If I sat very still and thought: Not me-not me-not me over and over, I could retrieve the feeling of being two girls, staring at each other through the glass of the mirror.

I didn't know then that I would eventually have that feeling all the time. Ego and image. Body and brain. The "mirror phase" of child development took on new meaning for me. "Mirror phase" essentially describes my life.

Mirrors began to appear everywhere. I was four, maybe five years old, in dance class. The studio, up above Main Street, was lined with mirrors that reflected Saturday morning sun, a hoard of dainty little girls in baby blue leotards, and me. I had on a brand-new blue leotard, not baby blue, but bright blue. I stuck out like an electric blue thumb, my ballet bun always coming undone. I was standing at the barre, looking at my body repeated and repeated and repeated, me in my blue leotard standing there, suddenly horrified, trapped in the many-mirrored room.

I am not a waif. Not now, not then. I'm solid. Athletic. A mesomorph: little fat, lot of muscle. I can kick a ball pretty casually from one end of a soccer field to the other, or bloody a guy's nose without really trying, and if you hit me real hard in the stomach you'd probably break your hand. In other words I am built for boxing, not ballet.[1] I came that way—even baby pictures show my solid diapered self tramping through the roses, tilted forward, headed for the gate. But at four I stood, a tiny Eve, choked with mortification at my body, the curve and plane of belly and thigh. At four I realized that I simply would not do. My body, being solid, was too much. I went home from dance class that day, put on one of my father's sweaters, curled up on my bed, and cried. I crept into the kitchen that evening as my parents were making dinner, the corner of the counter just above my head. I remember telling them, barely able to get the sour confession past my lips: I'm fat.

---

[1]There are few classes for four-year-old female would-be boxers, and I think my parents were trying to get me to be slightly more graceful (bull-in-china-shop syndrome).

Since I was nothing of the sort, my parents had no good reason to think that I honest-to-god *believed* that. They both made the face, a face I would learn to despise, that *oh please Marya don't be ridiculous* face, and made the sound, a terrible sound, that dismissive sound, *ttch*. They kept making dinner. I slapped my little-kid belly hard, burst into tears. My mother's face, pinched in distaste, shot me a glance that I would later come to think of as the bug zapper face, as if by looking at me, she could zap me into disappearance. *Tzzzt*. I kicked the cupboards near my feet, and she warned: Watch it. I slunk to my room.

And I remember the women's gym that my mother carted me along to. In front of the gym, I seem to remember a plastic statue of Venus de Milo, missing half a breast and both arms. The inside foreshadowed the 1980s "fitness" craze: women bopping around, butt busting and doggie leg lifting, sweating, wearing that pinched, panicky expression that conveyed the sentiment best captured by Galway Kinnell: "as if there is a hell and they will find it." The club also had something called the Kiddie Koral. The Kiddie Koral was a cage. It had bars all the way up to the ceiling, and the sticky-fingered little varmints clung to the bars sobbing for Mommy. Mommy was wearing some stupid bathing suit contraption, lurching around on the floor with a bunch of skinny ladies, getting all bony and no fun to sit on anymore. All the little kiddies in the kiddie cage wept and argued over the one ball provided for our endless entertainment. I managed to unhook the door of the cage, a door of wrought iron bars, and stand on it, swinging back and forth as I watched my mother and the rest of these women hop and lurch after some state of grace.

I remember watching my mother and the rest of these women's bodies reflected in the mirrors that lined the walls. Many many mad-looking ladies. Organizing them in my head, mentally lining them up in order of prettiness, hair color, bathing suit contraption color, and the most entertaining, in order of thinness.

I would do a very similar thing, some ten years later, while vacationing at a little resort called the Methodist Hospital Eating Disorders Institute. Only this time the row of figures I lined up in my head included my own, and, bony as we were, none of us were bopping around. We were doing cross-stitch, or splayed on the floor playing solitaire, scrutinizing one another's bodies from the corners of our eyes, in a manner similar to the way women at a gym are wont to do, as they glance from one pair of hips to their own. Finding themselves, always, excessive. Taking more than their fair share of space.

Discussion/Writing Prompts

- "I was never normal about food," Hornbacher confesses at the beginning of her story. What do you think she means? How, in your estimation, should a "normal" relationship to food be defined? Is this relationship one we see modeled in our larger culture? And how, finally, do our views about food influence the ways we define the appropriate or "normal" body?

- Hornbacher's examination of anorexia and bulimia is presented, quite self-consciously, as a childhood memoir. Is this fact significant? What point do you think she is trying to make (i.e., about the nature of these disorders; about their root causes or principal effects) by framing this account as a story about her own childhood? What would be different if she had begun this story by relating moments from her adult life?

- While in a very different vein, the Onion's satirical account of Oprah Winfrey's dieting history explores many of the same issues Hornbacher explores here: our culture's worship of thinness as a personal and social ideal; the connection between body image and self-worth. Choose a specific issue around body image that these two essays seem to share in common. Then write a one-page essay comparing the ways each goes about examining this issue. What sort of critique does each piece offer? Which commentary do you find more convincing? Why?

"Oprah Celebrates 20,000th Pound Lost" (Nov. 17, 2004), www.theonion.com

THE ONION

This mock news story sets about to satirize our ongoing fascination with celebrities, diet, and weight. Organizing its parody around perhaps the most outstanding example of this phenomenon—Oprah Winfrey—this piece invites itself to be read not just as a joke, but as a more serious commentary on the consequences of treating "stars" as role models for how we ourselves should look.

---- ✦ ----

> *"According to her spokesman, Winfrey has been on 674 diets, embarked on 255 fitness routines, and weighed herself 4,349,571 times during her 30-year career in broadcasting and film."*

CHICAGO—Talk-show superstar Oprah Winfrey celebrated losing her 20,000th pound in a star-packed gala at the Sutton Place Hotel in Chicago's Gold Coast Monday night.

"Tonight is an amazing personal milestone," Winfrey said. "I want everyone who has supported me through the years—my friends, my loved ones, and all of my wonderful fans—to share the joy I feel tonight in having shed my 20,000th pound."

According to her spokesman, Winfrey has been on 674 diets, embarked on 255 fitness routines, and weighed herself 4,349,571 times during her 30-year career in broadcasting and film.

Luminaries such as John Travolta, Bernie Mac, Patti LaBelle, U.S. Sen. Hillary Rodham Clinton (D-NY), Billy Crystal, Dr. Phil McGraw, and longtime boyfriend Stedman Graham joined the *Oprah Winfrey Show* staff in honoring the media icon's monumental achievements in weight loss.

The historic event was also showcased on Monday's episode of *Oprah*. Following a standing ovation from her studio audience, Winfrey explained that, during a weigh-in last Tuesday, she discovered that she had lost another pound, bringing her weight down to 139.

"I was recording my weight in my journal," Winfrey said. "You can imagine how excited and proud I was when I discovered that my one-pound loss that morning nudged my lifetime total to... 20,000 pounds!"

Over the audience's cheers, Winfrey added: "20,000 pounds! 20,000 pounds!"

The milestone follows Winfrey's recent loss of 33 pounds, following a protracted ballooning to 200 pounds, not long after a loss of more than 100.

"Oprah is absolutely extraordinary," said friend Gayle King, who helped organize the event. "Not only is she a talk-show host, actor, entertainment mogul, and philanthropist, but she's also a super-dieter. Oprah is so capable at what she does that she makes weight loss look easy. But it takes faith, staying power, and single-minded focus to keep losing thousands of pounds, gaining them back, and then losing them again."

Fans have lauded Winfrey for inspiring them to change their attitude toward weight loss.

"I felt horrible when I gained back the 60 pounds I'd worked so hard to lose," wrote one fan on an Oprah.com message board. "But Oprah has gained and lost that much countless times over. If she can do it, I can, too. Thanks, Oprah!"

Another fan wrote that she "share[s] Oprah's struggle."

"Pound number 428 and counting!" the post read. "Last week I gained five, and this week I lost two! Thanks, Oprah! Bless you for teaching me to be as fat or as thin as I can!"

The most eloquent tribute came from Maya Angelou, the celebrated author and poet, and a personal friend of Winfrey's. During the celebration, Angelou read a poem dedicated to Winfrey, "Water Into Air."

"As I lose, I gain," Angelou said. "I wing home to a place long forgotten. I swell as I recede, taking in all that has come before me. I molt. I shed. I diminish. But I feel no loss for I am free. My song slips its long confinement and joins the celestial roar. I was made of water, now I am air. I lose as I gain, but again I lose. I lose. I lose."

Far ahead of other celebrity weight-losers Rosie O'Donnell (15,860 pounds) and Roseanne Barr (7,229 pounds), Winfrey nevertheless appears determined to top her own record.

"I am going to ask my personal chef to whip me up some more of these breaded filet mignon appetizers," Winfrey said, piling her plate with filets during a post-celebration party. "Life is a process, people!"

The Onion is not intended for readers under 18 years of age © Copyright 2010 Onion Inc. All rights reserved.

Discussion/Writing Prompts

- Among other things, this satirical piece takes aim at the ways we have been taught to associate weight loss with such ideals as glamour, fame, wealth, and success. How do you understand this connection? Does it make logical sense to you to view thinness as a sign or symbol of such things? Does this logic prevail in your own experience, among your own acquaintances?

- The travails of weight gain and weight loss have become a signature focus within celebrity gossip culture. It is no more unusual nowadays to read about a given star's struggles with dieting than it is to follow any other aspect of their personal lives. Why do we care so much about the eating ups and downs of a figure like Oprah? What, in your view, accounts for the ongoing public fascination with tracking her weight loss efforts? Do you share this fascination? How or how not?

- The Onion article clearly aims to satirize our preoccupation with celebrity dieting. What aspects of our preoccupation is this article specifically trying to satirize? What aspects of our fan culture, what attitudes and ideas, is it attacking? And why? Do you agree?

"Food and Feelings"
(www.foodandfeelings.org)
LEORA FULVIO

A self-help program designed to help people overcome their emotionally debilitating relationship to food, this Web site offers a useful complement to those other selections in this chapter which examine the psychological dimensions of our contemporary eating practices.

◆

"Recovery Is Possible! You Can Start Loving Yourself as You Are Right Now!"

Are obsessive thoughts about food, diets and calories disrupting you from your life? Are fantasies of changing your body preventing you from living with joy in your current body? It doesn't have to be that way.

RECOVERY IS POSSIBLE!
You can stop dieting.
You can love yourself as you are right now.
Bulimia, binge eating, compulsive eating and obsessive
dieting don't have to run your life.

*Learn to love yourself and escape the trap of compulsive eating
and obsessive dieting*

Specializing in treating Binge Eating Disorder and Compulsive Eating
with Cognitive Behavioral Therapy, Psychodynamic Psychotherapy as
well as Transpersonal Psychotherapy and Hypnotherapy Techniques.
You CAN stop binge eating.
You CAN stop obsessively dieting.
You CAN learn to love yourself and be healthy.

Licensed Marriage & Family Therapist

Discussion/Writing Prompts

- As its title suggests, this self-help site assumes a key connection between our eating practices on the one hand and our emotional state on the other: that is, between food and feelings. What do you make of this conjunction? In what ways can eating be understood as an emotional act? What feelings are bound up in the choices we make about how, how much, and what to eat?
- The appeal of this program depends upon our willingness to see our eating habits and food choices in medical terms: as a pathology or disorder from which we need to "recover." In your own experience, how valid have you found this premise to be? Can you think of an action or attitude related to food that qualifies for this kind of designation?
- Both Martin and Hornbacher emphasize the emotional/psychological aspects of their respective relationships to food. Which of these two accounts do you think this "recovery program" might more effectively address? To what extent could this Web site's advice stand as a "cure" for the problems this account chronicles?

Tying It All Together: Assignments for Writing and Research

1. RHETORICAL ANALYSIS: "SELLING THE PERFECT BODY"

Choose an organization that attempts in one way or another to promote a particular body image. And think as broadly as you can about the type of organization that might fit the bill: health club, weight loss clinic, tanning salon, etc. In a four- to six-page essay, conduct a rhetorical analysis of the promotional material (i.e., Web site, print ads) this organization uses to represent itself and its overall mission. First, describe the specific body type this organization promotes as the ideal and the program it outlines for how to achieve it. Next, evaluate the particular rhetorical strategies it deploys in order to convince readers/viewers to identify with its program. What particular goals or benefits does it identify with following its instructions? And what, according to its presentation, supposedly makes them so worth pursuing? As you conduct this analysis, refer as much as possible to the concrete details within this material: particular words, phrases, images, etc. And finally, offer your own assessment of how effective or convincing this overall presentation is. In your view, does it succeed in getting readers/viewers to identify with the program it is promoting? How or how not?

2. PERSONAL REFLECTION: "PERSONAL MOTIVES: EATING JOURNAL"

One of the recurrent themes within these readings concerns the intimate, overlapping connection between physical well-being on the one hand and physical appearance on the other. When it comes to our motives for eating, how exactly do we distinguish our interest in being healthy from our desire to look good? For one week, keep a journal of all the individual eating choices you make: what foods you choose, in what amounts, at what times, etc. For each entry, offer a quick assessment of the concerns or goals that, in your view, prompted you to make this particular choice. Is your selection of an apple over a bag of chips for a snack simply a reflection of personal taste? Does it involve calculations about nutrition or health? Calories or body image? At the end of the week, spend some time looking over your journal entries. Do you notice any trends or themes? Do certain motives emerge as touchstones or guiding principles for how, when, and why you eat? Next, write a three- to five-page essay in which you reflect upon what this weeklong record tells you about your own attitudes toward eating and food. Based on these journal entries, would you say you have a reasonable or beneficial relationship to food? Do these entries raise any concerns or questions about your eating habits you might want to revisit? How?

3. COMPARE AND CONTRAST: "DISORDERED EATING/DISORDERED CULTURE"

In one way or another, each of the readings which chronicle the effects of a given eating disorder makes the point that diseases like these are as much cultural as they are medical: evidence of how "disordered" many of our societal norms regarding food and bodies have become. Choose three readings from this chapter that, in your view, present a critique of the disordered (i.e., flawed, problematic) connection between eating and body image in our culture. Then, in a three- to five-page essay, compare and contrast the particular analysis and argument each of these selections advances. What specific cultural message(s) does each pinpoint? And what danger or damage is associated with it? Next, present a brief explanation of which critique you find most effective or useful, and why.

4. VISUAL ANALYSIS: "READING BENEATH THE SURFACE"

One of the key contentions this chapter makes is that cultural definitions of the so-called perfect look can never be fully separated from equally powerful assumptions about food. To embrace and identify with one of our culture's ideal body types is always at the same time to acquiesce to certain rules telling us how and what we should eat. Choose an image from our current media that, in your view, presents a body type we are supposed to admire as an ideal. Then, in a three- to five-page essay, identify and analyze the specific ways it combines messages about physical appearance with underlying messages about eating. First, characterize the model of attractiveness you think this example promotes. How does the "perfect look" get defined here? What benefits or advantages does it imply we will gain by emulating this model? Next, reexamine this image for the embedded, unspoken messages it seems to contain about food, and eating in particular. Based on the physical ideal it presents, what sort of instructions does this image seem to offer concerning how (or how not) to eat?

5. ARGUMENT-BASED/PERSUASIVE WRITING: "DEFENDING/CRITIQUING THE IDEAL"

As noted above, the forms which the so-called ideal body can take in our culture are legion. Choose one such body type, a "look" that in your view gets presented and promoted within the media as a model to which we are all supposed to aspire. First, offer a short explanation of the specific appearance this body type proscribes, as well as where this type tends to get showcased. Then, write a three- to five-page essay in which you argue either for or against the benefits this particular look is supposed to yield. In your estimation, is this body image worth emulating? If so, what specific advantages make it so? If not, what particular problems outweigh these putative pay-offs? As you construct this argument, concentrate on responding to the claims that those on the opposite side might make. What ultimately makes your view of this ideal more valid? More persuasive?

CHAPTER 4

Ethics

EATING LOCALLY/THINKING GLOBALLY

When we ask ourselves "what do I feel like eating?" chances are we're not thinking of this as a question with especially moral implications. To assess a choice in moral or ethical terms is by definition to take into account the effects it may have on those around us. And certainly when viewed through the prism of our culture's mainstream messages about food, a question like "what do I want to eat?" tends to fall under the heading of the purely personal: a decision whose consequences extend no further than the boundaries of our individual bodies and individual taste. Indeed this very assumption (i.e., that eating is an essentially private act with solely personal consequences) could be said to exemplify the view we are taught to hold about our food-related choices more generally. Amidst the welter of diet books and cooking shows, kitchen ads and foodie Web sites that proliferate in our culture, the prevailing message we hear is that eating is about *us:* our health, our appearance, our needs, our pleasure.

To understand how a message like this has come to acquire the status of a self-evident truth, it might be helpful to look at a representative example from our current pop culture. Take, for instance, the restaurant review. Whether in the newspaper or on TV, over the radio or on the Web, we have all no doubt come across at least one essay that sets about to assess the merits and deficiencies of a given eating establishment. And even if we've seen only one or two, more likely than not we are also familiar enough with the form these reviews follow to know that certain aspects of the dining experience will be minutely dissected while others will be entirely overlooked.

We can rest assured, for example, that a typical review will include some evaluation of a restaurant's physical aesthetics: the decor, the layout, the ambiance. Just as reliably, we can also expect to find information about a meal's overall cost: the price for appetizers and entrées, a calculation of the average bill for two. And of course most dependably of all, we know we will be given a lengthy, detailed description of the meal itself: what key ingredients it includes, how competently and creatively it is prepared, how artfully it is presented, how satisfying it tastes.

Even an overview as cursory as this is enough to dispel any notions we might be tempted to harbor about this genre's supposed objectivity. No matter how much we may take its perspective for granted, the fact remains that it models a view of the dining experience that is both deeply skewed and highly circumscribed—one overwhelmingly biased in favor of what we might call the private aspects of eating. Without ever announcing its priorities out loud, this type of food writing treats "eating out" as an experience that revolves exclusively around the needs, tastes, and pleasures of the individual eater. In many respects, of course, this should hardly surprise us. The goal of the typical restaurant review, after all, is to *review*: that is, to offer readers pointed and credible advice as they consider whether to patronize a particular restaurant themselves. But restaurant reviews are more than simply consumer reports; on a deeper level, they also serve as guides or tutorials in how to think about eating more broadly. Even as they rank the quality of the decor, the service, or the food itself ("5 stars!"; "Thumbs down!"), these appraisals do the additional work of drawing the lines around how we are and are not supposed to think about food: firm (if unspoken) boundaries that separate those aspects of eating that matter, that merit our attention and concern, from those that do not.

Notice, for example, how many other considerations have to remain invisible, how many other questions have to go unasked, in order for our focus to stay fixed on the needs and pleasures of the individual eater. For the customer to remain front and center, the typical review can't really afford to direct readers' attention to all the activity that unfolds "behind-the-scenes." No extended portrait of the chores, routines, and squabbles that characterize the dynamics of the kitchen; no overview of the negotiations and conflicts that structure relations between managers and waitstaff; no back story informing us how the ingredients that go into a meal were grown, processed, or delivered in the first place. Even though they couldn't be more crucial to a restaurant's successful operation, and thus presumably essential to any accurate rendering of its overall quality, these sorts of details rarely rate a mention. The fact that we don't clamor for them to be included, furthermore, tells us something important about the power these unspoken boundaries have to bracket our own assumptions and expectations. Through sheer repetition and familiarity, it seems, we have grown entirely accustomed to the proposition that such "behind-the-scenes" material is stuff we simply don't need to look at. Indeed we might even go so far as to say that this material is kept off the table because its inclusion would force us to rethink the core belief that eating is an exclusively individual undertaking. To draw a connection between, say, the quality of a meal we are served and the wages paid to the employee serving it is to begin taking seriously the possibility that our personal eating choices may not be entirely personal after all. To start thinking of eating, in short, as an ethical act.

LOOKING BEYOND THE MENU: THE MULTIPLE CONTEXTS OF OUR FOOD-RELATED CHOICES

But what difference would such a shift in perspective make? If contemplating the ethics of how and what we eat means becoming more self-conscious and forthright about the fact that our food choices have consequences, what concrete changes might such newfound awareness bring about? Imagine for a moment that the typical restaurant review did include glimpses of such behind-the-scenes activity: that its evaluation of food, service, and ambiance were complemented by discussions of employee wage structure, labor/management relations, and/or kitchen staff routines. In the most immediate terms, if this alternative format were to become the norm, we might easily find ourselves inclined to alter how we behave as restaurant customers. Armed with such information, we might go to greater lengths to be courteous to our waitperson, might include a more generous tip, might think twice before sending a meal back to the kitchen. It is equally possible, furthermore, that this fuller understanding of restaurant work might prompt us to rethink the particular foods we choose to eat. If we were acquainted with the conditions under which a cow is raised, slaughtered, and processed on its way to becoming our steak, for instance, we might seriously reconsider the virtues vegetarianism. If we learned more about the chemical additives needed to produce the vibrant reds, greens, and yellows in our favorite "spring medley" salad, we might be prodded to look more closely at the environmental advantages of organic or "locally grown" produce. Looking beyond the context of our individual eating choices, this enlarged perspective could also bring about significant changes in the ways we approach broader (social, political, economic) issues. If the typical review linked its assessment of a restaurant's service to a more comprehensive description of a service worker's daily tasks or to a more candid accounting of this employee's wages and benefits, such data could well finds its way into our views on such topical issues as minimum wage or universal health care, workplace safety or the role of unions.

Indeed when we consider the many possible changes to which this alternative might give rise, it becomes all the more difficult to make sense of our cultural disposition toward viewing eating as an exclusively personal act. Difficult because over and against this media message stands a confounding counter-truth: namely, that our daily lives are in fact filled with food-related choices that reverberate far into the broader arenas of public life. From the environmental impact of buying fast food to the moral implications of eating meat to the economic benefits of "fair trade" coffee, it isn't hard to come up with a list of everyday eating decisions whose stakes are as much social as they are personal. From this vantage, the invitation to adopt a more explicitly ethical orientation to food comes to seem less like an innovation, a shift in attitude that is unprecedented or brand new, than a kind of return: a reminder that our eating choices always carry consequences that extend beyond our self-interest.

At the most fundamental level, an ethical understanding of eating hinges on precisely this acknowledgment: that we live in a world far more interconnected and interdependent than we are often led to believe, one in which our individual actions and personal concerns invariably carry collective consequences. Despite their differences, it is precisely this acknowledgment which informs each of the readings below. Examining our contemporary food culture from a variety of angles, these selections are linked by their shared desire to engender a broader and more mindful understanding of the ways our eating decisions affect the people, the landscape, and the other species with whom we share the planet.

What, for example, does our penchant for mass-produced or processed foods say about how we define our responsibility to the natural environment? How do cultural stereotypes about veganism encourage us to downplay or overlook concerns over animal welfare? What happens to our enthusiasm for the organic food movement when we take a closer look at the labor practices that sustain it? Put simply: does our contemporary food culture teach us to care about or to overlook the needs, the interests, and the conditions of anyone or anything other than ourselves? Given how vexingly subjective questions of wrong and right can be, we might reasonably ask whether it's possible, or even desirable, to assemble a set of guidelines for ethical eating that works for all. What type of moral calculus, what set of operating rules, would such guidelines employ? Rather than proscribe a one-size-fits-all solution, the selections assembled below are better viewed as a kind of "smorgasbord": a collection or constellation of individual responses, which taken together, capture for readers the breadth and scope, the richness and diversity, of ethical issues that a focus on eating raises.

"Whence the Beef?: The Gruesome Trip From Pasture to Platter," *Slate* (Feb. 26, 2004)

Laurie Snyder

Part of thinking ethically about how and what we eat involves educating ourselves about where exactly our food comes from: how it is grown, cultivated, processed, and/or slaughtered. Chronicling the odyssey by which different livestock (cows, pigs, chickens) are transformed into our dinner entrée, Snyder poses some hard questions about the moral implications of our modern industrial food chain, as well as our individual obligations to change it.

———————— ✦ ————————

"Leave it to the sweet-faced Holstein to remind us of the ugly work of bringing beef to the dinner table."
The gruesome trip from pasture to platter (and how to ensure that it's not so bad).

Leave it to a sweet-faced Holstein to remind us of the ugly work of bringing beef to the dinner table. When the nation's first confirmed case of mad cow disease cropped up in December, Americans received a crash course on the nastier aspects of the cattle business. We learned, for instance, that cows walking up the slaughterhouse line are often killed with a blow to the head, which can spew bits of brain into the muscle. That there's a process called "advanced meat recovery" in which the meat—later ground into tasty sausages or ballpark hotdogs—is sheared so close to the bone that there's a decent chance the meat contains spinal cord tissue. And that newborn dairy calves often survive on a formula fortified with protein from the blood of their brethren.

With the mad cow scare, many of these <u>practices are on their way out</u>, and the industrial farming industry has made strides in recent years toward improving animal welfare. Yet there's still plenty about the way meat is raised in the United States that can turn the stomach of even the heartiest carnivore. So, it's no surprise some companies have decided there may be a market for meat raised in less grisly conditions. Burgerville, a Northwestern chain, <u>announced</u> this week that it would buy beef solely from "a <u>cooperative</u> of 40 sustainable family ranches dedicated to raising cattle in harmony with nature, without the use of hormones, antibiotics, genetically modified grain or any animal by-products." All of this sounds very lovely to the consumer, but how much difference does it make to the cow? And just how bad do the animals that end up in the grocery store really have it?

To answer these questions, **Slate** presents this guide to what likely happened to your meat—whether it's beef, pork, or poultry—on its way to the table.

Industrial Beef: Life starts out serenely for most beef calves, who spend their first six months alongside their mothers, nibbling grass in open pastures, as described by Michael Pollan, who wrote an excellent *New York Times Magazine* piece, titled "Power Steer," on the cattle industry. But soon after that six-month mark, the stock is moved onto the feedlot and the factory farming begins.

Life on the feedlot is dismal: Several thousand head are crammed into the facility, where cattle spend days standing cheek to jowl, in mud and manure. At about 14 months, when cattle reach 1,200 pounds, they're ready for slaughter. (<u>Listen</u> to Pollan discussing this process with Terry Gross on *Fresh Air*.)

To get cattle to balloon in a span of months, ranchers stuff the feedlot cattle with a high-fat (and cheap) corn diet and administer growth hormones for an additional boost. Until recently, cattle also ate protein supplements made from ground-up chicken parts, "poultry litter" (feces and other debris swept off the chicken factory floor, including potentially cow parts that been ground up into chicken feed), and other mammalian byproducts. (Cattle also were fed cow and sheep bits, until the United States banned the practice in 1997 in an effort to keep mad cow disease out of American herds.)

As the Web site FactoryFarming.com points out, cattle's digestive systems are designed to process a grass-based diet, high in fiber and low in fat; the high-calorie corn diet creates <u>potentially fatal digestive problems</u> that must be treated with antibiotics. Drugs also keep down diseases that can thrive in such tight quarters. Animal rights activists warn, however, that the rampant use of these drugs in food production reduces their effectiveness in fighting human illness.

The Alternatives: To be certified "organic," cattle must be raised without hormones or antibiotics of any kind and must eat only pesticide-free vegetarian feed. Beef labeled "grass-fed" is the favorite of many animal rights activists. "Grass-fed" cattle likely spent months ambling in pastures before meeting the knife. (This beef is sometimes labeled "natural" rather than organic, since in order to meet that organic bar ranchers would have to certify that thousands of acres of rangeland, much of which may be federal property, is free of pesticides.) However, cattle raised in these fashions usually don't escape the factory farm experience entirely— they often spend a finishing period on feedlots before being slaughtered (a 90-day stay is typical). To avoid this, keep an eye out for labels that read "never confined to a feedlot." Ask butchers for specifics on how the animal was raised or check out producers' Web sites. Two for grass-fed beef are www.meadowraised-meats.com and www.eatwild.com. Expect to pay for this peace of mind, though; organic beef can cost 50 percent more than the standard fare; grass-fed New York strip steak sells for $9.99 a pound at a local Whole Foods; the conventional version at Safeway is a dollar cheaper.

Industrial Pork: If you pity burgers-to-be, you'll <u>pity pending pork chops</u>. Raised in huge warehouses lined with pens—called CAFOs or confined animal feeding operations—hogs live a grim existence. Pregnant sows live in narrow "gestation crates"—about 2 by 7 feet, too small to turn around in—with slanted floors that allow waste to drop through. As animal rights Food Animal Concerns Trust describes, sows are impregnated again and again, until they're sent to the slaughterhouse at around age 3 (in more natural conditions a pig can live into its teens). Each time a sow gives birth, she is briefly moved to a larger farrowing stall.

But after 15 days or so, the sow returns to the gestation crate to be inseminated again, and her piglets head to crowded pens. Once they reach 50 pounds, some are culled for breeding stock; the others are sent to a "finishing facility"—another set of crowded pens—until they reach typical slaughter-weight of 250 pounds, at six months. In these tight confines, cannibalism is common and the hogs often nonchalantly chew off their neighbors' tails. To prevent this from happening, hog producers clip the tails off.

The Alternatives: As with organic beef, organic pork is vegetarian, and antibiotic- and hormone-free, but may have spent months in cramped CAFOs. Some producers also sell what they call free-range or meadow-raised pork, meaning pigs that are pastured for much of the year. (These pigs certainly *look* happier.) But there are no restrictions on the use of these terms, so be sure to ask for the details. Also, in some states, there are efforts to ban the use of gestation crates in hog farming; for instance, Florida voters approved a ballot measure outlawing the practice.

Industrial Turkey: Turkeys live many to a pen, with about 3 square feet per bird. Farmers trim their beaks and toes to prevent the turkeys from attacking each other. The American love of white meat has pushed farmers to selectively breed their flocks for massive, bulging breasts and the ability to gain weight quickly. Commercial poults, or baby turkeys, go from 3-ounce newborns to 30-pound platter prizes in about 18 weeks, according to the industry group National Turkey Federation. This rapid weight may be behind many health problems, such as lameness and heart and lung trouble.

Modern turkeys are so breast-heavy they walk clumsily and cannot fly. Wild turkeys, admired by Benjamin Franklin for their athleticism, have a slim appearance, can run as fast as 18 mph, and bolt into the skies at highway speeds. Commercial toms, on the other hand, also have trouble raising their bodies high enough to have sex at all. Toms stay in one pen, hens in another, with farm workers ferrying the turkey sperm in between.

Industrial Chicken: Broilers (eatin' birds) live in similarly cramped pens. The eye-searing scent of urine on poultry CAFOs can wreak havoc on the birds' respiratory systems and can even cause blindness. Broilers are bred to pack on the pounds fast, too. The average broiler chicken weighs approximately 5 pounds when it heads to market at about 7-weeks-old.* The U.S. Department of Agriculture has sponsored studies that examine skeletal problems associated with rapid growth; an abstract of <u>one</u> mentions: "Approximately 30% of commercially raised broilers have leg disorders severe enough to impair their mobility."

Industrial Eggs: Chickens destined for egg production <u>fare worse</u> than the birds we eat. They often undergo beak- and toe-trimming and are kept in "<u>battery cages</u>" (as small as 16 by 18 inches) with five or six other birds, then the cages are <u>stacked floor to ceiling</u> in a warehouse-type facility. Animal rights groups charge that chicks born male are tossed alive into a meat grinder to be processed for cattle feed, gassed, or just dumped in trash bags to suffocate. (They're a different breed than what's used for broilers, so they can't be raised for meat.) The females live out their 2-year lives in sloped-bottomed cages that allow the eggs to roll down into troughs and be carried off on conveyor belts. When the hens reach a little over a year, producers withhold food to force molting, or feather loss. This process gives the hens a second wind, adding another 40 weeks to their egg-laying lives. The group Compassion Over Killing <u>contends that</u> nearly 10 percent of a typical flock die from disease or hang themselves on the cage bars. When the hens reach 2, they're sometimes slaughtered for pet food or processed food, such as chicken hot dogs.

The Alternatives: Fast-food giant McDonald's announced in 2000 that all producers who supply its eggs must give hens 72 square inches each (more than three times what they typically get), cannot use forced-molting, and should move toward stopping de-beaking chicks altogether.

But what about free-range poultry? According to activists, turkeys and chickens labeled "free range" <u>didn't necessarily enjoy</u> much more mobility than their CAFO-raised peers. In the United States, poultry can be labeled free-range as long as there's *some* access to the outdoors, for *some* of the birds in a flock. Free-range chicks may be de-beaked, and free-range egg-laying hens still spend their days in battery cages—they just have a bit more room to move about. One term to keep an eye out for is "cage free"—fowl raised in open spaces are likely a bit better off.

Discussion/Writing Prompts

- At the heart of Snyder's portrait of industrial farming is a concern for what she terms "animal welfare." How do you understand this term? In your view, what concerns should this term encompass? And where should the line dividing proper, reasonable, or legitimate concerns from their less valid counterparts be drawn? To what extent, in your estimation, should we use concerns over animal welfare to determine our own eating choices? Why?

- Snyder devotes part of her essay to itemizing the different practices that characterize industrial meat production. Take a closer look at this list. Then write a one-page essay in which you lay out the specific steps by which some aspect of this production process could be made more ethical. What concrete changes (i.e., in how animals are kept, treated, perhaps even ultimately slaughtered) would you institute? And what ethical difference would these changes make? How do your changes compare to the "alternatives" Snyder herself sketches?

- Snyder's essay also provides links to a number of different Web sites, some of which document the abuses of "factory farming" and some of which outline alternatives to current practices. Log on to one of the references, and spend a few minutes perusing its content. Then write a one-page review in which you evaluate how effective a commentary on the ethics of eating you think this Web site offers. Based on the abuses it chronicles or the solutions it advocates, in what ways can this Web site be read as a set of guidelines or instructions teaching us how to eat more ethically? And how convincing do you find this advice?

"Meatless Like Me: I May Be a Vegetarian, but I Still Love the Smell of Bacon," *Slate* (May 7, 2008)

Taylor Clark

Different eating practices carry different cultural connotations: images or stereotypes about the type of person who typically practices this eating style. But how accurate are such labels? And to

*what extent do they obscure rather than clarify our understanding
of what these eating practices might teach us? Turning a critical
eye toward the way vegetarianism has been defined in our world,
Taylor offers a personal testimony that complicates our culture's
clichés about this particular eating practice.*

───────────── ✦ ─────────────

*"Every vegetarian remembers his first time . . . the first
time he casually lets slip that he's turned herbivore,
prompting everyone in earshot to stare at him as if he just
revealed plans to sail his carrot-powered plasma yacht to
Neptune."*

I may be a vegetarian, but I still love the smell of bacon.

Every vegetarian remembers his first time. Not the unremarkable
event of his first meal without meat, mind you. No, I mean the
first time he casually lets slip that he's turned herbivore, prompting
everyone in earshot to stare at him as if he just revealed plans to sail
his carrot-powered plasma yacht to Neptune. For me, this first time
came at an Elks scholarship luncheon in rural Oregon when I was 18.
All day, I'd succeeded at seeming a promising and responsible young
man, until that fateful moment when someone asked why I hadn't
taken any meat from the buffet. After I offered my reluctant explanation—and the guy announced it *to the entire room*—30 people went
eerily quiet, undoubtedly expecting me to launch into a speech on the
virtues of hemp. In the corner, an elderly, suited man glared at me as
he slowly raised a slice of bologna and executed the most menacing
bite of cold cut in recorded history. I didn't get the scholarship.

I tell this story not to win your pity but to illustrate a point:
I've been vegetarian for a decade, and when it comes up, I still get
a look of confused horror that says, "But you seemed so . . .
normal." The U.S. boasts more than 10 million herbivores today,
yet most Americans assume that every last one is a loopy, self-
satisfied health fanatic, hellbent on draining all the joy out of life.
Those of us who want to avoid the social nightmare have to hide
our vegetarianism like an Oxycontin addiction, because admit it,
omnivores: You know nothing about us. Do we eat fish? Will we
panic if confronted with a hamburger? Are we dying of malnutrition? You have no clue. So read on, my flesh-eating friends—I believe it's high time we cleared a few things up.

To demonstrate what a vegetarian really is, let's begin with a simple thought experiment. Imagine a completely normal person with completely normal food cravings, someone who has a broad range of friends, enjoys a good time, is carbon-based, and so on. Now remove from this person's diet anything that once had eyes, and, *wham!*, you have yourself a vegetarian. Normal person, no previously ocular food, end of story. Some people call themselves vegetarians and still eat chicken or fish, but unless we're talking about the kind of salmon that comes freshly plucked from the vine, this makes you an omnivore. A select few herbivores go one step further and avoid *all* animal products—milk, eggs, honey, leather—and they call themselves *vegan*, which rhymes with "tree men." These people are intense.

Vegetarians give up meat for a variety of ethical, environmental, and health reasons that are secondary to this essay's goal of increasing brotherly understanding, so I'll mostly set them aside. Suffice it to say that one day, I suddenly realized that I could never look a cow in the eyes, press a knocking gun to her temple, and pull the trigger without feeling I'd done something cruel and unnecessary. (Sure, if it's kill the cow or starve, then say your prayers, my bovine friend—but for now, it's not quite a mortal struggle to subsist on the other five food groups.) I am well-aware that even telling you this makes me seem like the kind of person who wants to break into your house and liberate your pet hamster—that is, like a PETA activist. Most vegetarians, though, would tell you that they appreciate the intentions of groups like PETA but not the obnoxious tactics. It's like this: We're all rooting for the same team, but they're the ones in face paint, bellowing obscenities at the umpire and flipping over every car with a Yankees bumper sticker. I have no designs on your Camry or your hamster.

Now, when I say that vegetarians are normal people with normal food cravings, many omnivores will hoist a lamb shank in triumph and point out that you can hardly call yourself normal if the aroma of, say, sizzling bacon doesn't fill you with deepest yearning. To which I reply: We're not *insane*. We *know* meat tastes good; it's why there's a freezer case at your supermarket full of woefully inadequate meat substitutes. Believe me, if obtaining bacon didn't require slaughtering a pig, I'd have a BLT in each hand right now with a bacon layer cake waiting in the fridge for dessert. But, that said, I can also tell you that with some time away from the butcher's section, many meat products start to seem gross. Ground beef in particular now strikes me as absolutely revolting; I have a vague memory that hamburgers taste good, but the idea of taking a cow's leg, mulching it into a fatty pulp, and forming it into a pancake makes me gag. And hot dogs . . . I mean, *hot dogs?* You *do* know what that is, right?

As a consolation prize we get tofu, a treasure most omnivores are more than happy to do without. Well, this may stun you, but I'm not any more excited about a steaming heap of unseasoned tofu blobs than you are. Tofu is like <u>fugu blowfish sushi</u>: Prepared correctly, it's delicious; prepared incorrectly, it's lethal. Very early in my vegetarian career, I found myself famished and stuck in a mall, so I wandered over to the food court's Asian counter. When I asked the teenage chief culinary artisan what was in the tofu stir-fry, he snorted and replied, "Shit." Desperation made me order it anyway, and I can tell you that promises have rarely been more loyally kept than this guy's pledge that the tofu would taste like shit. So here's a tip: Unless you know you're in expert hands (Thai restaurants are a good bet), don't even try tofu. Otherwise, it's your funeral.

As long as we're discussing restaurants, allow me a quick word with the hardworking chefs at America's dining establishments. We really appreciate that you included a vegetarian option on your menu (and if you didn't, is our money not green?), but it may interest you to know that most of us are not salad freaks on a grim slog for nourishment. We actually enjoy food, especially the kind that tastes good. So enough with the bland vegetable dishes, and, for God's sake, *please* make the Gardenburgers stop; it's stunning how many restaurants lavish unending care on their meat dishes yet are content to throw a flavorless hockey puck from Costco into the microwave and call it cuisine. Every vegetarian is used to slim pickings when dining out, so we're not asking for much—just for something *you'd* like to eat. I'll even offer a handy trick. Pretend you're trapped in a kitchen stocked with every ingredient imaginable, from asiago to zucchini, but with zero meat. With no flesh available, picture what you'd make for yourself; this is what we want, too.

For those kind-hearted omnivores who willingly invite feral vegetarians into their homes for dinner parties and barbecues (really! we do that, too!), the same rule applies—but also know that unless you're dealing with an herbivore who is a prick for unrelated reasons, we don't expect you to bend over backward for us. In fact, if we get the sense that you cooked for three extra hours to accommodate our dietary preferences, we will marvel at your considerate nature, but we will also feel insanely guilty. Similarly, it's very thoughtful of you to ask whether it'll bother me if I see you eat meat, but don't worry: I'm not going to compose an epic poem about your club sandwich.

Which leads me to a vital point for friendly omnivore-herbivore relations. As you're enjoying that pork loin next to me, *I am not silently judging you.* I realize that anyone who has encountered the breed of smug vegetarian who says things like, "I can hear your lunch screaming," will find this tough to believe, but I'm honestly not out to convert you. My girlfriend and my closest pals all eat meat, and they'll affirm that I've never even raised an eyebrow about it. Now, do I think it strange that the same people who dress their dogs in berets and send them to day spas are often unfazed that an equally smart pig suffered and died to become their McMuffin? Yes, I do. (Or, to use a more pressing example, how many Americans will bemoan Eight Belles' fatal Kentucky Derby injury tonight at the dinner table between bites of beef?) Would I prefer it if we at least raised these animals humanely? Yes, I would.

Let's be honest, though: I'm not exactly St. Francis of Assisi over here, tenderly ministering to every chipmunk that crosses my path. I try to represent for the animal kingdom, but take a look at my shoes—they're made of leather, which, I am told by those with expert knowledge of the tanning process, comes from dead cows. This is the sort of revelation that prompts meat boosters to pick up the triumphant lamb shank once again and accuse us of hypocrisy. Well, *sort of.* (Hey, *you* try to find a pair of non-leather dress shoes.) My dedication to the cause might be incomplete, but I'd still say that doing something beats doing nothing. It's kind of like driving a hybrid: not a solution to the global-warming dilemma but a decent start. Let's just say that at the dinner table, I roll in a Prius.

Finally, grant me one more cordial request: Please don't try to convince us that being vegetarian is somehow wrong. If you're concerned for my health, that's very nice, though you can rest assured that I'm in shipshape. If you want to have an amiable tête-à-tête about vegetarianism, that's great. But if you insist on being the aggressive blowhard who takes meatlessness as a personal insult and rails about what fools we all are, you're only going to persuade me that you're a dickhead. When someone says he's Catholic, you probably don't start the stump speech about how God is a lie created to enslave the ignorant masses, and it's equally offensive to berate an herbivore. I know you think we're crazy. That's neat. But seeing as I've endured the hassle of being a vegetarian for several years now, perhaps I've given this a *little* thought. So let's just agree to disagree and get on with making fun of Hillary Clinton's inability to <u>operate a coffee machine</u>.

Because, really, peace and understanding are what it's all about: your porterhouse and my portobello coexisting in perfect harmony—though preferably not touching. We're actually not so different, after all, my omnivorous chums. In fact, I like to think that when an omnivore looks in the mirror, he just sees a vegetarian who happens to eat meat. Or, no, wait, maybe the *mirror* sees the omnivore through the *prism* of flesh and realizes we all have a crystalline animal soul, you know?

This is excellent weed, by the way, if you want a hit. Hey, while you're here: Have I ever told you about hemp?

Discussion/Writing Prompts

- Clark is clearly taking aim at some of the clichés used to stereotype vegetarians. How effective or convincing do you find his critique? What profile of the vegetarian eater does this essay present? And how does it differ from some of the stereotypes that prevail in our culture?
- In Clark's view, vegetarianism still exists outside the mainstream social norms around eating. To practice vegetarianism, as he notes, is to run the risk of seeming something other than "normal." Do you agree? To what extent, in your view, does vegetarianism place one outside the boundaries of the mainstream?
- Snyder and Clark both invite us to consider the effects our eating choices have on the other species with whom we share the planet. To what extent do you think Snyder would find herself in sympathy with the definition and defense of vegetarianism Clark offers? Which of the ideas Clark presents seem, in your view, most in line with the changes in industrial food production Snyder calls for?

"Causes of Hunger Are Related to Poverty," in *Global Issues: Social, Political, Economic, and Environmental Issues That Affect Us All*, www.globalissues.org (2009)

ANUP SHAH

In this Web site, Shah presents a clearinghouse of information documenting the many connections between global poverty and global hunger. Organized as a list of statistics, this resource provides readers with a firm, factual foundation for inquiring more deeply into the ef-fect our own eating habits and food economy have on worldwide mal-nutrition.

———————— ✦ ————————

"Over 9 million people die each year worldwide because of hunger and malnutrition. 5 million are children . . . In the US, 40–50% of food ready for harvest never gets eaten."

- Almost half the world—over 3 billion people—live on less than $2.50 a day.
- The GDP (Gross Domestic Product) of the 41 Heavily Indebted Poor Countries (567 million people) is less than the wealth of the world's 7 richest people combined.
- Nearly a billion people entered the 21st century unable to read a book or sign their names.
- Less than one per cent of what the world spent every year on weapons was needed to put every child into school by the year 2000 and yet it didn't happen.
- 1 billion children live in poverty (1 in 2 children in the world). 640 million live without adequate shelter, 400 million have no access to safe water, 270 million have no access to health serv-ices. 10.6 million died in 2003 before they reached the age of 5 (or roughly 29,000 children per day).

—More Facts (and Sources)

Poverty is the state for the majority of the world's people and nations. Why is this? Is it enough to blame poor people for their own predicament? Have they been lazy, made poor decisions, and been solely responsible for their plight? What about their govern-ments? Have they pursued policies that actually harm successful development? Such causes of poverty and inequality are no doubt real. But deeper and more global causes of poverty are often less discussed.

Behind the increasing interconnectedness promised by glob-alization are global decisions, policies, and practices. These are typically influenced, driven, or formulated by the rich and pow-erful. These can be leaders of rich countries or other global actors such as multinational corporations, institutions, and influential people.

In the face of such enormous external influence, the governments of poor nations and their people are often powerless. As a result, in the global context, a few get wealthy while the majority struggle.

These next few articles and sections explore various poverty issues in more depth:

POVERTY FACTS AND STATS

Most of humanity lives on just a few dollars a day. Whether you live in the wealthiest nations in the world or the poorest, you will see high levels of inequality.

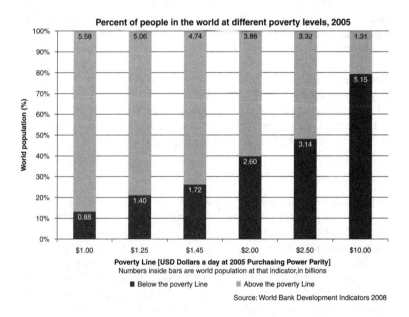

Percent of people in the world at different poverty levels, 2005

Poverty Line [USD Dollars a day at 2005 Purchasing Power Parity]
Numbers inside bars are world population at that indicator, in billions

■ Below the poverty Line   ■ Above the poverty Line

Source: World Bank Development Indicators 2008

The poorest people will also have less access to health, education and other services. Problems of hunger, malnutrition and disease afflict the poorest in society. The poorest are also typically marginalized from society and have little representation or voice in public and political debates, making it even harder to escape poverty.

By contrast, the wealthier you are, the more likely you are to benefit from economic or political policies. The amount the world spends on military, financial bailouts and other areas that benefit the wealthy, compared to the amount spent to address the daily crisis of poverty and related problems are often staggering.

Some facts and figures on poverty presented in this page are eye-openers, to say the least.

STRUCTURAL ADJUSTMENT—A MAJOR CAUSE OF POVERTY

Cutbacks in health, education and other vital social services around the world have resulted from structural adjustment policies prescribed by the International Monetary Fund (IMF) and the World Bank as conditions for loans and repayment. In addition, developing nation governments are required to open their economies to compete with each other and with more powerful and established industrialized nations. To attract investment, poor countries enter a spiraling race to the bottom to see who can provide lower standards, reduced wages and cheaper resources. This has increased poverty and inequality for most people. It also forms a backbone to what we today call globalization. As a result, it maintains the historic unequal rules of trade.

POVERTY AROUND THE WORLD

Around the world, in rich or poor nations, poverty has always been present. In most nations today, inequality—the gap between the rich and the poor—is quite high and often widening. The causes are numerous, including a lack of individual responsibility, bad government policy, exploitation by people and businesses with power and influence, or some combination of these and other factors. Many feel that high levels of inequality will affect social cohesion and lead to problems such as increasing crime and violence.

Inequality is often a measure of relative poverty. Absolute poverty, however, is also a concern. The latest World Bank figures for world poverty reveals a higher number of people live in poverty than previously thought. For example, the new poverty line is defined as living on the equivalent of $1.25 a day. With that measure based on latest data available (2005), 1.4 billion people live on or below that line. Furthermore, almost half the world—over three billion people—live on less than $2.50 a day and at least 80% of humanity lives on less than $10 a day:

TODAY, OVER 25,000 CHILDREN DIED AROUND THE WORLD

Over 25,000 children die every day around the world.
That is equivalent to:

- 1 child dying every 3.5 seconds
- 17–18 children dying every minute
- A 2004 Asian Tsunami occurring almost every 1.5 weeks
- An Iraq-scale death toll every 16–38 days
- Over 9 million children dying every year
- Some 70 million children dying between 2000 and 2007

The silent killers are poverty, easily preventable diseases and illnesses, and other related causes. In spite of the scale of this daily/ongoing catastrophe, it rarely manages to achieve, much less sustain, prime-time, headline coverage.

WORLD HUNGER AND POVERTY

Meaningful long-term alleviation of hunger is rooted in the alleviation of poverty, as poverty leads to hunger. World hunger is a terrible symptom of world poverty. If efforts are only directed at providing food, or improving food production or distribution, then the structural root causes that create hunger, poverty and dependency would still remain. While resources and energies are deployed to relieve hunger through technical measures such as improving agriculture, and as important as these are, interrelated issues such as poverty means that political solutions are likely required as well for meaningful and long term hunger alleviation.

Discussion/Writing Prompts

- Broadly speaking, the information presented in this Web site falls into two categories: statistics on the rate of malnutrition and/or hunger in developing countries and statistics on rates of food production/consumption in developed countries. Why do you think Shah chooses to organize the information in this particular way? What message about hunger—its causes, conditions, and possible solutions —do you think this organizational strategy is designed to suggest?

- As its title makes clear, this Web site's key contention is that there exists a fundamental, formative connection between hunger and poverty. Choose an example from your own experience (i.e., a story you've read or heard from a friend, family member, or acquaintance) that illustrates how this connection works. An example where economic circumstances clearly play a role is in how someone is forced to go hungry. First, describe these circumstances as fully as you can: what specific factors (i.e., joblessness, homelessness, health- or family-related challenges) most directly account for why this person goes hungry? Next, outline what you believe would be the most effective way to correct or remedy this situation.

- One of the greatest strengths of this Web site, the fact that it has so much factual information at its disposal, could also be said to pose one of its greatest challenges. To cast the problems of poverty and hunger in statistical terms is to run the risk of overlooking the more personal, individual, or "human" side of this tragedy. In a one-page essay, compare the relative benefits and downsides to addressing these issues in so abstract a way. What are the advantages of organizing this discussion around statistics? What vantage on these problems does such an approach give us? And how do the benefits of this vantage compare to the risks or limitations? What aspects of poverty or hunger, in other words, does this perspective encourage us to overlook?

"The Ethics of Eating: Consider the Farmworkers," *Civil Eats* (May 22, 2009), www.civileats.com

Eric Haas

We've all heard about the environmental benefits of "going" organic. But what about the social consequences? When viewed through the experience of the workers upon whose labor this movement depends, does eating organic still come across as an unalloyed good? Chronicling the lives of the migrant farmworkers who toil at the bottom of the "Slow Food" movement, this essay challenges us to consider more critically whether the benefits wrought by the organic food industry are as widely shared as we are sometimes led to believe.

———————— ✦ ————————

"And then, because we were eating, I found myself wondering about the people who had grown the vegetables on my plate. What were their lives like? What hardships did they endure?"

On a recent Saturday, I took a trip out to rural Oregon with about 20 other Slow Food Portland members. We woke early and drove through the dreary morning rain, leaving behind the streets of Portland for the vast agricultural fields of nearby Marion County. We were seeking the origins of our food.

I helped organize the event, which was billed as an opportunity to "Share a Meal With the People Who Feed Us." The idea was to meet with migrant farmworkers and to learn more about the different places they live: either in housing provided by their employers, or in housing created by a local nonprofit, the Farmworker Housing Development Corporation (FHDC). FHDC staff agreed to take us on a tour of the farms and of their development in Woodburn, after which we would share a potluck lunch with the residents there.

The day was inspired largely by Carlo Petrini, the founder of Slow Food, who insists that our food be "Good, Clean, and Fair." By this he means that our food should be fresh and healthy, it shouldn't depend on chemicals that destroy the environment, and the people who grow it should be compensated well for their work.

His ethics, I think, are admirable. They are simple and elegant. But they can be quite difficult to put into practice.

Many of us know that the ways in which we typically grow, process, distribute, and consume food in this country are harmful to our health and the environment. As a nation, we are coming to understand that the production and consumption of a "conventional" tomato, for example, means degraded soils, polluted waterways, poisoned air, and toxins in our bodies. Given the state of our health-care system, as well as the threat of global climate change, this conventional tomato affects us in ways that are increasingly difficult to ignore.

It's no wonder, then, that the "good" and "clean" elements of Petrini's ethic have become major preoccupations in the American mind. And because of our increased awareness, I think, we've already developed some relatively good ways to address our concerns; on the West Coast, at least, it's easy to find fresh and locally grown organic produce almost any time of year.

The problem is that this doesn't necessarily account for how "fair" the food is.

Long hours and low pay are the industry standard, even for many organic and small-scale farms. In the worst cases, farmworkers are held against their will and forced to labor as indentured servants—continually paying off debts to their employers—in a system legally defined as slavery. In Florida, for example, a state that one federal prosecutor recently called "ground zero for modern-day slavery," at least five operations involving more than 1,000 workers have been prosecuted for violation of anti-slavery statutes since 1997.

It's unclear how pervasive these conditions are, or where exactly they exist. It *is* clear, however, that they're far more common than we'd like to admit. They represent an egregious extreme of abuse, but they are also part of a continuum: the mistreatment of agricultural workers is a deeply entrenched problem in this country, and has been for a long time. In 1972, for example, the average life expectancy for a farmworker was 47 years; in 2008, it was 49.

According to FHDC staff, rates of cancer, asthma, birth defects, and tuberculosis for farmworkers all hover somewhere around 25 percent above national averages. In general, hard work, toxic chemicals, and poor nutrition degrade workers' immune systems; unsanitary and crowded housing exposes them to disease; and low pay makes decent medical treatment extremely difficult to find. The few laws that prohibit these scenarios are rarely enforced, and the undocumented-immigrant status of many workers prevents them from reporting abuses or advocating for their rights.

A large proportion of migrant laborers live on the borders of the fields where they work, typically paying their employers about $50 per week to stay in run-down shacks and trailers. The statistics on just how many people live this way don't exist, because the studies haven't been conducted; as a rule, these farms hide the housing far from view and guard it with private security forces. Entry onto the property is illegal, even for union organizers, unless a worker has given them an explicit invitation to enter. Such invitations are virtually impossible to receive, of course, since it would mean instant dismissal and deportation for whomever made it.

Our tour

The harvest season in Marion County won't start for another few weeks, so the farms we visited on Saturday were empty; they were also unguarded, however, which gave us the rare opportunity to see housing facilities up close.

Even with a fresh coat of paint on their exteriors, the buildings were obviously dilapidated. Inside, concrete walls were stained with black mold and rust. Bedrooms were crammed with bunk beds, and the mattresses were nothing more than wooden planks or sheets of carpeting. The air was dank and sickly. The floor was smeared with a brown layer of bacterial mud.

At both farms we visited, it looked as though someone might've made a recent effort to clean. The dirt was smudged, and the stains had been scrubbed. In both cases, however, the years of accumulated grime remained. Set against a bright blue-and-white sky, nestled near a blossoming field of tulips, these conditions seemed particularly horrendous.

Fire extinguishers were mounted in every doorway at the first farm we saw, and a sign was posted in the kitchen at the second, imploring workers to clean up after themselves —as though safety and sanitation were genuine concerns.

Who built these hovels, and how could they charge rent to the people who live here? Is it simply a matter of farmers trying to meet the bottom line? Are the economics of agriculture really so dire?

And what do these conditions say about us, the people who pay money to support them? What does it mean that we feed ourselves with food grown from filth and suffering?

The people who live here

On Saturday, we weren't able to meet anyone currently living on the farms, but we did meet many who had lived on farms like these recently, or whose parents had.

During lunch at the FHDC development, which is called *Nuevo Amanecer,* or "New Dawn," I spoke with a woman who had moved from a farm in eastern Oregon, where she had shared a single trailer with 10 other workers. "Oh, and with their children," she added as an afterthought, as though it hardly made a difference. "There must have been four or five children, too."

What could life possibly be like for 15 or 16 people living inside one trailer?

And then, because we were eating, I found myself wondering about the people who had grown the vegetables on my plate. What were their lives like? What hardships did they endure?

I asked the woman, who prefers to go unnamed, whether she ever thought about such things while she ate. "I'm not stupid," she said. "I know where my food comes from. What can I do about it? I've got to eat something."

The things I encountered on Saturday were hard and ugly; they were difficult to understand. They were so distant from my daily experience that I've had to fight the impulse to forget, or even to disbelieve what I saw. I continually have to remind myself, as another FHDC resident explained to me, *"Es muy duro, pero es una realidad."* It's very hard, but it's a reality.

Transforming reality

Before I went to Marion County, my awareness of these problems was abstract; I read about them and was troubled, but only in a vague way, the way that any injustice might prod my conscience. As a consequence, the solutions I sought were similarly vague. I thought of grappling with labor law, immigration reform, NAFTA, CAFTA, and the Farm Bill. Ultimately, however, the prospect of affecting such a mess of legislation was debilitating, and I didn't do anything at all.

But after visiting Nuevo Amanecer, I've become convinced that even relatively small and incremental changes can be enormously significant. The FHDC's accomplishments in Oregon—like those of the UFW in California, or the CIW in Florida—provide a clear example of a way in which a few dedicated people can make a tangible difference in others' lives.

The apartments at Nuevo Amanecer are quiet and comfortable. They're small, but they're clean, they're affordable, and they even seem to foster a sense of communal pride among residents. The people who live here are all farmworkers. Most of them are seasonally unemployed, and they all make less than $16,000 annually. If it weren't for an intricate combination of federal funds and private donations subsidizing rent, these families would be living in the fields.

Nuevo Amanecer has a community center where teachers offer lessons in computer skills and English; there's green grass for kids to play on, and a community garden for growing food. The residents I spoke with regularly called their situation a "gift from God," a "blessing," and a "relief." The development provides them with a respite from grinding poverty and all that it entails—illness, fatigue, gang violence, an overwhelming sense of isolation—which can otherwise destroy the fragile ties holding peoples' lives together.

FHDC has spent almost 15 years establishing its facilities in Woodburn, but even so, there's far from enough housing available. At present, there's a waiting list with 250 families on it, and the staff estimates it would take them more than 57 years to meet existing demand. And that's only in Woodburn.

Clearly, this isn't a panacea. But it is a model that can be replicated elsewhere, and it's doing incalculable good for those who can live there. It's a reason for hope.

The label approach

As hopeful as it is, Nuevo Amanecer does little to address the systemic nature of the problem at hand. As any of the staff there will tell you, it is only one small component of the nationwide efforts that are necessary. Given the historical difficulty of effecting large-scale change on this issue, however, the specifics of such a solution are far from clear. And new strategies seem to be in order.

Can we use what we've learned from the efforts to make food "good" and "clean" to also make it "fair"? Could we use a combination of market forces and government regulations like those that created the organic label to develop a "humane" label, perhaps—something like a domestic version of fair trade?

The idea seems promising. The danger, however, is that any standards—like their organic counterparts—would be extremely difficult to enforce, and we'd be creating powerful economic incentives for farmers to violate them.

Moreover, the integrity of the standards—again, like their organic counterparts—would be susceptible to the influence of large corporations, who continually exert pressure on government officials to include as many questionable practices as possible under the "ethical" label.

An Oregon Tilth inspector recently informed me that 23 percent of organic produce was found to have toxic chemical residue on it. He was proud of this statistic, as though it were proof of the efficacy of enforcement. While it is certainly better than the 73 percent found in conventional produce, it's hardly good enough for my tastes; I told him as much, and he was offended.

"Grow your own," he said. "Nothing's perfect."

Sadly, I think he's right. Whether the contamination is willful or inadvertent, caused by the spray from neighboring fields, it seems obvious that no scheme of classification and inspection will ever be foolproof.

We don't feel comfortable leaving minimum-wage regulations or fire codes up to consumer choice, so why should we allow the market to dictate the lives of migrant farmworkers? This is a matter of human rights, and relying solely on a label to effect change would still allow injustice to continue—by sanctioning it, in fact, as "conventional."

Growing your own

Ultimately, it may be true that the only way to understand where your food comes from, and to feel good about it, is to grow it yourself.

Discussion/Writing Prompts

- As Haas relates, the motto of the Slow Food movement is that food be "safe, clean, and fair." In light of what we learn about the conditions under which its hired farmworkers operate, how faithfully would you say this movement lives up to this stated goal? Can you think of a specific example from the essay where this ideal gets fulfilled? Where it falls short?

- According to Haas, there is an inevitable tension between creating a food production system that is environmentally safe and sustainable and creating one that is fair to its workers. In Haas' view, why are these goals so often in tension? And do you share this view yourself? Do we truly live in a world where we have to choose between "going green" and "being fair"? How or how not?

- While it documents the lives of those on the production end of the organic food chain (i.e., the workers who grow, harvest, and process the food), this essay is also clearly intended as a wake-up call to those of us on the other end: the consumers of organic food. In a one-page essay, outline the particular message you think this essay aims to communicate to those of us who eat organic food. In what ways does this portrait of migrant farmwork invite us to rethink the ways we think about, shop for, and consume this type of food?

Tying It All Together: Assignments for Writing and Research

1. RHETORICAL ANALYSIS: "ALL ABOUT US?"

One of this chapter's key contentions is that our media encourage us to adopt a deeply self-focused attitude toward food: to view eating and eating-related questions as being, always and exclusively, about us. Choose an example from our larger pop culture (i.e., an ad, Web site, cooking show, diet book) that, in your view, attempts to promote precisely this message. In a three- to five-page essay, analyze the particular tactics this example uses to convey this idea. What aspects of eating or food does it showcase? And how does it work to represent their consequences and/or benefits as purely personal? Next, offer an assessment of the larger contexts this focus omits. What broader effects—social, environmental, economic — does this example encourage us to overlook? And how would including a discussion of such effects change its overall message?

2. PERSONAL REFLECTION: "MORAL MENUS"

From the livestock raised to the produce grown, from the labor of farmworkers to the decisions of multinational corporations, a number of the selections above challenge us to think more critically about where our "finished" meals actually come from. Choose a recipe for a meal that you've either eaten in the past or would like to eat. What are the necessary ingredients? What steps are required for preparing it? What is the average overall cost? Once you've answered these questions, take a second look at the recipe you've chosen. How much do you know about how these ingredients are grown or processed, manufactured or marketed? To answer this question, write a three- to five-page essay in which you conduct some research into where the ingredients for your recipe actually come from. Once you've presented the "back story" for each key ingredient of your recipe, offer some evaluation of the ways this additional information changes your understanding of or feelings about this meal. Does knowing this back story cause you to want to cook or eat in a different way?

3. COMPARE AND CONTRAST: "EAT THE RIGHT THING"

Regardless of their respective subject matter, all of the readings above are underwritten by some working definition of what it means to eat in the "right way." In a three-to five-page essay, choose two of these selections and compare their models of "correct" or "ethical" eating for which each is arguing. What forms of eating does each include? What types of foods, in what amounts? And just as importantly, what larger ideas about or attitudes toward food does each encourage? What larger values or ideals, in other words, does each attach to its model of eating?

4. VISUAL ANALYSIS: "UNINTENDED CONSEQUENCES"

From advertisements to restaurant reviews, our media landscape is replete with images of the different foods we are told we simply "have" to eat. Rarely, however, do these images encourage us to think more deeply or broadly about the effects this eating choice might have on others. Choose an image from our current media that showcases and attempts to market a specific food. In a three- to five-page essay, first analyze the particular ways this food is presented as something desirable, even necessary, to eat. What visual or textual elements are used to highlight its particular appeal? Next, conduct an analysis in which you speculate about the effects (social, economic, ethical) this eating choice might have on others. In your view, does highlighting these potential effects undermine or enhance the promotional message(s) this image is designed to convey?

5. ARGUMENT-BASED/PERSUASIVE WRITING: "FOOD FIGHTS"

Choose a debate or controversy that is currently being waged in public life. It can involve issues that are political, social, economic, or cultural; and it can be local, regional, national, or international in scope. The only requirement is that it be a debate with no overt or immediately discernible connection to eating. In a three- to five-page essay, first outline the basic elements of this debate: the questions or issues it revolves around; the different attitudes and stances, values and ideals, it puts into conflict. Next, return to the specifics of this debate and offer an analysis in which you argue for the ways this debate can, in fact, be understood as one that is related to eating. When you look beneath the surface of the issues being raised or the competing claims being made, in what ways can it be said to have food-specific significance?

CHAPTER 5

Work

WILL WORK FOR FOOD: EATING AND EMPLOYMENT

Consider the following scenario. As the lunch hour approaches, you find yourself increasingly daydreaming about biting into a cold, crisp apple. After searching your cupboards, fruit bowls, and refrigerator, however, you realize that you are fresh out. Undaunted, you decide to make a quick trip to the grocery store, where you wander for several minutes through aisles stacked high with countless varieties of fruits and vegetables. After browsing the selections for a few moments, your eyes settle on a neatly stacked pyramid of apples, fire-engine red, glistening under the store's bright lights. In short order, you throw a half-dozen or so into a bag, proceed to the checkout counter, pay your money, hop back into your car, and make your way home—secure in the knowledge of a job well done.

In looking over the above account, it's easy to assume that this is a story in which you—the apple-obsessed grocery shopper—and you alone play a starring role. What else does it present, after all, if not the heartening tale of an individual eater satisfying her personal taste all on her own? Consumer wants apple; consumer finds apple; consumer buys apple; consumer eats apple. A simple, elegant tale of one person's search for the perfect snack.

But is it? When we scrutinize the details of this grocery store vignette a bit more closely, do we really see nothing more than the actions of a solitary eater, single-mindedly pursuing her goals without any assistance from a supporting cast? To answer this query, we might begin by posing some questions of our own. Questions like: where did all those apples come from in the first place?

How did they come to present themselves so alluringly on that shelf, symmetrically stacked and burnished to such a high gloss? And while we're at it, who planted and tended the orchards from which they were harvested? By whose hand were they watered and sprayed, plucked and packaged? What workers stacked the boxes or drove the trucks in their journey from orchard to store? And once there, how many additional employees—from produce managers to checkout cashiers—played a role in shepherding these apples from produce shelf to home?

From our vantage as consumers, it's easy to imagine that food is largely about individual choices or personal lifestyles. For thousands upon thousands of people, however, food is also a job. We may be habituated to think of eating as a kind of solo act, but the truth is that behind this conception lies another vision: that of countless workers plying their trade up and down the industrial food chain, laboring in ways large and small to ensure that our supposedly "personal" eating choices feel exactly so. From farmers to fast-food servers, chefs to short-order cooks, restaurant managers to nutritionists, our world abounds with jobs that in one way or another are connected to how and what we eat. Ironically, the very fact that they proliferate in such number may partly explain why we so often take these jobs for granted. Their contributions are so omnipresent, their influence so pervasive, that it's easy to begin treating such work—and the workers who perform it—as invisible. And while this tendency is perhaps understandable, it is also one we would do well to move beyond. Whether it be what restaurant to patronize or what produce to buy, what meal to cook or what diet to follow, the truth is we enjoy such an array of food choices only because so many other people labor to make them possible.

What happens, this chapter asks, when we acknowledge this truth more forthrightly; when we begin, consciously and critically, to take into account the ways our individual eating practices intersect with the lives and livelihoods of all those who "work for food"? Seeking to address this question, the selections assembled here survey the landscape of our modern food industry, presenting readers with a representative sampling of eating-related jobs: the tasks they involve; the conditions they impose; the sacrifices they demand. Because the forms that food work takes vary so widely, this chapter organizes these readings around a specific set of questions: what types of labor do these jobs involve? How much control do individual workers have over the form this labor takes?

How alternately rewarding or exploitative do these jobs feel to those who perform them?

Next, we use these employment portraits as a framework or lens for taking a closer look at the reciprocal, symbiotic relationship that obtains in our society between food consumers and food workers. As we've already noted, virtually every one of our individual eating practices depends upon the efforts and contributions of some workers within the food industry. But the obverse of this is equally true; the conditions and character of modern food work derives in no small measure from the expectations, needs, and demands we have developed as an eating public. Farmworkers put in 14-hour days harvesting lettuce in order to satisfy the public demand for 24-hour fresh produce; waiters and kitchen staff adhere to breakneck schedules because we have become conditioned to waiting no more than 15 minutes for our meal; delivery trucks drive through the night so that grocery store customers won't find themselves dismayed by the spectacle of empty frozen food shelves the next day. Just as our options as eaters are made possible by the jobs food workers perform, so too are these jobs determined by the options we as eaters have come to feel entitled to expect.

The goal behind this approach is twofold. First, to better acquaint ourselves with the vast and various universe of food work. And second, to prod ourselves into a deeper consideration of the responsibility this newfound knowledge carries. If it's true that the jobs undertaken by food workers—from growing and harvesting, to processing and packaging, to serving and selling—is ultimately work undertaken on our behalf, then it could be argued we have an obligation not only to understand exactly what this work involves, but also to factor such insight into the actions and decisions we take as eaters. Such heightened awareness of the interconnection between food consumption and food work could well lead us to become more mindful of the expectation and assumptions that guide our actions as eaters. To remember that real people doing actual work are responsible for the meals we order or the groceries we buy is to redefine eating itself not as an individual or self-contained act but as an opportunity to recognize how interconnected and interdependent we all are. In this sense, food could be said to hold larger lessons about the nature of work in our society more generally. When we look at the vast array of jobs gathered under the rubric of food service, it turns out we discover a fairly accurate picture of the broader American employment scene. To investigate the conditions, questions, and controversies that attend the modern food industry is thus on one level to confront some of the most fundamental issues regarding work altogether: what work means to us and what it does to us; the ways it connects us and the ways it divides us; the rewards it proffers and the costs it extracts.

"My Week as a Waiter," *New York Times* (Jan. 25, 2006)
FRANK BRUNI

Of all the food-related jobs we tend to take for granted, none ranks higher on the list than "server." Whether at the supermarket checkout, the fast-food counter or the restaurant table, we have become so accustomed to being served by somebody else that it's easy to stop thinking about the effort and sacrifice this type of job involves. Seeking to redress this oversight, New York Times food critic Frank Bruni tells the story of his weeklong experiment working as a waiter in a Boston-area restaurant. Chronicling the major challenges and minor humiliations posed by this job, he offers readers a bracing reminder of life on the other side of the service divide.

———————— ✦ ————————

"[L]ast week I traded places and swapped perspectives, a critic joining the criticized, to get a taste of what servers goes through and what we put them through, of how they see us and survive us."

IT'S 7:45 p.m., the East Coast Grill is going full tilt and I'm ready to throttle one of the six diners at Table M-8.

He wants me to describe the monkfish special. For the fourth time. I hoarsely oblige, but when I return yet again to my riff on the apricot lager mustard, which comes right before my oratorical ode to the maple pecan mashed sweet potatoes, his attention flags and he starts to talk to a friend.

Does he mistake me for a recorded message, paused and played with the push of a button? Doesn't he know I have other tables to serve?

I need to go over and massage the mood at R-5, where one of the two diners has a suspiciously shallow pool of broth in her bouillabaisse, perhaps because I spilled some of it near M-2.

And I need to redeem myself with the two diners at X-9, who quizzed me about what the restaurant had on tap and received a blank stare in response. I'm supposed to remember the beers? Along with everything about the monkfish, these oddly coded table references, more than 10 wines by the glass and the provenance of the house oysters?

I had no idea.

I usually spend my nights on the other side of the table, not only asking the questions and making the demands but also judging and, I concede, taking caustic little mental notes. And it's been 20 years since I walked in a waiter's shoes, something I did for only six months.

But last week I traded places and swapped perspectives, a critic joining the criticized, to get a taste of what servers go through and what we put them through, of how they see and survive us. My ally was Chris Schlesinger, a well-known cook and author who owns the East Coast Grill, in Cambridge, Mass., and has no business interests in New York. So that my presence in the restaurant wouldn't become public knowledge, he introduced me to his staff as a freelance writer named Gavin doing a behind-the-scenes article to be placed in a major publication.

In some ways this restaurant, which opened in 1985 and specializes in fresh seafood and barbecue, was an easy assignment. Its service ethic is casual, so I didn't have to sweat many niceties. Its food is terrific, so diners don't complain all that much.

But its pace can be frenetic, and servers have little room to maneuver among 100 or so tightly spaced seats.

From Monday through Saturday, I worked the dinner shift, showing up by 3:30 and usually staying past 11. I took care of just a few diners at first and many more as the week progressed.

And I learned that for servers in a restaurant as busy as the East Coast Grill, waiting tables isn't a job. It's a back-straining, brain-addling, sanity-rattling siege.

MONDAY

Pop Quiz and Chop Chop

Every day at 4 p.m., the servers take a pop quiz. This afternoon's questions include ones on how the restaurant acquires its oysters and the color, texture and taste of mahi-mahi.

Before and after the quiz they tackle chores: moving furniture, hauling tubs of ice from the basement, folding napkins. I pitch in by chopping limes into quarters and lemons into eighths. I chop and chop. My fingers go slightly numb.

The servers range in age from their early 20's to their late 40's. Some go to school or hold other jobs on the side. Many would like to do less physically demanding work. All would like to earn more money.

If they put in a full schedule of four prime shifts a week, they might make $45,000 a year before taxes. Almost all of it is from tips. They wonder if diners realize that.

Bryan, a young server with whom I'm training, brings me up to speed on the crazy things diners do. They let their children run rampant, a peril to the children as well as the servers. They assume that the first table they are shown to is undesirable and insist on a different one, even if it's demonstrably less appealing. They decline to read what's in front of them and want to hear all their options. Servers disparagingly call this a "menu tour."

I acquire a new vocabulary. To "verbalize the funny" is to tell the kitchen about a special request. "Campers" are people who linger forever at tables. "Verbal tippers" are people who offer extravagant praise in lieu of 20 percent.

The doors open at 5:30 and soon two women are seated at L-3. They interrogate Bryan at great length about the monkfish, which, in changing preparations, will be a special all week long. He delivers a monkfish exegesis; they seem rapt.

They order the mahi-mahi and the swordfish.

"It's amazing," Bryan tells me, "how unadventurous people are."

How unpredictable, too. During a later stretch, Bryan has a man and a woman at L-3 and two men at L-4. The tables are adjacent and the diners receive the same degree of attention. The men at L-4 leave $85 for a check of $72 a tip of about 18 percent.

L-3's check is $58, and Bryan sees the man put down a stack of bills. Then, as the man gets up from the table, the woman shakes her head and removes $5. The remaining tip is $4, or about 7 percent.

TUESDAY

Ice, Ice Baby

I'm shadowing Tina, who has worked at the East Coast Grill for decades and seen it all. She is handling the same section Bryan did. She offers a psychological profile of a woman sitting alone at

L-3, who declared the chocolate torte too rich and announced, only after draining her margarita, that it had too much ice.

"Some people are interested in having the experience of being disappointed," Tina says.

Some people are worse. Arthur, a young server who is fairly new to the restaurant, recalls a man who walked in and announced that he had a reservation, a statement Arthur distrusted. The East Coast Grill doesn't take reservations.

Arthur tried to finesse the situation by saying he was unaware of the reservation but hadn't worked over the previous three days.

"You haven't worked in three days?" the man said, according to Arthur's recollection. "You're going to go far in life!"

At about 9:30, a half-hour before the kitchen stops accepting orders, I take my first table, two women and a man. I ask them if they want to know about the half-dozen specials.

"We want to know everything," the man says.

The statement is like a death knell. I mention the monkfish, but forget to say that it comes with a sweet shrimp and mango salsa. I mention the fried scallops, and I'm supposed to say they're from New Bedford, Mass. But that detail eludes me, so I stammer, "Um, they're not heavily breaded or anything." They seem puzzled by my vagueness and poised to hear more. I've got nothing left.

What unnerves me most is trying to gauge their mood. Sometimes they smile when I circle back to check on them. Sometimes they glare.

In addition to dexterity, poise and a good memory, a server apparently needs to be able to read minds.

WEDNESDAY

Who Really Needs a Drink?

I'm under Jess's wing. She's young, funny and generous with her encouragement. That final quality turns out to be crucial, because after I greet four diners at M-7, I'm informed that one of them has an affiliation with the Culinary Institute of America.

As I walk toward them with a bowl of house pickles, which is the East Coast Grill's equivalent of a bread basket, my hand shakes and several pickles roll under their table. I can't tell if they notice.

But I can tell they don't trust me. I'm tentative as I recite the specials, and I ask one of them if he wants another Diet Coke. He's drinking beer. They all look at me as if I'm a moron.

Jess tells me that enthusiasm is more important than definitive knowledge, that many diners simply want a server to help them get excited about something.

"You've got to fake it until you make it," she says.

I take her pep talk to heart, perhaps too much so. I handle three men at M-6, one of whom asks, "Between the pulled pork platter and the pork spareribs, which would you do?"

I tell him I'd change course and head toward the pork chop.

"It's that good?" he says.

"It's amazing," I say. I've never had it, but I've seen it. It's big, and so is he.

He later tells me, "Dude, you so steered me right on that pork chop."

I serve four young women at M-9. They order, among other dishes, the "wings of mass destruction." Per the restaurant's script, I warn them away from it, pronouncing it too hot to handle. They press on and survive.

One of them later wonders aloud whether to have the superhot "martini from hell," made with peppered Absolut. I didn't even know it was on the menu before she mentioned it.

"Why worry?" I say. "With those wings, you climbed Everest. The martini's like a bunny slope."

She orders it and drinks it and she and her friends leave a 22 percent tip (which, like all the tips I receive, will be given to the other servers). The three men at M-6 leave 20 percent.

Have I become a service God?

THURSDAY

I'm Really Allergic to Tips . . .

Divinity must wait.

It's on this night that I spill bouillabaisse, confront my limited beer knowledge and silently curse Mr. Monkfish at M-8. I move up to an evening-long total of eight tables comprising 20 diners; on Wednesday I served five tables and 17 diners.

I encounter firsthand an annoyance that other servers have told me about: the diner who claims an allergy that doesn't really exist. A woman at X-10, which is a table for two, or a "two top," repeatedly sends me to the kitchen for information on the sugar content of various rubs, relishes and sauces.

But when I ask her whether her allergy is to refined sugar only or to natural sugars as well, she hems, haws and downgrades her condition to a blood sugar concern, which apparently doesn't extend to the sparkling wine she is drinking.

She orders the sirloin skewers, requesting that their marginally sweet accouterments be put on a separate plate, away from her beef but available to her boyfriend. He rolls his eyes.

Pinging from table to table, I repeatedly forget to ask diners whether they want their tuna rare or medium and whether they want their margaritas up or on the rocks. I occasionally forget to put all the relevant information—prices, special requests, time of submission—on my ordering tickets.

At least everyone at M-8, including Mr. Monkfish, seems content. As I talk to one of the women in the group, another server noisily drops a plate bound for a nearby table. A rib-eye steak special skids to a halt at the woman's feet.

"Is that the cowboy?" she says, using the special's advertised name. "That looks really good!"

About an hour later M-8's spirits aren't so high. They're motioning for me, and it's a scary kind of motioning. The two credit cards I've returned to them aren't the ones they gave me.

One of my last tables is a couple at X-1. They take a bossy tone with me, so when the woman asks if it's possible to get the coconut shrimp in the pu pu platter á la carte, I automatically apologize and say that it's not.

It turns out that I'm right. (I guiltily check a few minutes later.) It also turns out that servers make such independent decisions and proclamations, based on the way diners have treated them, all the time.

FRIDAY

Do Not Jump the Shark

Apparently everything up to now has been child's play. Business will double tonight. People will stand three deep at the bar, closing lanes of traffic between the kitchen and some of the tables.

"Like a shark," Chris Schlesinger tells us, "you've got to keep moving or you die."

My chaperone is Christa, who's as down to earth and supportive as Jess. She's supposed to watch and inevitably rescue me as I try to tackle an entire section of five tables, each of which will have at least two seatings, or "turns."

By 7:30, all of these tables are occupied, and all have different needs at the same time. One man wants to know his tequila choices. I just learned the beers that afternoon.

Another man wants directions to a jazz club. Someone else wants me to instruct the kitchen to take the tuna in one dish and prepare it like the mahi-mahi in another. That's a funny I'll have to verbalize, a few extra seconds I can't spare.

I've developed a cough. It threatens to erupt as I talk to three diners at M-6. Big problem. I obviously can't cough into my hand, which touches their plates, but I can't cough into the air either. I press my lips together as my chest heaves. I feel as if I'm suffocating.

The kitchen accepts orders at least until 10:30 on Fridays and Saturdays. I'm dealing with diners until 11. By then I've been on my feet for more than six hours.

Over the course of the night I have surrendered only two tables and six diners to Christa. I have taken care of 11 tables and 32 diners myself. Except I haven't, not really. When my tables needed more water, Christa often got it. When they needed new silverware, she fetched it, because I never noticed.

Truth be told, I wasn't so good about napkin replacement either.

SATURDAY

Feeding the Hordes

My last chance. My last test. The restaurant ended up serving 267 diners on Friday night. It will serve 346 tonight.

Between 5:30 and 5:50, I get five tables, each of which needs to be given water, pickles, a recitation of the specials and whatever coddling I can muster.

The couple at one table want a prolonged menu tour. I'm toast.

Once again I try to tackle an entire section, seven tables in all. Dave is my minder. He tells me to make clear to diners that they need to be patient.

"If you don't control the dynamic, they will," he says.

I don't control the dynamic. Around 6:30 I ask him to take over a table I've started. As some diners leave and new ones take their places, I ask him to take over a few more tables.

I deliver a second vodka on the rocks with a splash of Kahlúa to a woman at L-9. Before I can even put it down, she barks, "There's too much Kahlúa in that!" Nice to know you, too, ma'am.

I do some things right. I point a couple at L-6 toward the tuna taco, because by now I've tasted it and I know it's fantastic. They love it and tell me they love me, a verbal tip supplemented by 17 percent. The next couple at L-6 barely talk to me, seek and receive much less care and leave a tip of over 50 percent. Go figure.

I do many things wrong. I fail to wipe away crumbs. I don't write the time on one ticket. I write M-12 instead of L-12 on another, creating a table that doesn't exist.

Around 8:45, my shirt damp with perspiration, I hide for five minutes in a service corridor, where I dip into the staff's stash of chocolate bars. Then I suck on a wedge of lemon, a little trick I learned from Bryan, to freshen my breath.

By the end of the night I've served a total of 15 tables comprising 38 people. Some of these people were delightful, and most tipped well, keeping my weeklong average for a comparatively light load of tables—at about 18 percent.

Some weren't so great. They supported an observation that Dave made about restaurants being an unflattering prism for human behavior.

"People are hungry, and then they're drinking," he noted. "Two of the worst states that people can be in."

I recall a young woman at a six-top who bounced in her seat as she said, in a loud singsong voice: "Where's our sangria? Where's our sangria?" Her sangria was on the way, although she didn't seem to need it, and the bouncing wasn't going to make it come any faster.

Around 11:30 all the servers are treated to a shot of tequila. I drink mine instantly. I'm exhausted. I'll still feel worn out two days later, when I chat briefly on the telephone with Jess, Christa and Dave, who by that point know the full truth about me.

"I think you got a good sense," Dave says.

I think so, too, if he's talking about trying to be fluent in the menu and the food, calm in the face of chaos, patient in the presence of rudeness, available when diners want that, invisible when they don't.

It's a lot, and I should remember that. But I'd still like frequent water refills. And a martini from hell. Straight up.

Discussion/Writing Prompts

- One of the terms often used as a substitute or synonym for "waiter" is "server." How do you understand the difference between these two descriptors? To what extent does "waiter" conjure a different view of this job than "server"? Based on Bruni's description of his own experience as a waitstaff member, how accurately does the idea of "serving" capture what this job seems to involve? Does this term give you a positive or negative view of such work? How specifically?

- Of all the lessons Bruni claims to have learned during his week as a waiter, none is more fundamental than this: "I learned that for servers in a restaurant as busy as the East Coast grill, waiting tables isn't a job. It's a backstraining, brain-addling, sanity-rattling siege." First, choose one of the specific experiences

Bruni relates (i.e., an interaction with a customer, a conflict with kitchen staff, his performance of a particular task) that, in your view, exemplifies the "lesson" summarized above. Next, write a one-page essay in which you outline the particular ways this experience illustrates this larger lesson. What aspects of the job does Bruni highlight here? And how does he use these details to advance his view of serving as a kind of siege. And finally, offer a quick assessment of how convincing you find this effort.

- One of the unspoken goals behind this piece is to prod readers into considering different ways of looking at, thinking about, and interacting with those whose job is to serve food. How successful is Bruni in this effort? In what specific ways does this portrait of serving encourage or incline you to alter your own views, your own behavior, regarding these workers? Can you think of another selection in the chapter that similarly attempts to affect or alter our views? How do the two efforts compare?

"Working in the Shadows: America's Dirty Food Jobs," *Salon* (Feb. 11, 2010)

FRANCIS LAM

We all know what a package of frozen chicken breasts or hamburger patties looks like. But how many of us can tell the story of where these packages come from? Offering an overview of the work required to make this food available, Lam acquaints readers with some of America's "dirtiest food job." Along the way, she poses hard questions not only about the ways the industrial food system treats animals, but also about the conditions it mandates for the workers who labor on its behalf.

✦

> "It's great that, in the age of locavorism, more people are asking where their food comes from, but Gabriel Thompson asked a different question: Who does your food come from?"

We all know what a package of frozen chicken breasts or hamburger patties looks like. But how many of us can tell the story of where these packages come from? A writer joins an army of immigrant workers at the bottom of our nation's food industry, offering in the process an overview of the work required to make this food available. Along the way, she poses hard questions not only about the ways the industrial food system treat animals, but also about the conditions it mandates for the worker who labor on its behalf.

I t's great that, in the age of locavorism, more people are asking where their food comes from, but Gabriel Thompson asked a different question: *Who* does your food come from? Cute little farmers' markets aside, the vast majority of us still eat lettuce harvested by immigrant labor, packed in Arizona, and shipped to our supermarkets all over the country. And it's the stories of those often invisible workers in lettuce fields, in chicken plants, on delivery bikes, that Thompson finds while living and working with them for months at a time in his new book, "Working in the Shadows."

In these jobs, he meets people who have no other options, but also people who are grateful for the economic stability work offers them, people who take great pride in their skills with lettuce, and people who can't tell if it's their fingers or their minds that are more numb while tearing apart chicken breasts on an icy assembly line.

Salon spoke with Thompson about the relations of immigrants and locals in these industries, how he managed to not realize he was writing a book on food, and about how breaking your back while harvesting lettuce can be kind of . . . fun.

The part of the book on working in Yuma, Ariz., lettuce fields is called "Salad Days." At first that just sounds like an ironic joke, but that time does seem to be the most positive experience in your project.

Yeah, there was something very lighthearted in it. The work itself was the most physically demanding, and I contemplated walking away from it more than the others because of the pain in my hands and back. But there were things that made it more pleasurable.

One, people, our crew, was always looking out for me. And not just me—people would jump in and help each other out. No one used the word "solidarity," but there was a sense of worker solidarity, that we're all in this together. My crew was at first concerned that I was some kind of undercover agent, but then later was just worried that I had some sweating problem I should have checked out. For my last day, they put together a huge meal for me, and the foreman gave us twice as long as normal for lunch, a full hour.

Two, there's something about working outside versus in a depressing plant that just feels psychologically healthier, even though in two months in the fields, I never saw a single insect. They had that much fumigation going on.

And three, there was a sense of pride in the workers in their abilities. "We want you to tell your friends what it's like out here, how their salad got there," they told me."It's the toughest work around, and we're *good* at it." It helps a lot if you have pride in what you do. If you believe it's important and not many people can do it, you can put up with a lot of crap.

Can you talk about that pride? What are lettuce skills?

Well, first, you don't pick lettuce, you cut it. So you have to bend down and stab it to separate it from the ground, then trim the outer leaves off before it starts to look like something you'd recognize. It would sometimes take me 30 seconds, and others would have it cut and bagged in just a few seconds. In low points, dribbling sweat all over the stuff, I would just slice the heads up and crush them like they were defective. At one point my co-worker called me the "Lettuce Assassin."

I thought it was just going to be backbreaking work. Well, after a while, my endurance was increasing, and yet my maximum speed for cutting one row was like everyone else's relaxed pace for cutting two. So what I thought was an "unskilled" job is in fact very skilled. With every new head of lettuce cut I learned something new, so the chance to constantly try new theories, like different movements, made it interesting.

Towards the end I was getting a little nostalgic, but the last two days we harvested more than 40 tons of lettuce, and that beat the nostalgia right out of me.

Did work in the chicken plant ever seem challenging in that good way?

In the poultry plant—and this is purposeful—all the jobs have been deskilled to the point where anyone can be bored within five seconds; it's something a monkey can do. The turnover is so high, they don't want to train anyone new. One week I was there, they had rehired 10 percent of the entire workforce. You'd think it was easy, but it's much more difficult, because you go a little crazy. You're just grabbing a chicken breast and tearing it in half 7,000 times a day. You can't have conversation because you've got headphones on from the machine noises. You have to stand still. Half of my orientation class left within *one week*.

One day, I had a revelation: that chicken breasts look like the butts of white babies. And that was probably my single thought in that five-hour session.

Was there much of a sense among the people you worked with that they had other economic options?

What was most shocking of all to me was rural poverty for Americans. Russellville is where people bounce between two jobs—Walmart or the poultry plants. You just can't work in the poultry plant very long before you have health problems. It's just designed very clearly without the health of workers in mind. Lots of repetitive stress injuries in this push for everything being cheap: Who can get the cheapest chicken to McDonald's?

There had been a KKK march before I showed up, so I expected lots of animosity between locals and immigrants. But the Guatemalans were treated almost like foreign exchange students, more with curiosity than animosity. And it turns out that no one believed that immigrants were taking jobs away from Americans. People didn't have the jobs because they couldn't stand them.

One night, we were tearing breasts in half, and the supervisor comes over and says, "You have to work as hard as possible, this is really important!"

And Kyle said, "What is this, national security?" There was this sense that this stuff is cheap and we are treated like we are cheap.

You wrote a book about life in lettuce fields, working in a chicken plant, and being a restaurant delivery boy. So how is it that you didn't set out to write a book about food?

Well, my general take on food was always: "Where is it, and can I have some?" So, honestly, it wasn't until groups like Slow Food started asking to talk with me that I thought that maybe this book can help people in the food movement go beyond "Is this food safe for my kids?"

For me, it's as much about the woman who couldn't stay awake, falling asleep while standing because she worked the night shift and took care of her kid during the day. I wrote this, to the best of my ability, as a portrait of immigrant work, which is the subject of lots of loud, abrasive conversation, but which people have so little sense of in their everyday lives. I just hope that the book will let people pause for a minute and think about the work they do that supports us.

Before I got to Arizona, to get ready, I was doing push-ups and I bought a biography of John Steinbeck. I read about him talking about wanting to write, supporting himself through hard manual labor, like digging ditches. And what he realized after not too long was that he didn't have any creative energy at the end of the day to write. That was one of the lessons to me early on, how privileged I am. In Yuma, I was in bed, exhausted, every night by 8. Creative work can be angst-filled, but it's a privilege to have the energy to even think of doing it.

Discussion/Writing Prompts

- Many observers of the contemporary food scene have argued for the importance of knowing exactly where our meals come from, of tracing the process by which various raw materials are transformed into a finished product. To what extent does Lam's exposé accomplish this goal? And what is the upshot or consequence of learning this information? Does this essay affect or alter your view of what it means, for example, to eat a chicken dinner? If so, how?
- In the most immediate terms, this essay aims to highlight the hardships experienced by food industry workers: the physical, emotional, and psychological toll these kinds of jobs exact. In a one-page essay, offer an assessment of

how effective you find this critique to be. In your view, does this essay do a convincing job of presenting these workers as victims of the industrial food system? How or how not?

- As the employers of thousands of food industry employees, multinational corporations like McDonalds and Tyson Foods go to great lengths to burnish their public image. To what extent can Lam's essay be read as an attempt to challenge this type of public image? What specific aspect(s) of the corporate public relations campaign does this "insider story" serve to discredit? And how effective, finally, do you find each?

"Rethinking Work: Cooking as Labor," *AlterNet* (March 10, 2010)

SARAH JAFFE

We often hear that we now live in an era in which all of the old re-strictions and prejudices around work—especially those regarding gender—have fallen away. But when it comes to the work around cooking, how much of this conceit is truth and how much fantasy? Taking up this question, Jaffe invites us to consider what happens to our assumptions about gender and class when we start thinking about cooking as "labor."

———————— ✦ ————————

"[F]oodies want to return to a world where food isn't just an afterthought or something we pay others to do. But too often these food evangelists forget a couple of important factors. One of them being cooking is work."

F ood politics are sweeping the United States. The local food move-ment, the slow food movement, all of it embodied in periodic sweeping pieces from lead guru Michael Pollan, whose writing is lush and pretty enough to make you feel the sensual pleasure he takes in his food—from procuring to cooking to eating, though rarely growing/killing.

Pollan and other foodies want to return to a world where cook-ing isn't just an afterthought or something we pay others to do. But too often these food evangelists forget a couple of important factors. One of them being that cooking is work.

In a mostly-lovely *New York Times Magazine* piece last summer, Pollan sang the praises of Julia Child (revived by the Oscar-nominated Meryl Streep in "Julie and Julia"). He wrote:

> Child was less interested in making it fast or easy than making it right, because cooking for her was so much more than a means to a meal. It was a gratifying, even ennobling sort of work, engaging both the mind and the muscles.

Kate Harding noted Pollan's call for a return to cooking, though, sounds an awful lot to some of us like a call for women to get back in the kitchen. His acknowledgement of cooking as work that could be satisfying, in other words, leaves out the fact that it is also work that many people hate. She suggests:

> I wasn't around in the '60s, but I'm guessing [feminists] made ridiculous, man-hating arguments like, "Dude, Julia Child gets paid to cook."
> And for women, having the option of feeding ourselves and our families without working pro bono all day is part of what allows us to function as (mostly) equal citizens.

Pollan may not have been making an explicitly gendered argument toward people getting back in the kitchen, but he did note that televised cooking has shifted from Julia Child's glamorous-yet-comforting how-to style to daytime "dump 'n' stir" and nighttime competition that moves at a breakneck pace—and is made to appeal to men.

Delicious. But. . .

It's been an argument made for years that cooking, when it is glamorous and well-compensated, is something for men. Chefs are male, but the everyday cooking in the household is something for women to do. When men do the work, in other words, it is labor to be compensated (if chefs do often make very little in comparison to the waitstaff at fancy restaurants) and congratulated; when women do it, it is part of everyday life.

Out of the kitchen and into the workforce arguments always had a class (and race) division to them: many women had already been working and didn't find it particularly liberating. Many of them, often women of color, worked as domestic laborers as well—getting paid, if not very well, to do the same work they then did for free at their own home. Well-off women were already recognizing in their own way that cooking was work, and we still recognize this when we watch cooking shows on TV or go to restaurants, fancy or otherwise. Now back-in-the-kitchen arguments have their own class dimension. They imply the time to spend in the kitchen as well as the money to buy fancy ingredients. Ethically produced local food tends to be more expensive partly because the people who produce it are being paid decently, so despite the lack of middlemen we pay much more for organic produce from the farm around the corner.

Raj Patel, in *Stuffed and Starved*, connects the dots from the labor of people on the consuming end of food to the labor of those who produce it, and notes that the creation of the unhealthy food economy that Pollan and company so despise squeezes those at the producing end as much as the consuming end. Cheap food, after all, is necessary in a world where most people (again, often people of color) have little income to spare to spend on fresh food, let alone delicacies, and little spare time to prepare things. Cheap food that is still profitable for corporations requires cheap labor. And so we go around the vicious circle.

Examining our social relation to food has to include the work necessary to prepare it—in a piece on health and "obesity" (the convenient stand-in for unhealthy eating that mistakes bodily characteristics for behaviors), *Mary Ferguson* wrote:

> Recent research shows that social class measured by income and education can be more powerful than genetics in predicting future health problems, including obesity.

Though the piece focused on physical activity as a way to prevent obesity rather than on healthy eating at any weight, a much more important goal, sentences like this one explain just as much about why people don't cook for themselves and eat cheap, fast, unhealthy food as they do about lack of exercise:

> "A lot of minority women can't relate to the word 'leisure-time,'" Dr. Amy Eyler, a researcher at the School of Public Health in St. Louis, Mo., said in an interview with Reuters. "And when you ask them about it they say, 'I don't have any.'"

Over and over, new food evangelists arise with the latest solution to the problem, often in the form of a book they want you to buy, as if the problem doesn't go deeper than something you can purchase. The problem, after all, is our entire system, built on squeezing some group or other for more work to make more profits.

Adding more work to the end of our already overworked days on its own is not going to be enough, and it doesn't help that the people who tend to be spokespeople for the food movement do enjoy the work of cooking.

It seems to be shocking, even to feminist foodies like *Lisa Jervis*, who understand not just the food part of food politics, but the class and gender issues at play, that some people simply do not enjoy cooking and will do almost anything to avoid it. She says:

> I would want to know what they don't like about it. Do they feel like they're going to produce something that's not good? Are they nervous about the result? Does their hand cramp when they hold the knife? Are they afraid they're going to cut themselves? Are they too tired at the end of the day? Maybe it's lonely in the kitchen. There are solutions to a lot of those problems.

Or perhaps it's just work that people don't want to do for free. One of the feminist arguments for work as liberation, after all, wasn't just the right to be fairly compensated—it was the right to choose the form of our labor.

While that choice is not nearly as wide-open as the myths of the free market make it seem, it's still an important choice for people— not just women—to make. Fixing our food system is one of the most important things we can do for our collective health, but ordering people to do work for free that they don't enjoy isn't going to fix it.

Discussion/Writing Questions

- What do you make of the conventional distinction in our culture that defines cooking as "woman's work"? Does this stereotype seem accurate in your own experience? To what extent does this view reinforce other stereotypes in our culture?

- From parenting manuals to cookbooks, our world abounds with material that encourages us to view the kitchen as women's domain. Choose an example of this material, and write a one-page assessment of the ways it uses cooking to define woman's work. How does it define the concept of woman's work? In your view, is this definition accurate or helpful? Unfair or problematic? And how?

- How does Jaffe's discussion of cooking compare to Lam's exposé of "dirty food jobs"? What are the similarities and differences between these respective portraits of food labor? And which portrait do you find more compelling? Why?

"Competitive Eating: The Most American Sport?" *Salon* (March 25, 2010)

THOMAS ROGERS

What happens to our assumptions about food when we start to think of eating as a job? Outlining the strange career of professional competitive eating, Rogers invites us to think about the effects and the meaning of this increasingly popular phenomenon.

————————— ✦ —————————

"It's crude, it's rude, and it's all about eating disturbing amounts of food."

Amid the push toward healthier food the popularity of eating contests continues to soar. But what happens when such popularity leads us to begin thinking of eating itself as a kind of job? Outlining the strange career of professional competitive eating, Rogers invites us to think about the effects and the meaning of this burgeoning new sport.

Competitive eaters face off in annual "Wing Bowl"

It's crude, it's rude, and it's all about eating disturbing amounts of food. This week, the trailer for "Nacho Mountain," the first fiction film about the world of competitive eating, has been circulating on food blogs. The low-budget independent film tells the story of Keefer, a man who loses his job and begins participating in underground eating competitions.

Unfortunately, based on the trailer, the gross-out comedy (which has yet to get distribution) isn't all that much to get excited about (it appears to be an even less funny version of "I Hope They Serve Beer in Hell"). But it serves as a testament to the extent to which competitive eating has managed to insinuate itself into American culture over the past decade. In the past few years, the eating contest has turned from a fairground novelty into an organized circuit—with a supervising body, professional competitors, and hundreds of thousands of dollars in prize money.

It has managed to do this at a time when worries about obesity and overeating have prompted everything from salt-regulation legislation to Jamie Oliver anti-obesity reality shows. To find out why competitive eating continues to have such a hold over American culture—and what it says about Americans' attitude toward food—we called Ryan Nerz, a competitive eating announcer and the author of "Eat This Book: A Year of Gorging and Glory on the Competitive Eating Circuit."

The competitive eating world has grown dramatically over the past few years. Where did this widespread popularity come from?

The real start of this modern era of competitive eating was in 2001 when Takeru Kobayashi won the hot dog eating contest in Coney Island by doubling the record and eating 50 hot dogs in 12 minutes. It really started catching on in 2004, 2005, when the number of eating contests per year went from 30 or 40 to about 100. The International Federation of Competitive Eating (now known as Major League Eating) has done a fantastic job of relentlessly going after brands to sponsor these contests—casinos and food companies. Now there's probably about $250,000 of prize money a year.

And there's been lots of documentaries on the Travel Channel, Discovery, Spike TV; there's this movie ["Nacho Mountain"]; all these guys have blogs, and Facebook pages and fans and, believe it or not, groupies. It's not the Olympics yet, despite Major League Eating's real intention of having it be in the Olympics. These days, Nathan's famous contest gets as many viewers as some of the games in the Stanley Cup finals. If you consider how absurd many feel the contest of competitive eating is, it already has become a successful sport, but I feel like it's plateauing, frankly. I'm shocked that it's gotten where it is.

Why don't you think it will get much more popular?

I just think it's too redundant. They just keep eating. That's all they do. For an announcer it becomes frustrating. Sometimes one person is eating faster than the other, or the person has some sort of technique to break apart a chicken wing, but after a certain point, I just want to be like, "They're eating and they're eating and you're watching and I'm talking." It's just the same thing over and over again. There are no passes or dribbles or fouls. It's just eating. There's an inherent ceiling.

Why do so many people like watching people gorge themselves?

It's this uniquely American spectacle that is half sport and half magic. People can't wrap their heads around the idea of eating 69 hot dogs in 10 minutes, so it does have an element of magic. Though, if you want to be pessimistic about competitive eating, it's also a kind of a freak show. It's a little bit like watching a train wreck and you try to hide your eyes and peek through your fingers.

What makes it uniquely American?

Well, that's not entirely accurate. Japan also embraces it and I've announced mince pie eating contests in England, a chicken satay contest in Singapore, and a dumpling one in the Czech Republic. But I think Americans are just insanely competitive people, and as such we want everything to become a competition. If you look at where new sports really stem and proliferate from, America is pretty up there—snowboarding and all these newfangled sports. In America we're so inundated with different sports and media that we have an appetite for a new and esoteric sport that allow a small number of people to be experts in it.

I also think Americans have a slightly different attitude about food than many other countries. Americans often think of food in utilitarian terms—eating as fast as possible at Burger King. It's not as much about taste and atmosphere as it is in many other countries.

I think there's a degree of truth to that. Certainly if there's any group of people that I've talked to who are confused, disturbed and outraged by competitive eating it's the French and the Italians. We have fast food places where you eat by going through a drive-through and grabbing some fries and a burger—that's a pretty utilitarian process. It's not much of a leap of logic from eating in that way to timing yourself for 10 minutes and seeing how much you can eat.

In the past few years, there's been an increasing move to regulate the way people eat—limiting trans fats and posting calorie counts on menus. Do you think the popularity of competitive eating is a backlash against that?

There's a little bit of a working-class mentality where guys are like, "Fuck you, I'm going to eat a bacon double cheeseburger because I'm a man." It shirks this new paternalism in the same way that New Yorkers, I think, cut back on smoking at first when it was banned indoors and it came back with some enthusiasm and now there are places where you know you can smoke after midnight. To me competitive eating is probably more of a curiosity [than a political statement].

What's your favorite competitive eating event?

The best contest was probably a one-minute raw onion-eating contest in Maui, where they ate sweet onions like apples. I like the deep-fried asparagus contest in Stockton, Calif. It happens in late April. There's tens of thousands of people there to celebrate asparagus—they drink things like aspara-tea—and it's just a really weird and oddly pure sort of event. The record I love the most is the mayonnaise record, 8 pounds in 8 minutes.

On the other end, there's the Wing Bowl, in which 30,000 kids in Philadelphia's Wachovia Center watch fat dudes eat wings while being flanked by naked women. I found it to be a version of hell on Earth. I needed to go home and take several showers to get the Wing Bowl out of me, but a lot of people think it's a very American thing.

Discussion/Writing Prompts

- What is your reaction to regarding eating as a professional sport? Does this view strike you in any way as odd or incongruous? What changes when we start to think about eating as a competitive activity undertaken for financial gain?
- First, create a list of the qualifications you think are most essential for a person seeking to become a professional competitive eater. When you're done, create a similar list of qualifications for a second job, one that strikes you as more typical or conventional. Then, write a one-page essay in which you describe and assess how these two lists compare. When read against a more conventional job description, how do the qualifications for competitive eating appear? Is there anything about these qualifications that, in your view, makes this job seem less like "real work" than other jobs? How?
- Unlike the other selections in this chapter, which tend to focus on the ways food is produced, processed, or marketed, this piece takes a closer look at how food is consumed. In your view, is this perspective a useful or important one to take into account? In a one-page essay compare the lessons we learn about our modern food culture in this reading to those we learn from one of the other selections in this chapter. How similar or different do you find their respective commentaries? And which piece, in your view, has something more valuable to teach us? Why?

Tying It All Together: Assignments for Writing and Research

1. RHETORICAL ANALYSIS: "EXPLORING THE FOOD CHAIN"

One of the unspoken messages behind this chapter is that the decisions about how and what we eat affect more than just ourselves. As the selections assembled above make clear, our actions and choices as eaters are but one link in a much larger chain, one that connects us to the work and livelihoods of countless fellow citizens. Choose an example from our larger pop culture (i.e., an ad, Web site, cooking show, diet book) that, in your view, makes the connection between food and work more explicit. Then write a two- to three-page essay in which you analyze the specific ways this connection is presented. What example of food or eating does your selection showcase? And how does it use this depiction to make larger statements about the work which makes this example possible? Next, evaluate whether or not you find this particular presentation useful or effective. Does your selection offer us a way of thinking about eating and food that is valuable? Necessary? How or how not?

2. PERSONAL REFLECTION: "YOUR SERVER WILL BE"

Whether or not we've ever held a job in the food service industry, chances are we've all experienced this world from the other side: that is, as customers or consumers. Every one of us has shopped at a convenience store, patrolled the aisles of a supermarket, or eaten a meal at a restaurant. And more likely than not, we have also developed fairly established expectations about how this experience is supposed to go. Less obvious, though, are the ways these expectations are made possible by the work others perform on our behalf. In a two- to three-page essay, reflect back on a recent experience as a consumer within the food service industry: as a shopper, customer, restaurant patron, etc. What did it feel like to find yourself "served" by others? What expectations, what unspoken rules, governed the interaction? And did the interaction itself leave you feeling comfortable? Satisfied? Frustrated? Embarrassed? Why? And finally, based on this assessment, how would you define the ideal customer/server relationship?

3. COMPARE AND CONTRAST: "(DE)VALUING WORK"

As is true of the workplace more generally, the jobs within the food industry encompass a wide range of activities and contexts, skill sets and income. Just as wide-ranging are the ways these jobs are evaluated in the eyes of our larger culture. Some types of food-related employment carry significant social cache while others carry very little. Choose two food-related jobs that, in your view, represent the opposing ends of this spectrum: one that ranks high and one that ranks low on our society's conventional scale of value. In a two- to three-page essay, offer an assessment of how these two jobs compare. What are the key tasks and responsibilities that define each? What purpose is each designed to fulfill? How is each compensated? Once you've sketched out these differences, reflect upon why these jobs are conventionally valued in such different ways. In your view, do these assessments seem accurate? Fair? If you could, how would you change the standards we use to evaluate these kinds of work?

4. VISUAL ANALYSIS: "IMAGINING FOOD WORK"

From news reports to sitcoms, our media landscape is filled with countless depictions of different workers. How often, though, do these portraits draw a connection to food? While food-related jobs abound in the real world, they seem far less in evidence when we scan our popular culture. Choose an image from our current media that showcases an example of food-related work. Then write a three- to five-page essay in which you analyze the particular messages in this example about what food-related work is like. In your estimation, does it present a portrait that is accurate or misleading? Positive or critical? And finally, how compelling or convincing do you find this depiction to be? Why?

5. ARGUMENT-BASED/PERSUASIVE WRITING: "WORKING IT OUT"

A number of the selections above highlight a particular controversy related to food work: from exposés of slaughterhouse workplace conditions to critiques of fast-food service jobs. Write a three- to five-page essay in which you identify and analyze one such controversy. What key issues, questions, and/or conflicts does it involve? Whom does it seem most to affect? Once you've addressed these questions, present your own argument about how this particular controversy could be resolved. What in your view would constitute a fair and feasible solution to this problem?

CHAPTER 6

Technology

EATING WHAT COMES NATURALLY

Of the countless labels affixed to our food these days, none is more ubiquitous than the one reassuring us that such-and-such item—whether it be breakfast cereal or ground beef, tortilla chips or baby food—is "100 percent natural." Along with taste, nutrition, and cost, *naturalness,* it seems, has now joined the ranks of the priorities at the very top of our food culture pyramid. Roam any supermarket aisle and more likely than not you'll find yourself amidst a thicket of signs, logos, and labels, each one straining to outdo its rivals in trumpeting the "natural" bona fides of its given product—from organic peanut butter to bgh-free milk, "shade-grown" coffee to wild-caught salmon, grass-fed steak to preservative-free salad dressing. And while this sort of experience has grown more and more commonplace—so familiar at times as to feel like a "natural" feature of our shopping lives in its own right—it is far from clear exactly *why* this is so. What is it that explains our current obsession with eating 100% natural foods? Why have we come to regard naturalness as such a vital and necessary aspect of what we eat? Do we see it as a guarantor of physical health? Or does it stand as a symbol for other values and virtues? And while we're at it, what is it precisely about the prospect of eating something *less* than 100% natural that we have come to regard as so unsettling?

One way to answer these questions is to think of this trend not just as a celebration of naturalness per se, but as an extended response to all the different ways our food system in general has been modernized: a strategy we have turned to in order to make sense of the myriad advancements (scientific, technological, and industrial) that, over the last fifty years, have so drastically re-shaped both how and what we eat. From the pesticides sprayed on our produce to the growth hormones infusing our meat, from ge-netically engineered peaches to frozen pizzas, the last half century has witnessed breathtaking changes in the ways our food is pro-duced, packaged, preserved, and distributed. And while these transformations have led to undeniable improvements in our daily eating lives, they have also given rise to pronounced anxieties. Whether measured in terms of convenience or cost, accessibility or variety, it is difficult on the one hand to argue that our food sys-tem has not made huge strides over this period. Food, in greater abundance and diversity, is now more widely available, at more af-fordable prices, than at any other time in our history. And yet these very same developments have led to what many decry as the grow-ing *artificialization* of what we eat. While food is both plentiful and cheap, it is also true that virtually every one of the products stock-ing the shelves of our grocery and convenience stores has in some way been processed, fortified, or otherwise adulterated by some chemical, scientific, or industrial process.

A BRAVE NEW MEAL: SCIENCE, TECHNOLOGY, AND FOOD

When it comes to the role science and technology have played in refashioning food, what exactly are we to think? Breakthroughs in food chemistry have not only led to a proliferation of new food, they have also succeeded in enhancing the flavor and appearance, the nutritional and caloric content of old food. Advancements in technology have enabled producers to transport fresh food halfway across the globe and consumers to store food for years on end. Innovations in industrial production have led both to staggering increases in the amount of food available and a marked decrease in its overall cost. By these lights, the artificialization of modern food looks to have proven itself an unalloyed boon.

At the same time, however, such progress has led to other de-velopments whose consequences are far from benign. While new additives and preservatives have succeeded in extending the shelf life of different foods, they have also been linked to a marked in-crease in the rates of different diseases. The ascendance of the in-dustrial food economy has made countless foods more affordable, more abundant, and more accessible; yet such convenience has come at a steep price, both to our health and to the environment. The phenomenal success of the fast-food industry over the last half century, to cite just one example, is not only reflected in the millions of Americans who now struggle with obesity and high-blood pressure, but also in the millions of acres of rainforest clear cut to supply the meat for these burger-making behemoths. To weigh such deleterious costs against the unambiguous gains is to confront the welter of conflicting feelings—from confidence and comfort to uncertainty and outrage—which the modernization of food has come to engender. To put it mildly, the verdict on the role of science, technology, and industry is decidedly mixed.

All of which brings us back, one last time, to "natural foods." To capture the way this movement stands as a kind of Rorschach test for our feelings about modernization, consider a representative natural food product, one that has increasingly become a fixture on supermarket dairy shelves: organic milk. To be sure, grocery stores have been selling milk for as long as they have been in existence. But only in the last decade or so have most stores begun to regularly offer customers an organic alternative alongside the conventional gallons and half-gallons on display. Why choose organic over regular milk? In one sense, the answer seems obvious: a product so obviously more natural is also presumably far healthier to drink. Our choice of organic over "regular" milk could thus be viewed as one way to express our suspicions or worries about the kinds of additives or preservatives conventionally used. Continuing in this vein we might even go so far as to speculate about the psychological, even the symbolic, dimensions to our choice. Opting for organic milk not only expresses our desire for a more healthful beverage; it also makes a statement about the kinds of values most important to us: the natural over the artificial, the pure over the manufactured, perhaps even the expensive over the cheap.

The picture becomes more complex, however, when we start to account for all the ways this natural item owes its existence to the very technical/scientific/industrial practices its most enthusiastic advocates decry. Despite its reputation as an alternative to industrialized food, the organic movement has long since become a multibillion dollar, multinational industry in its own right. The major players in organic food are themselves corporations, with production, distribution, and marketing organizations that rival the scale of any of their industrial counterparts. With this additional information in hand, we might well be tempted to revise our forgoing analysis. In light of this fuller picture, our choice of organic milk seems less an unambiguous rejection of the forces of the modernization of food than a complicated negotiation with them. A choice that does not so much hearken back to an era before corporate, technological, and scientific change, but one that rather seeks to make this change compatible with the idea(l) of "naturalness."

At the other end of the spectrum, we might look briefly at a counterexample: the Twinkie. Cream-filled and shrink-wrapped, a staple of countless of grade-school lunch boxes, this torpedo-shaped pastry has come in many respects to stand as the quintessential American snack food. Shot through with additives and chemicals, laced with preservatives that render it impervious to the elements, however, this iconic edible has also long served as a touchstone for all the ways our modern eating habits have been remade by science and technology. If we are looking for an object that captures and crystallizes our complicated feelings about food and technology, we could do a lot worse than the Twinkie. Loaded with preservatives, reflecting a yellow hue rarely found in nature, this classic munchable has enjoyed a long career as the ultimate example of "fake" food. And yet—as its enduring popularity with successive generations of children attests—the Twinkie is also a food that many of us love. Even as we decry its wholly manufactured character, even as we reflexively make it the butt of our jokes or the scapegoat of our critiques, the Twinkie endures, continuing to stock the pantries in millions of American homes. What this apparent contradiction suggests is that our feelings about the role of technology/science in our eating lives are more complicated than it first appears. While the increasingly manufactured quality of our food, its sometimes distressingly artificial semblance, often troubles us, it also suits us. We have grown extremely accustomed to having what we want—at any time, in any amount—when we want it. In this sense, the Twinkie represents the fulfillment, not the failure, of our ideals: a ready-made food so ingeniously engineered as to be perpetually, if paradoxically, "fresh."

Between the gallon of organic milk and the package of Twinkies is the terrain this chapter endeavors to survey. Taking direct aim at the complex and conflicting feelings we seem to harbor about modernization, this chapter uses food as a lens for more closely examining the ways we've learned to think about technological, scientific, and industrial change. When we take a closer look at all the ways our food system has been modernized (by advancements/innovations in technology, science, industry) over the last half century, to what extent do our attitudes and assumptions about food stand as an index of how we feel about modernization more generally?

"The Udder Truth," *Salon* (Jan. 19, 2007)

HANNAH WALLACE

One of the most powerful and enduring fantasies is the dream of returning to our origins, our most essential, natural, and authentic state. Taking direct aim at this dream, Wallace presents a probing examination of the true health benefits that come from eating raw food.

———————— ◆ ————————

"Raw milk really is a wonder tonic, say devotees, who meet secretly to buy it and swear it reverses chronic diseases. But is it safe to drink? The official word. No."

Thirty-four-year-old Brigitta Jansen, a statuesque brunette with radiant skin, is no stranger to unpasteurized milk. She grew up in a tiny German village, where she and her grandmother, pails in hand, would fetch milk fresh from a neighbor's farm. But over the years, after moving to a bigger town and then, ultimately, to New York City, she unthinkingly switched to pasteurized milk, which was more convenient and easier to find.

Two years ago, however, while pregnant with her first child, the eczema that had always plagued her got a lot worse. "My skin grew so sensitive. I would stand in the shower and scratch my arms and legs," Jansen says. After a lengthy Internet search, she came across the Weston A. Price Foundation, which promotes the nutritional philosophies of a Canadian dentist who advocated eating traditional foods such as grass-fed beef and raw dairy products. Price's 1939 book, "Nutrition and Physical Degeneration," showed—with photographic evidence of implausibly straight and cavity-free teeth—how the nutritionally rich diets of so-called primitive cultures were far healthier than the diets of Western industrial nations.

Jansen bought "Nutrition and Physical Degeneration" and read it cover to cover. After that, "I had to have raw milk," she says. And through the New York City chapter of the WAPF, now 600 members strong, she found a farmer who produced it. After a few months of drinking the milk on a daily basis, Jansen's eczema was gone. She guzzled it throughout her pregnancy and now that she's breast-feeding, craves it even more. "I drink about a quart a day," Jansen says, laughing.

Jansen is part of a growing movement of health-conscious consumers who say that unpasteurized milk—as long as it's from grass-fed cows—is capable of reversing chronic diseases from asthma to irritable bowel syndrome. According to raw milk devotees, pasteurization—which zaps the milk to 145 degrees (or even higher with ultra-pasteurization)—destroys vitamins A, B12 and C as well as beneficial bacteria such as lactobacillus, enzymes such as phosphatase (which facilitates proper calcium absorption), and an anti-arthritis compound called the Wulzen Factor. Lactobacillus, in turn, breaks down into lactase, an enzyme that helps people digest lactose, making raw milk easier for even the lactose-intolerant to imbibe.

Many people come to raw milk as a last resort; one man I spoke to for this article had terrible asthma, one woman had debilitating arthritis, and another had osteoporosis (which pasteurized milk hadn't improved)—and all saw complete reversals of their diseases after a few months of drinking it. Their stories were persuasive, but in an age where E. coli is turning up at Taco Bell and even in organic spinach, I wondered: Is it really safe to drink unpasteurized milk?

In a word: no. A scan of the CDC's Web site turns up several recent bacterial outbreaks traced to raw milk: Last year in Washington and Oregon, four children were sickened by E. coli O157:H7; in 2002, there was a multi-state outbreak of Salmonella enterica serotype typhimurium; and in Wisconsin, in 2001, 70 people were infected with Campylobacter jejuni. Such outbreaks were the reason pasteurization was introduced in the first place, of course (it was only an added benefit that the process also extended milk's shelf life). As early as 1908, cities such as Chicago and New York required the pasteurization of milk—and in 1948, Michigan became the first state to ban raw milk. Today, though pasteurization is not compulsory on a national level, it is required of any dairy hoping to ship its wares across state lines and has become the law in states that have adopted the Food and Drug Administration's pasteurized milk ordinance, an operating manual for the handling and production of milk. Public health officials unanimously agree that pasteurization has dramatically reduced infectious diseases.

Still, despite the risks, remarkable recovery stories like Jansen's abound—and demand for raw milk is increasing. The Weston A. Price Foundation, founded by nutrition activist Sally Fallon in 1999, already has 400 chapters around the world and more than 9,000 members. According to Fallon, anywhere from 2,000 to 3,000 people join each month. "People are sick and searching for answers—and they're getting better," Fallon says. Pam Laine, a 45-year-old from Silicon Valley, was headed toward diabetes when she began drinking raw milk. "It eliminated all my cravings for sweets, refined foods and alcohol," she told me. "My blood sugar levels are now normalized." A 53-year-old New Jersey man I spoke to was so impressed with his own turnaround on raw milk (he was diagnosed with hepatitis C, with viral counts at 15 million, and after nine months of drinking it, the virus was undetectable) that he starting giving it to his four grandchildren, all of whom had asthma. "This is the first winter they're not getting sick," says the man, who asked to remain anonymous, since raw milk is illegal in New Jersey. "They don't need their inhalers anymore."

> It's a Wednesday night in a brick office building near Manhattan's Union Square, and a cross-section of New Yorkers—a Dominican family from the Bronx, an African-American woman in her 30s and a young mother with an Australian accent—are traipsing up a stairwell with empty bags and boxes in hand. On the second floor, a hipster couple in their 30s inquire about a delivery of colostrum, while an elderly woman steps gingerly over a cooler full of half-gallon jugs of milk.

A few times a month, members of this private "milk club" come here (and to several other drop-off locations across the city) to pick up raw milk and other natural foods—like grass-fed meat, organic vegetables and fermented foods such as kim chee, sauerkraut and kvaas—that they've ordered directly from local farmers. Their reasons for seeking out the milk are as diverse as the members themselves—some are chefs who crave the quality and rich flavor, or immigrants who miss the raw dairy of their homeland, or people of all income levels with health problems, or problems digesting pasteurized milk, who find that raw dairy helps. The timing of deliveries is not publicly advertised, and members learn about drop-offs and sites a few weeks in advance on the club's Web site.

While such clubs may be reminiscent of Prohibition-era speakeasies, what their patrons are doing is not technically illegal. Each state has the right to regulate its own raw milk—though the FDA banned the sale of raw milk across state lines in 1987—and in New York state, on-farm purchases of raw milk are legal. The difference is that, rather than commute to the country fields for their weekly fix, milk club members place their orders over the phone with the dairy and mail their checks. The club then hires a middleman to deliver the prepaid orders to the city.

Today, raw cow's milk is legal in at least 22 states—and is legally available through inventive arrangements in a handful of others. In Florida and Arizona, raw milk can be sold as pet food, as long as it is labeled as such. Dairy farmers in other states are getting even more resourceful in skirting the law while also meeting demand: Cow-share programs, in which consumers buy a share in a cow (usually an annual fee of $25) and then pay a "boarding fee" when they come to fetch their share of the animal's milk, are thriving in Ohio, Virginia and Michigan. "There is no law against drinking milk from your own cow," Fallon explains.

But some states—and even the FDA—have begun cracking down on such creative loopholes. Wisconsin banned shares a few years ago, after an outbreak of Campylobacter jejuni was traced to raw milk. In October, state troopers pulled over Michigan dairy farmer Richard Hebron as he was making a delivery and seized more than 400 gallons of his raw milk. And one month earlier, in California (where it's been legal since 1930 and is to this day sold in retail outlets), agriculture officials shut down the nation's largest raw milk dairy, Fresno-based Organic Pastures, after five children who drank the milk became infected with E. coli. (Intensive investigations since then have not turned up any E. coli at the farm, in the milk or even in the cows' manure.) Finally, last fall, an Amish dairy farmer who ran a cow-share program in northeastern Ohio was busted when an undercover state inspector came to his door, feigning interest in raw milk.

One of the most outspoken critics of unpasteurized milk is John Sheehan, director of dairy and egg safety for the FDA's Center for Food Safety and Applied Nutrition. Drinking it, Sheehan says, "is like playing Russian roulette with your health." He's even devised an anti-raw-milk PowerPoint presentation. When I ask Sheehan if he's familiar with the theory that pasteurized milk is a nutritionally depleted beverage, his response is terse: "Such claims are wholly without scientific support." Sheehan's slide show enumerates the hazards of drinking raw milk (especially by those who are immuno-compromised) and appears to be a direct rebuttal to a similar slide show that can be found on the Weston A. Price Foundation's Campaign for Real Milk site. (One of Sheehan's slides: Myth No. 1: Raw milk kills pathogens. No it doesn't.")

Mark McAfee, the owner of Organic Pastures, says his dairy has been under intense scrutiny since September, when the E. coli outbreak prompted state investigators to shut the company down for a few weeks. Two of the five children infected with E. coli were hospitalized—and one nearly died. Still, McAfee maintains there is no proof that the E. coli strain that infected the five children came from Organic Pastures milk. (Indeed, that strain was also separate from the E. coli O157:H7 traced to Earthbound Farm's spinach, which infected nearly 200 Americans in 26 states in September.) Even before this scare, McAfee's dairy was aggressively inspected by the California Department of Food and Agriculture, the Fresno County Health Department and even the FDA.

"I'm probed like you cannot believe," he says. "There's no notice—they just show up in their white suits with their hairnets and booties." Though disruptive, these inspections are essential if he is to keep his Grade A status. "And they've never found a pathogen," McAfee says, with obvious pride. "Anytime, anyplace."

He isn't surprised. McAfee's Holsteins and Jerseys, all 300 of them, feed year-round on fresh, organic grass—Sweet Clover, Bermuda and Johnson—and are kept immaculately clean. McAfee has even invented a mobile milking barn for his cows that allows them to graze rotationally and keeps them away from crowded, manure-filled barns.

Another reason no pathogens have ever been found in his milk, McAfee believes, is that it contains a host of active antibacterial components—not just proteins like lactoferrin, but enzymes, bacteriocins, colicins and at least 25 beneficial bacteria, including lactobacillus and bifidus, the same probiotics that are found in most yogurt. And all of those components, McAfee says, are destroyed during pasteurization. (In her book "Nourishing Traditions," WAPF founder Fallon concurs: "Pasteurization destroys these helpful organisms, leaving the finished product devoid of any protective mechanism should undesirable bacteria inadvertently contaminate the supply.") To prove his theory, a few years ago, McAfee sent his milk and colostrum to a private lab and had both injected with high levels of the three pathogens. The bacterial counts of all three bugs decreased over time. And the conclusion of the scientist at BSK Labs? "Raw colostrum and raw milk do not appear to support the growth of Salmonella, E. coli O157:H7, and Listeria monocytogenes," stated the lab report. McAfee is so proud of his below-normal bacteria counts that he posts annual averages on his Web site.

"Pasteurization is an excuse to produce dirty milk," says Los Angeles raw milk activist Rahman Dalrymple, citing the outbreaks of salmonella, listeria and Campylobacter that have all been traced to pasteurized milk. In California, accepted bacteria levels for Grade A raw milk are fewer than 15,000 colony-forming units per milliliter; accepted levels for raw milk destined for pasteurization is 50,000. (Post-pasteurization, milk in California can contain 15,000 CFUs per milliliter. States that adopt the FDA's Pasteurized Milk Ordinance allow pasteurized milk 20,000 CFUs per milliliter, one-quarter more than California's raw-milk limit.) Dalrymple, who credits raw milk with curing his asthma, emphasizes that he would never drink raw milk that's destined for pasteurization by a large industrial dairy. Not all raw milk is created equal, Dalrymple says. "Raw milk *is* dangerous—if you get it from one of these industrial dairies that have fecal matter and pus and blood in their milk. I would absolutely not drink that!"

This distinction—between raw milk that's destined for pasteurization and raw milk from a small, spotlessly clean dairy that's kept to higher standards precisely because the milk won't be pasteurized—is a crucial one, and it's lost on public health officials like Sheehan, who seem to lump all raw milk into the same pathogen-contaminated vat. Industrial farms are dirty—as the recent agri-exposés "Fast Food Nation" and "The Omnivore's Dilemma" have proved. When Sheehan thinks of raw milk, in other words, he's thinking of milk from cows crowded together in barns, eating a diet of corn, and standing in their own manure. All the raw milk advocates I spoke to are against drinking this type of raw milk.

Perhaps even more convincing is the argument, made by raw milk advocates, that safe raw milk must come from grass-fed cows. That distinction, too, is ignored on the FDA's Web site, in remarks that Sheehan made last May to Ohio's House Agriculture Committee, and in his anti-raw-milk PowerPoint presentation. Cows, like all other ruminants, are meant to eat grass. Yet, at the vast majority of U.S. dairies—even organic ones—cows subsist on corn feed. In "The Omnivore's Dilemma," Pollan explains how eating a high-starch diet acidifies a cow's rumen, making the animal sick and cventually allowing bacteria to enter its bloodstream. A cow's corn diet can also make *us* sick: E. coli O157:H7 has been around only since the early '80s, when it likely evolved in the acidic guts of corn-fed cattle. (E. coli O157:H7 is so lethal because human stomachs, too, are acidic. We can kill off microbes that evolve in the neutral pH of a grass-fed cow's rumen, but not the acid-resistant strains such as E. coli O157:H7.) Grass-fed cows also produce milk that is intrinsically more nutritious: Whole milk, butter and cream from grass-fed cows contain conjugated linoleic acid, an omega-6 fat that has been shown to inhibit breast, skin, stomach and colon cancers. (CLA is found in both raw and pasteurized grass-fed milk—it does not appear to be damaged by pasteurization.)

Like irradiation, which has been proposed as a way of ensuring the safety of meat and vegetables in our food supply, pasteurization is an after-the-fact measure that does little to prevent contamination in the first place. Rather than trying to force industrial dairies to clean up their act in order to improve the health of their herds, the FDA has put its support behind higher-temperature pasteurization. As described on Cornell University's Dairy Science Web site, this process is even more lethal to bacteria, further extending milk's shelf life. According to the International Dairy Foods Association, the most common method of pasteurization today is high-temperature short time (known as HTST), in which milk is heated to "at least" 161 degrees Fahrenheit for just 15 seconds. But IDFA spokeswoman Susan Ruland says that dairies are increasingly moving toward ultra-pasteurization (UP), during which milk is heated to 280 degrees Fahrenheit for two seconds, and ultra-high temperature (UHT), a method so intense, it effectively sterilizes milk so it doesn't even require refrigeration. Horizon, the largest organic milk brand in the United States and a subsidiary of dairy giant Dean Foods, uses only HTST, UP and UHT. Such high-temperature, shorter-time methods are ideal for specialty products such as cream or organic milk that don't move off the shelves as quickly as regular milk.

Raw milk advocates say the higher-temperature pasteurization methods have a much greater impact on milk's nutrient content than even traditional vat pasteurization, which heats the milk to 145 degrees Fahrenheit for 30 minutes. But according to Kerry Kaylegian, a food scientist at Cornell University who specializes in dairy chemistry, though HTST, UP and UHT inactivate more enzymes and nutrients in raw milk, this inactivation is minimal. "Pasteurizing milk does not affect the nutritional properties of the fats, the proteins or the lactose," says Kaylegian, who is spearheading Cornell's Milk Facts Web site. Though Kaylegian acknowledges that lactobacillus is destroyed by pasteurization, she dismisses the assertion that raw milk from small, pristine dairies is somehow safe to drink. "Raw milk, even from healthy cows under sanitary conditions, still runs the risks of having pathogens in it," Kaylegian says.

But raw milk proponents like Dalrymple are quick to argue that pasteurization isn't a panacea for pathogens, either—and that plenty of outbreaks have recently been traced to pasteurized milk and pasteurized cheese. In most cases, as in the 2000 case of multidrug-resistant Salmonella typhimurium in Pennsylvania, Delaware and New Jersey, pathogens contaminate the milk after pasteurization when containers, surfaces or hands are not properly washed or the milk or cheese isn't sufficiently pasteurized. (All of which, raw milk advocates would agree, is terrible: When insufficiently pasteurized, some of the protective, good bacteria is killed off, yet the pathogens remain.) Another worry for the dairy industry is heat-resistant pathogens, such as Mycobacterium avium subspecies paratuberculosis, a hardy bacterium that causes Johne's disease (pronounced "yo-knees"—a disease common in U.S. herds that has been controversially linked to Crohn's disease in humans). At least one study, conducted in 2004 by Dr. Jay Ellingson, of Marshfield Clinic Laboratories, in Marshfield, Wis., has shown that MAP can survive pasteurization.

> So, what to make of Jansen's vanishing eczema or Dalrymple's complete recovery from his asthma? Ditto the New Jersey man whose four grandchildren no longer need their inhalers?

A compelling new study, published in the June 2006 issue of the Journal of Allergy, Asthma and Immunology, seems to lend support to what these three already know to be true. Researchers at the University of London analyzed the diet of 4,700 children in Shropshire and found that those who lived on farms and drank raw milk had significantly fewer symptoms of asthma, hay fever and eczema. Children who drank raw milk were 40 percent less likely to develop eczema and 10 percent less likely to get hay fever than their non-raw-milk-drinking peers. Blood samples showed that they had 60 percent lower levels of immunoglobulin E, an antibody released by the immune system when it's confronted by allergens. (IgE, in turn, causes cells to release histamines, which is what causes an allergic reaction.) In their conclusion, study authors Michael Perkins and David Strachan surmised that the lactobacilli found in raw milk protect against eczema. They also stated, "Unpasteurized milk is known to be rich in a variety of gram-negative species and their lipopolysaccharides, and it is plausible that a persistent exposure to a diverse milieu of bacteria from an early age is likely to have an effect on the developing immune system."

In the end, it seems, raw milk is a lot more complicated than the FDA and the AMA would have consumers believe. Like sushi, raw milk is a nutritionally rich food that can be contaminated if it's not fresh and prepared in an immaculate, sterile environment. Just as raw milk devotees buy their milk from farmers they know and trust, so sushi connoisseurs tend to patronize the same few high-end restaurants—and know which days the fish is freshest. But the government isn't lobbying to make raw fish illegal (yet). That may have everything to do with sushi's status as an exotic Japanese import—a food usually enjoyed (in this country) by city-dwelling adults. Milk, on the other hand—wholesome, nourishing cow's milk—is more than just a healthy beverage; it's a symbol of the American heartland. It's a drink Americans of all income levels feed their children unthinkingly. And the behemoth dairy industry—in 2006, it made $20 billion from milk alone, according to the National Milk Producers Federation—would like to keep it that way. As Dalrymple put it: "Milk is big business. When you think milk, think Exxon."

Still, to suggest that there's a conspiracy afoot seems absurd. Small dairy farmers—some of whom can't even legally advertise that they sell raw milk—make up a fraction of the country's market. David Gumpert, a columnist at BusinessWeek.com who has covered the recent crackdowns on raw milk farmers on his blog, The Complete Patient, doesn't think Big Dairy is threatened—yet. "Raw milk is not huge right now, but if it ever caught on . . ." Gumpert's voice trails off. Most dairy farmers sell their milk to pasteurization cooperatives for roughly $1 a gallon. But Mark McAfee can get as much as $10 a gallon for his raw milk—and he sells direct to stores and consumers. Though Organic Pastures is a relatively small operation, it doesn't take an econ major to figure out that those numbers could quickly add up.

Meanwhile, the FDA has just announced that it's safe to eat meat and drink milk from cloned animals. In such an Orwellian universe, where raw milk from cows that have two biological parents is considered dangerous, while pasteurized milk from cloned cows is safe— is it any wonder that a growing band of consumers don't trust FDA decisions? Raw milk drinkers don't appreciate being treated like drug addicts, reduced to buying their milk at clandestine outlets or joining a cow share just so they or their farmer won't be harassed. But their goal is not to make raw milk ubiquitous, they say—only legal. "We're not pushing for in-store sales of milk," says Fallon. "We want to make sure that farmers can sell it at the farm gate."

Discussion/Writing Prompts

- This blog lays out a number of specific benefits it claims eating raw food will yield. To what extent is it possible to read this celebration of "rawness" as an implicit or unspoken critique of so-called modern food practices? Take a closer look at the list of benefits Fry claims for the raw food movement. For each, write two or three sentences on the ways it can be read as a critique of our modern food system. What particular technological, industrial, or scientific practice does each seem to offer up for criticism?
- Take a closer look at the excerpted quotation above. How do you understand the relationship between rawness and health? In your view, does the raw food movement represent an advance in the way we think about and try to foster public health? How or how not?
- Much of the support for the raw food movement rests upon the assumption that such foods are more authentic. To what extent does Wallace's exposé challenge this assumption? How sympathetic do you think Lionette would be to Wallace's argument?

"Mass Production of Food Is Ruining Our Health," *The National Expositor* (Dec. 10, 2007), www. nationalexpositor.com

JAMEY LIONETTE

While the modern food industry has succeeded in supplying us with food in stunning abundance, it is far from clear whether this success has been matched by a comparable increase in food quality. Making the opposite argument, Lionette, a farmer by trade, presents a stinging indictment of the ways the organic food movement has become increasingly commercialized and industrialized.

———————— ◆ ————————

*"Chain supermarkets are 'listening to their customers' and
capitalizing on cheap organic food. But the chain-supermarket owners are some of the same people who screwed up
our food supply in the first place. How can we trust them?"*

South End Press—I am not a scientist, journalist, or other spe-
cialist. I sell food. I help run a family-owned and operated
neighborhood market and café that buys and sells predominantly
local, clean, and sustainable food. I cannot speak about the reality of our food supply around most of the world. I can only can
speak of what is happening in the first world, where, unfortunately, only the privileged elite can choose to put real food on
their dinner tables.

Lately it seems every mass media newspaper or magazine,
from the *New York Times* to *Rolling Stone*, has an article digging
into the true filth that most food in the U.S. really is. Some people
are actually questioning mass produced and monoculture organic
food. Even *Time* magazine proclaimed "Local Is the New Organic"
on its cover. Everywhere I turn people tell me that there is a new
wind in the U.S.; that people are now concerned about eating
local, clean, and sustainable food. From my vantage point in the
market, behind the counter, I just don't see it. Yes, in Massachusetts there are more farms today than in the last 20 or so years, but
fewer total acres than ever recorded. Farmers markets are becoming popular or perhaps trendy. Chain supermarkets are "listening to their customers" and capitalizing on cheap "organic"
food. But the chain-supermarket owners are some of the same
people who screwed up our food supply in the first place. How
can we trust them?

Outdoor food markets are a mainstay in most cultures in the
world and were once a given in our culture. Now most people go
there to shop for the luxury food treats (locally grown food) and
get their staples at the supermarket. I think that because of the Depression (when there was no money to spend on food) and World
War II (when there was rationing and everyone was focused on the
war effort) Americans lost their taste-buds. Along came the mass-
produced foods of the 1950s at cheap prices. Supermarkets were a
"progressive" thing, as suburban living was progressive. Rural culture and production was frowned upon as old-fashioned and primitive. Food from all over the world suddenly became available and
at prices lower than local food. Protecting America's foreign interest, the beginning of what we now call globalization, became a

new form of colonialism. Foreign resources, raw materials as well as labor, were now easily exploitable by the nation's new super-power status. As the economy grew, money filtered down to the managerial and to some of the working class and was coupled with an influx of cheap products made cheaply and available to most classes of the U.S. Consumerism took off. Our food changed as well, especially with faster transport and technologies trickery to extend the shelf life of food. Seasonal produce became available year round; exotic food (such as bananas and oranges in Boston) became readily available and affordable. Everything was cheaper, the shopping was more convenient, and exotic foods became staples in our diet. Small and local farms shut down or were forced into monoculture farming. A disconnect sprouted between our diets and our food sources. An orange, once a special and rare treat, became an everyday commodity.

Supermarkets are part of mainstream America's identity. Working-class people have little choice but to shop at conventional supermarkets. Middle-class people can shop at places like Whole Foods and appease their consciences with the notion that that food is safer and tastier than conventional supermarket food. And those of the flat earth society—middle- and upper-class people who do not believe that their climate is changing, that a global market is a bad thing, or that our food systems are in trouble—favor the conventional supermarket. However, both conventional and progressive supermarkets operate on the same model: mass-produced foods, made cheaply, and sold at cheap prices.

Supermarkets sell commodities. They buy mass-produced food from big business. This model of efficiency, which mirrored the production of things like automobiles and VCRs, is what created the mess our food supply is in. Efficient ordering and deliveries, no seasonal variety of stock, little to no blemishes (whether natural or from human error), significant quantities—enough to keep all those shelves constantly filled with whatever the customer might want. I describe this model as "I want what I want when I want it," and it goes against everything about food that is local, clean, and sustainable. It cannot be done at a mass level. [. . .]

People first bought cheap food because they either did not have enough money or felt like they were beating the system by spending less than they budgeted for food that week. Over time our budgets became based on the price of cheap food, so that now, during the rare moment of seeing real food, the price tag appears exorbitant. Our wages and salaries, our rent and utilities, all are tied to our cheaply priced food.

Many people who can actually afford local, clean, sustainable food buy it only when it is trendy, sold at boutique shops, or for a special occasion. Those from the class which struggles to afford mass-produced food certainly cannot afford the real price of food in the U.S. One often-overlooked agent of gentrification and, after rent increases, one of the best ways to ruin a neighborhood is by shopping at chain supermarkets. Local neighborhood markets close or survive by becoming convenience stores. Farmers' markets become a trendy place to buy a few novelty items: "Oooh look at this peach. I bought it from a farmer!" Once the small markets are gone, only supermarkets are left. We are so out of touch with the struggle to get food, because of how much cheap food is available in the country, that we do not see a pattern of destruction.

The more we buy mass-produced foods, the more it empowers agro-business and the fewer farms there will be. The more we shop at supermarkets, the fewer neighborhood markets there will be. Already we are almost trapped by agro-business and its sales outlets. Soon, there will be no escape. As it stands right now, only a privileged few can afford real, clean, and sustainable food; soon, even the privileged will have little access to such food. The fewer local farms we have, the more expensive their food becomes and the more difficult it is for local farms to feed the local population. Once the farms are gone, only mass-produced food is left.

Hadley, Massachusetts, is known as having the best asparagus in the world. Though just an hour or so outside of Boston, it is near impossible to find asparagus grown in Hadley in Boston. Futures of the asparagus are sold; mostly to France and Japan, I am told. Instead of a wonderful spring vegetable for a local dish, Hadley asparagus has become a boutique item for other parts of the world. Yet in spring, summer, winter, or fall, asparagus flown in from Peru is half the price of in-season asparagus grown on a family farm in New England. And I must admit it seems a bit shameful to complain about such a situation in the U.S., when so many peoples around the world local resources have been diverted to produce food for Americans.

The late summer is tomato season in New England. The glory of a local tomato salad on a warm summer night in Boston is something which we can only enjoy a couple of months a year. The flavor of our farmers' tomatoes are spectacular. Especially when bought at a local shop or farmers' market, where we actually speak with the people involved in harvesting and distributing our food, people who are part of our community. These tomatoes were not sprayed with anything; the soil was not ruined by chemicals or monoculture farming. These tomatoes traveled only a few dozen miles and were grown outside, thus using only a little energy and creating little pollution. The farmer, part of our community, was deservedly paid and did not exploit anyone or the land. No one was ripped off during the whole transaction, and the tomatoes were available to everyone in Boston during the late summer months.

Yet the rest of the year we still expect to have fresh tomatoes available, and they are called for in many dishes. Fresh tomatoes are considered year-round staples. There is never any questioning tomatoes in March, their integrity or their source. We have become used to hydroponic tomatoes flown in from Mexico or Holland. Instead of focusing our efforts on bringing in tomatoes year-round to Boston, we should focus making the Northeast corridor able to feed itself now and in the future. At the very least, these factory-grown tomatoes do make our local tomatoes taste even more wonderful. We are so used to the mealy, flavorless (or artificially flavored) hydro-tomato that when we taste a real one, it seems so special. This is one reason why local farmers are not perceived as the people who raise our food, but as the producers of specialty items.

Another reason farmers are considered purveyors of specialty foods is their prices. Let us end the idea right now that local, clean, and sustainable foods result in a high profit for the producer and the retailer—trust me, there is absolutely no money in sustainable food. When food is handled as sustenance—not as a commodity—there is little profit to be had. That is why real food is so rare and so hard to come by now. The perverted twist is that it would seem logical that food transported for days around the world would cost more than something fresh and local. But quite the opposite is true. Nobody considers what the true price of real food is. Nobody is outraged that what most working-class people can afford, and even the middle class can afford, is nothing more than mass-produced, cheapened food.

There are, of course, the Whole Foods, Wal-Marts, Trader Joes, and other chain supermarkets trying to sell organic foods. Everyone knows these places are cheaper than local markets and farmers' markets, but rarely do people think about how supermarkets work. People are generally aware of the smaller mark-up chain supermarkets can afford, as compared with an independent neighborhood market, as well as all the corporate capital and funding behind them. But few often think about what is involved in producing enough of a particular food for every shelf of their hundreds or thousands of outlets across the region or country. You can't see the devastating effects of monoculture farming in the sterile and lifeless supermarket. The food looks so perfect and seems so abundant. And with such cheap prices, why ask questions? Sustainable farming does not have the ability to be mass produced; it cannot be sold at the level of a chain supermarkets. Corners must be cut to keep costs low, production must increase to fill the shelves, the laws of nature must be beaten by science to allow for year round production, and if the weather cannot yet be defeated, then the product should be mass-produced and imported from another part of the world.

Listen, Thanksgiving 2006: Whole Foods Boston was selling a "fully pastured naturally raised" turkey for $1.99/lb. That is painfully cheap. Was it trying to compete with the half-dozen small town turkey farmers still left in Massachusetts or the handful of farmers selling turkeys to their regular customers at the farmers' markets or through community-supported agriculture (CSA)? Probably not. Such consumers of locally raised food still have an appreciation for the tradition of buying a turkey from the same place every year or still get pleasure from buying their turkeys directly from their friend, the farmer, or a neighborhood shop. Whole Foods was trying to compete with the other big supermarkets, who sell cheap food.

Whole Foods (and the supermarkets imitating it) will be the death of the movement for clean, local, and fair food for many reasons, but this is an important one. By dropping the price so low, and using claims and slogans designed not by farmers but by slick salespeople, it has set the expectation that clean food can be as cheap as, or just slightly more expensive than, filthy food. Many people could afford to make the jump from Butterball to a Whole Food bird and, with that jump, assume that the bird was safer, more sustainable, and cleaner. So now any farmer charging a real price is seen as greedy or overpriced. Like Wal-Mart's cheap organic, Whole Foods has cheapened (in integrity, as well as price) naturally raised meats and clean food. It lowers the bar by allowing cheap mass-production and corner-cutting, all to sell cheap food that you think is something it is not. There is tokenistic buying of local food and various labels to suggest a certain quality to the consumer. Because we have so few local farms left, it is easy for a chain supermarket to buy some local food and appear to be supportive of local farms. For most people, this is the easy and convenient way to feel as though they are doing the right thing. But it was the supermarket in the first place that helped reduce the number of farms and transformed our understanding of what local farms are.

Organic food is by no means synonymous with clean food. What should we expect, considering a food supply which is mass-produced will be shipped all over the world? And how did the E. coli get into the spinach? Nobody knows. The apparatus is too big. We are concerned, but we are overwhelmed and more importantly completely removed from our food; we have no idea how to eat locally. I am sure nearly half of Boston goes months without ever eating a single bite of local food.

Are people buying store-brand organics duped or misled? Not exactly. The argument for mass-produced organic food is that at least it is a lesser of two evils. I would agree that mass-produced organic or mass-produced naturally raised is not as bad as mass-produced conventional food, but it is still bad. Are we content with eating bad food? Where is the outrage at choosing between bad and worse? Within the first world, on a day-to-day basis, there is barely a struggle to obtain food. But obtaining clean food is a struggle. And to complicate matters are savvy marketing and confusing legal and nonlegal claims. Do the research on what the USDA allows for the claim "free-range" or "organic." They are by no means what you would expect. To be labeled free-range, the law states only that once a bird is old enough to safely venture outside (fair enough, small chicks are at risk outside to predators, weather, diseases, etc.) that they can be kept inside as long as they have access to the outdoors. Often this means a small hole in the wall leading to a small, lifeless patch of land, which the bird never bothers going out to. And for organic—just a few hours outdoors (not necessarily free of a cage) and nothing but USDA certified organic feed. Great, but that feed may not be what that animal wants to eat at all. Mass-produced food and monoculture farming does nothing good for the land. It burns it up. It is not sustainable. Organic or conventional—if it is produced in favor of profit over sustainability it cannot last forever. [. . .]

This is our society. A society that has no interest in banning feedlots or the excessive/exclusive feeding of grains, hormones, animal by-products, and antibiotics to cows and seemingly covers up

any connection with these practices to E. coli. Worse, our health officials and beef industry leaders come up with a chemical injection
to kill possible E. coli and dabble in using pro-biotic injections to
make our food "safe." What did you expect? These are the same
people who actually believed that forcing cows to be cannibals in
confined quarters-which gave us mad-cow disease-for the sake of
cheap beef and high profits was not a bad idea. If you could witness
how most of our food is produced, you would not eat it; you would
be outraged. We are so far removed from our food.

People think that by washing the vegetable with water that all
the chemicals are washed off. Even more absurd, many of these
same people will buy bottled water because they don't trust the tap
water to drink (but they think it is clean enough to rinse their food
with?). People don't worry about chemicals possibly absorbed into
the food and seeping into the land. People choose shiny fruit covered in wax and pesticide over the uglier, mishapen, dull-colored
clean fruit from a farm because they believe it will taste better or
is safer. How ludicrous is it when mass-produced food is just called
"tomato" or "beef," but real food must be called "NOFA Certified
Organic-locally grown on a small, clean, sustainable farm, free of
all pesticides heirloom tomato" or "100 percent grass-fed/grass finished, hormone-free, antibiotic-free, animal-by-product-free, fully
pastured, naturally raised on a small, local, sustainable family-
farm beef." This is a society that has organic corn syrup! There is
fair reason to be disgusted and outraged at our current food supply and culture of convenience that has created and perpetuated
this mess.

It is nice to believe that eating is a revolutionary act, but
sooner or later someone is going to have to call this system out.
When a few people start ruining our food, we must take action
against those people. When a system has failed, we must change
that system. When we are perpetuating that system because of
our laziness and lust for convenience, then we must change, or
else we will collapse. I cannot think of any point in history when
a food supply has been so dangerous. Food's place in our culture
and community has faded into cheap traditions. Our planet's fer-
tile land has decayed, been poisoned, and been transformed into
factories while we have been too busy and out of touch with our
food to notice. The people who know how to use the land to produce food have lost their place on the land, and we did not notice
because we no longer know who produces our food. Our food supply is being linked to long-term damage such as heart disease and

cancer. And now our food is killing us instantly. Not a week passes it seems that there is not some kind of deadly outbreak. What are you doing about it? We can easily envision a society based on sustainable food; most cultures throughout history have had sustainable farming practices. Basically, Grandma had it right and the progressive supermarkets had it all wrong. We do not necessarily have to turn back the clock and return to an agrarian society, but let's understand what Grandma was doing and realize that she was a lot smarter than we are today. She may not understand the complexities of the internet, but we are the fools who cannot even preserve our summer vegetables so we don't starve in the winter.

We must address the classic American attitude of individuality. Our culture, probably more than any other culture in the world, is based on the individual. Our economic system fuels this individuality. Look at our eating habits. Rather than supporting our community, we buy cheap food from far-away places in chain supermarkets. We do not realize what we are doing to our own community, because we no longer think about our community—we think only of ourselves. Eating can no longer be an individual act. It is not about whether an individual wants to get fat or die from gluttony.

Antibiotics are becoming less and less efficient as pathogens and virus mutate. It seems clear that this is directly related to the excessive use of antibiotics in our food supply. Roughly 75 percent of all antibiotics in this country are given to our livestock. Again, I am not a scientist, but it seems quite clear that even people who only eat antibiotic-free meats will find their medicine useless, as a mutated virus will resist antibiotic treatment regardless of what kind of meat was eaten. The use of pesticides can be equally harmful to the strict organic eater, as a personal choice at the dinner table can do nothing to stop the chemicals of conventional farms from seeping into the rivers and soil. We should all have a right to eat clean, healthy, and sustainable food. It should be a privilege to eat exotic and out-of-season food. Right now, however, we have the right to eat exotic and out-of-season food, and the privileged few can eat clean, healthy, and sustainable food.

When we fully realize or finally admit the effects of climate change, peak oil, and globalized food as our primary source of food, food from international sources will be more expensive than local food. How do we get back to where local food is normal and affordable, and food from far away is exotic and truly expensive?

We have successfully wiped out most of the farms and do not have many farmers left. I can only hope that we can start supporting our local farmers-real support, not the tokenistic once in a while local treat. We must face the reality that urban sprawl must give way to farmland. We must realize that we cannot eat beef every day, but, at least when we do it won't kill us. This will involve spending more of our money, but soon the amount we spend on food will feel normal and not expensive. Americans pay less per capita than anyone else in the world for food.

It should be really easy for privileged people to buy fewer luxury items and spend the same percentage of income as other people in the world do on food, but the same cannot be said for the majority of people in the U.S. Most people in this country are dependent on their weekly wages and live paycheck to paycheck. Wages are set to allow people to survive so they can show up to work. There is little extra money put into that equation for clean, sustainable food.

We could hope that more farms will appear and there will be more farmers to provide enough real food for everyone at an affordable price. We could hope that supermarkets and agrobusiness would just take care of the problem for us and magically make good, clean, fair, sustainable food cheap enough to fit into our current model. Or hope that these same businesspeople who have ruined our food supply and who are wrecking our land will take their millions of dollars of profit and happily give it back to the farmers and small producers-people who see food as sustenance, not commodity. But that just is not going to happen.

As our food entered our economic systems it was transformed from sustenance to commodity, and I do not see how we can take it back while maintaining this economic system. We have to ask ourselves what we want, food or our current economic system. We need to realize that our system itself is not sustainable and has failed.

Buy gold online—quickly, safely and at low prices

Discussion/Writing Prompts

- Among proponents of our modern, industrial food system, one of the most oft-cited benefits revolves around the question of convenience. To what extent do you think Lionette's essay can be read as a challenge to our critique of this particular claim? What specific aspects of our industrial food system does this essay underscore that, in your view, complicate or undermine this celebration of convenience?

- This essay also takes aim at another one of the benefits frequently cited by proponents of organic food: variety. In a one-page essay, write an assessment of how closely Lionette's critique compares to your own experience as a shopper. In what ways have you found yourself surveying the variety of organic produce or "all natural" breakfast cereal aisle only to discover a hidden uniformity underneath? To what extent, in your view, does this question of sameness pose a problem?

- In many ways, Dixon Lebeau's history of the frozen TV dinner can be read as a response to Lionette's critique of industrialized food. In her view, the rise of so-called artificial food has brought as many benefits as costs. Put yourself in the position of Dixon Lebeau, and in a one-page essay lay out the kind of response or critique you think she would offer to Lionette's argument. Which of his specific claims, in your view, would she most directly challenge? What alternative view of industrial food would she advance?

"At 50, TV Dinner Is Still Cookin'," *Christian Science Monitor* (Nov. 10, 2004), www.csmonitor.com

MARY DIXON LEBEAU

The butt of countless jokes, the frozen TV dinner has nonetheless proven itself to be a remarkably resilient staple of the modern American diet. Taking a closer look at the history of this quintessential meal, Dixon Lebeau not only tells the story of where our enthusiasm for frozen food originated, but also makes the case for why it remains a hallmark of so many American kitchens.

◆

Although technology moved on, the original aluminum tray did not. In 1986, it took its place in the Smithsonian Institution, immortalized right next to Fonzie's jacket, the two most appropriate symbols of television's happy days."

It began as a solution to that All-American holiday problem—what to do with the leftover turkey. But executives at C.A. Swanson & Sons weren't talking about just the remainders of the family meal. They were talking 520,000 pounds of poultry.

The Omaha, Neb., frozen food company had overestimated the demand for and undersold its 1953 Thanksgiving supply. Having insufficient warehouse facilities to store the overage, brothers Gilbert and Clark Swanson loaded the turkeys into 10 refrigerated railroad cars, which had to keep moving to stay cold.

As the turkeys traveled from Nebraska to the East Coast and back again, the Swanson brothers handed their staff a challenge—make good of this "fowl" situation.

Enter Gerry Thomas, a company salesman. Visiting the food kitchens of Pan American Airways in Pittsburgh, he caught sight of the single-compartment aluminum trays the cooks used to keep food hot. Thomas requested a sample, then spent his flight home designing a three-compartment tray that was a step up from the serviceman's mess kit. He decided his design might be just what Swanson needed to sell off that turkey.

Back in Omaha, Thomas presented a turkey dinner-filled tray to the Swanson brothers. Then he suggested tying the dinners to the nation's latest craze, television. Packages were designed to resemble a TV screen, complete with volume control knobs—and the TV dinner was born.

Swanson didn't actually invent the frozen dinner. That can be credited to (or blamed on) Clarence Birdseye, who in 1923 invested $7, purchased an electric fan, buckets of brine, and some ice, and invented a system of packing and flash-freezing waxed cardboard boxes of fresh foods.

But it was that packaging—the compartments for individual servings—that put Swanson on the frozen food map.

"The segmented plate was enormously powerful, and remains so," says Betty Fussell, food historian and author of "My Kitchen Wars."

"The childlike packaging makes it appealing," she adds. "The food is segmented, just the way we separate food on our plates when we're children and don't want things mixed. It's a form of comfort to us. Everything is in its place."

It was 50 years ago that Swanson contributed to an American food revolution by selling its first TV dinner—packaged in Thomas's segmented tray—for 98 cents. It let customers feast on turkey with corn bread stuffing, buttered peas, and sweet potatoes—right in front of their television screens.

The Swansons, a bit skeptical about the new—fangled idea, ordered a first run of only 5,000 meals. But they quickly learned that they had greatly underestimated the demand. In 1954, more than

25 million TV dinners were served in front of 33 million television sets in living rooms across America. [**Editor's note**: *The year of the introduction of the TV dinner is disputed.*]

It came, it thawed, it conquered. Americans loved those prepackaged turkey meals almost as much as they loved Lucy. As families gathered around their 8-inch black and white Philcos to watch "You Bet Your Life" and "The Bob Hope Show," they ate from those familiar trays.

The demand soared, and the Swansons—finally recognizing a good thing when they saw it—added fried chicken, Salisbury steak, and meatloaf to their TV dinner menu.

Still, not everyone was thrilled about the new dinnertime innovation. Despite the popularity of the convenient meals, Swanson did receive "hate mail"—mostly from disgruntled husbands who were suddenly coming home to find precooked, reheated dinners instead of their favorite home cooking

"You can't blame the TV dinner for taking the family away from the table," Ms. Fussell points out. "The TV did that. And, actually, it was another form of togetherness—eating tray next to tray in front of the TV."

"Society had changed a lot since World War II," says Deborah Duchon, a nutritional anthropologist who appears on the Food Network program "Good Eats."

"People were working and living urban lives," Ms. Duchon explains. "Cars made us mobile, and teenagers had their own lives. Convenience became a priority for us. In the '50s, society became very futuristic. We wondered what our lives would be like in the year 2000, and were very interested in technology and machinery. People embraced TV trays and TV dinners not because the food was good—it was awful—but because it was futuristic and convenient."

In that way, "food was an expression of the values of society," she says.

Still, futuristc and convenient weren't all Americans wanted. They didn't want to skip dessert for the sake of the future. In 1960, as TV viewers enjoyed the homegrown stories of Mayberry, Swanson sweetened their meals by adding desserts—and a fourth compartment—to the dinner trays.

Then another idea occurred to the marketing department: If frozen prepackaged meatloaf was good for dinner, wouldn't it work just as well at lunch? In 1962 Swanson dropped the "TV Dinners" name to suggest that the meals were good any time of day. To reinforce this point, Swanson Breakfasts were introduced in

1969, and children around the country met Big Bird, Ernie, and the "Sesame Street" crew while eating reheated eggs that year.

IMITATORS GALORE

Just like real television programming, TV dinners had sequels and copycats. Many companies tuned into convenience foods.

Today, 50 years after that first segmented tray appeared in the frozen food sections of US grocery stores, shoppers can find just about any type of cuisine in frozen form.

There's 24-hour programming in the form of frozen food for any meal or occasion, from breakfast to snacks. And cooking times became faster than a game show lightning round, since the aluminum tray was canceled and replaced with plastic-crystallized polyethylene, which is ideal for the microwave.

Today's highest ratings go to family-size or individual meals that offer large portions of meat. For the most part, dessert has disappeared (Swanson cut them from the lineup in 2001) in favor of diet foods, which now make up a third of the market.

Even without the brownie, Americans keep eating frozen meals. Dollar sales grew an average 7.5 percent per year from 1998 to 2003, according to research by the Mintel International Group.

TRAYS AS CULTURAL ICONS

Although technology moved on, the original aluminum tray was not forgotten. In 1986, it took its place in the Smithsonian Institution, immortalized right next to Fonzie's jacket, the two most appropriate symbols of television's happy days. [**Editor's note**: *The tray is currently on loan to the Copia museum in Napa, Calif.*]

Hollywood followed suit in 1997 when an aluminum tray— along with handprints of Swanson salesman Gerry Thomas—was placed in the cement outside Mann's Chinese Theatre alongside the marks of Lassie, Uncle Miltie, and other TV legends. In 1999, Hollywood produced a commemorative sequel, giving the tray its own star on the Hollywood Walk of Fame.

As Americans mark the 50th anniversary of the sale of the first TV dinner, the concept of a convenient frozen meal has become ingrained in the culture. For 66 percent of families, the act of eating in front of the TV screen, which Swanson was the first to capitalize on, has been syndicated and is rerun nightly.

Discussion/Writing Prompts

- As the title of this essay makes clear, the appeal of frozen food has been long and enduring. In your view, what accounts for the enduring popularity of this particular technology? What are the specific advantages it offers to eaters? To cooks? Now, address this question from the opposite perspective. What might you argue is problematic, even harmful, about having frozen foods occupy such a prominent place in our modern food culture?

- As Dixon Lebeau points out, the success of the TV dinner occurred simultaneously with (perhaps even helped contribute to) a number of other transformations in American life: the emergence of television as the dominant cultural medium, the rise of the suburbs, the increasing fragmentation of the nuclear family. Choose one of the larger social changes Dixon Lebeau references. Then, write a one-page essay in which you speculate about why this particular change would have coincided with the rise of the TV dinner. In your view, does it make sense to see the ascendance of this new meal as the cause for this larger change? If so, how?

- For better or worse, the TV dinner has clearly cemented itself within the public imagination as a touchstone of modern life. How do you think Wallace might respond to this fact? Based on Wallace's discussion of "raw food," what meaning do you think she would find in the fact that the TV dinner has achieved such iconic status?

"The Green Monster Could Frankenfoods Be Good for the Environment?" *Slate* (Jan. 28, 2009)
JAMES E. MCWILLIAMS

Few innovations over the last few years challenge our received attitudes toward eating more directly than those made in the field of genetically modified organisms (GMO), colloquially referred to by its many critics as Frankenfood. Surveying the contentious debates swirling around GMO, journalist McWilliams offers some pointed observations about the way science has affected how we both think about and argue over food.

———————————— ✦ ————————————

"Whether or not [critics'] concerns warrant a ban on GMO—as many environmentalists would like to see—is a hotly debated topic. The upshot to these potential pitfalls, however, is beyond dispute: A lot of people find this technology to be creepy."

I'm sitting at my desk examining a $10.95 jar of South River Miso. The stuff is delicious, marked by a light, lemony tang. The packaging, by contrast, is a heavy-handed assurance of purity. The company is eager to tell me that the product I've purchased is certified organic, aged for three weeks in wood (sustainably harvested?), unpasteurized, made with "deep well water," handcrafted, and—the designation that most piques my interest—*GMO free.*

GMO refers to "genetically modified organisms." A genetically modified crop results from the laboratory insertion of a gene from one organism into the DNA sequence of another in order to confer an advantageous trait such as insect resistance, drought tolerance, or herbicide resistance. Today almost 90 percent of soy crops and 80 percent of corn crops in the United States sprout from genetically engineered seeds. Forty-five million acres of land worldwide contain genetically engineered crops. From the perspective of commercial agriculture, the technology has been seamlessly assimilated into traditional farming routines.

From the perspective of my miso jar, however, it's evident that not all consumers share the enthusiasm. It's as likely as not that you know GMOs by their stock term of derision: *Frankenfoods.* The moniker reflects a broad spectrum of concerns: Some antibiotech activists argue that these organisms will contaminate their wild cousins with GM pollen and drive native plants extinct. Others suggest that they will foster the growth of "superweeds"— plants that develop a resistance to the herbicides many GMOs are engineered to tolerate. And yet others fear that genetic alterations will trigger allergic reactions in unsuspecting consumers. Whether or not these concerns collectively warrant a ban on GMOs—as many (most?) environmentalists would like to see— is a hotly debated topic. The upshot to these potential pitfalls, however, is beyond dispute: A lot of people find this technology to be creepy.

Whatever the specific cause of discontent over GM crops, popular resistance came to a head in 2000, when the National

Organic Program solicited public input on the issue of whether they should be included. In response, sustainable-food activists deluged officials with a rainforest's worth of letters—275,000, to be exact—beating the measure into oblivion. Today, in the same spirit, environmentalists instinctively deem GMOs the antithesis of environmental responsibility.

Many scientists, and even a few organic farmers, now believe the 2000 rejection was a fatal rush to judgment. Most recently, Pamela Ronald, a plant pathologist and chair of the Plant Genomics Program at the University of California-Davis, has declared herself one such critic. In _Tomorrow's Table: Organic Farming, Genetics, and the Future of Food_, she argues that we should, in fact, be actively merging genetic engineering and organic farming to achieve a sustainable future for food production. Her research—which she conducts alongside her husband, an organic farmer—explores genetically engineered crops that, instead of serving the rapacity of agribusiness, foster the fundamentals of sustainability. Their endeavor, counterintuitive as it seems, points to an emerging green biotech frontier—a hidden realm of opportunity to feed the world's impending 9 billion a diet produced in an environmentally responsible way.

To appreciate how "responsible genetic modification" isn't an oxymoron, consider grass-fed beef. Cows that eat grass are commonly touted as the sustainable alternative to feedlot beef, a resource-intensive form of production that stuffs cows with a steady diet of grain fortified with antibiotics, growth hormones, steroids, and appetite enhancers that eventually pass through the animals into the soil and water. One overlooked drawback to grass-fed beef, however, is the fact that grass-fed cows emit four times more methane—a greenhouse gas that's more than 20 times as powerful as carbon dioxide—as regular, feedlot cows. That's because grass contains lignin, a substance that triggers a cow's digestive system to secrete a methane-producing enzyme. An Australian biotech company called Gramina has recently produced a genetically modified grass with lower amounts of lignin. Lower amounts of lignin mean less methane, less methane means curbed global warming emissions, and curbed emissions means environmentalists can eat their beef without hanging up their green stripes.

Another area where sustainable agriculture and genetic modification could productively overlap involves nitrogen fertilizer. A plant's failure to absorb all the nutrients from the fertilizer leads to the harmful accumulation of nitrogen in the soil. From there it leaches into rivers and oceans to precipitate dead zones so choked with algae that other marine life collapses. In light of this problem, Syngenta and other biotech companies are in the process of genetically engineering crops such as potatoes, rice, and wheat to improve their nitrogen uptake efficiency in an effort to diminish the negative consequences of nitrogen fertilization. Early results suggest that rice farmers in Southeast Asia and potato farmers in Africa might one day have the option of planting crops that mitigate the harmful effects of this long-vilified source of agricultural pollution.

Animals, of course, are just as modifiable as plants. Livestock farmers have been genetically tinkering with their beasts for centuries through the hit-or-miss process of selective breeding. They've done so to enhance their animals' health, increase their weight, and refine their fat content. Breeding animals to reduce environmental impact, however, hasn't been a viable option with the clunky techniques of conventional breeding. But such is not the case with genetic engineering.

Case in point: Canadian scientists have recently pioneered the "enviropig," a genetically modified porker altered to diminish the notoriously high phosphorous level of pig manure by 60 percent. Like nitrogen, phosphorous runoff is a serious pollutant with widespread downstream consequences. But with the relatively basic insertion of a gene (from E. coli bacteria) that produces a digestive enzyme called phytase, scientists have provided farmers with yet another tool for lessening their heavy impact on the environment.

When commercial farmers hear about GM grass, increased nitrogen uptake, and cleaner pigs, they're excited. And when they hear about other products in the works—genetically modified sugar beets that require less water and have higher yields than cane sugar; a dust made from genetically modified ferns to remove heavy metals from the soil; genetically modified and *edible* cotton seeds that require minimal pesticide use—they're also excited. And they're excited not only because these products have the potential to streamline production, but also because GM technology allows them to play a meaningful role in reducing their carbon footprint.

However, with the exception of the modified sugar beets, the GMOs mentioned in this article are not currently on the market.

The cutting-room floors of research laboratories all over the world, in fact, are littered with successful examples of genetically engineered products that have enormous potential to further the goals of sustainable agriculture. Demand for these products remains high among farmers—it almost always does—but food producers fear the bad publicity that might come from anti-GMO invective.

Given the potential of these products to reduce the environmental impact of farming, it's ironic that traditional advocates for sustainable agriculture have led a successful campaign to blacklist GMOs irrespective of their applications. At the very least, they might treat them as legitimate ethical and scientific matters deserving of a fair public hearing. Such a hearing, I would venture, would not only please farmers who were truly concerned about sustainability, but it would provide the rest of us—those of us who do not grow food for the world but only think about it—a more accurate source of scientific information than the back of a miso jar.

Discussion/Writing Prompts

- Take a moment to consider the term "Frankenfood." What images or associations does it conjure in your mind? In your view, what specific aspects of the genetic food movement does it seem designed to critique? And how much sympathy do you feel personally for this critique?
- Ranged against the many objections critics level against GMO (e.g., threats to existing species, health risks to individual consumers), McWilliams lays out the case for the particular benefits such science might yield: "a hidden realm of opportunity to feed the world's impending 9 billion on a diet produced in an environmentally responsible way." Choose one of the objections to GMO that McWilliams cites. Then write a one-page essay in which you assess the danger and/or cost it poses against the potential benefits of GMO that the essay also references. In your view, what is the best way to weigh the pros and cons of this emerging technology against each other?
- The most vivid counterpoint to the research into genetically modified organisms is probably the raw milk movement. In a one-page essay, lay out what you see as the key differences between these two contrasting approaches to food. What are the underlying assumptions and overall objectives that motivate each of these movements? And which set of values and goals do you find more compelling? Why?

"Fast-Food Assistant 'Hyperactive Bob' Example of Robots' Growing Role," *Pittsburgh Post-Gazette* (June 16, 2006), www.post-gazette.com

CORILYN SHROPSHIRE

Have technological advances in the food industry reached a point where the human role itself is becoming obsolete? Contemplating this unnerving possibility, journalist Shropshire reports on one attempt to integrate robot workers into the fast-food business. In the process, her article raises complex questions about where the new limits around industrialized food are being drawn and whether they have gone too far.

———————— ✦ ————————

"'Hyperactive Bob' has been tested in a number of national fast-food restaurants, including McDonalds and Burger King."

Kerien Fitzpatrick may be a die-hard roboticist, but he isn't too steeped in the technology to let a good business opportunity pass him by.

The former Carnegie Mellon University researcher co-founded North Side-based HyperActive Technologies in 2001 to put the "fast" back into fast food.

"HyperActive Bob"—which looks more like a control center than a stereotypical robot—is designed to help chains "deliver food as fast as they want to," said Mr. Fitzpatrick, who'll join about 700 fellow robot enthusiasts at the RoboBusiness Conference and Exposition that kicks off Tuesday at the Sheraton Station Square.

The 3-year-old annual business development conference gathers investors, entrepreneurs and scientists to size up and show off the latest in robotics.

Catering to the fast-food masses with "HyperActive Bob" is a decidedly commercial application for robotics, whose roots are steeped in the military. But industry watchers expect an increasingly consumer, mass-market-focused future.

That was always HyperActive's mission, according to Mr. Fitzpatrick. "I was always more interested in having something that left the university and got used."

Using a small mounted camera on the restaurant's roof, "Bob" spots vehicles entering the parking lot. It then considers how much food is already prepared and how many employees are needed before telling the kitchen when and what to throw on the grill or put in the fryer. "Bob" also sizes up the vehicles—a big SUV could mean more food to prepare, a run-of-the-mill sedan likely would mean less.

More than half of the work involved in creating "Bob" was in making it user-friendly, Mr. Fitzpatrick said. The roughly $5,000 computer system comes equipped with touch-screens and easy-to-follow instructions.

"HyperActive Bob" has been tested in a number of national fast-food restaurants, including McDonald's and Burger King. The company recently landed its first big customer, Zaxby's, a franchise chain with more than 300 outlets in the South.

What makes "Bob" a robot is that it's smart enough to analyze its environment, make a decision and then act.

It's what separates the robots from mere machines and ensures that these complex and expensive systems will someday be as commonplace as a desktop computer, according to William Thomasmeyer, president of the National Center for Defense Robotics, a subsidiary of the North Side-based Technology Collaborative, an economic development group.

Despite proclamations more than half a century ago, with the exception of Boston-area based iRobot's "Roomba" vacuum, robots have yet to perform such everyday tasks as house cleaning and lawn mowing.

That's because there's still a disconnect between transforming largely government-funded robotics research into consumer-friendly products, according to Dan Kara, the RoboBusiness conference chairman. He's also president of trade show and publication company Robotics Trends Inc., based in Northborough, Mass. In the United States, robots still are largely the territory of the military, which has spent billions fueling projects aimed at taking soldiers out of harm's way with unmanned machines that are both smart and agile.

Plus, Mr. Kara added, like any other emerging technology, robotics remains too complicated, costly and futuristic—at least until a breakthrough eventually brings commercial success.

That's what Mr. Fitzpatrick hopes "HyperActive Bob" will deliver for the industry and for the city dubbed "Roboburgh" by the Wall Street Journal in 1999.

Pittsburgh has the ingredients to sprout a vibrant robotics cluster, Mr. Kara said. The city was the "next logical choice" for the upcoming conference because of its researchers, technology and growing crop of 60-plus robotics companies and a business community eager to invest.

Another sign of Pittsburgh's potential, added Mr. Thomasmeyer, is that several local firms already are venturing from government-funded projects into the commercial marketplace. Local robotics firms are split about 50-50 between military and commercial customers, he said.

Other Pittsburgh-based robotics companies pursuing the commercial market include RedZone Robotics, Automatika and Nomad Networks.

RedZone has developed a robot that can clean and repair cities' water and sewage pipes, while Nomad Networks is fine-tuning a wireless security system that spots intruders.

Mr. Thomasmeyer said he expects robotics' commercial momentum to build over the next decade, producing more companies and products.

"It's a nascent marketplace. But on the verge of spectacular growth," Mr. Kara said.

Discussion/Writing Prompts

- To be sure, the food industry is not the first venue that comes to mind when we think about robotics. Why do you think this is? What is it about food and eating in particular that makes it seem so incompatible with this sort of technology? And how, in your view, might our preconceptions about food change if this technology were to become even more commonplace?
- Here is how this article characterizes the work performed by "Hyperactive Bob," the robotic worker: "Using a small camera mounted on the restaurant's roof, 'Bob' spots vehicles entering the parking lot. It then considers how much food is already prepared and how many employees are needed before telling the kitchen when and what to throw on the grill or put in the fryer. 'Bob' also sizes up the vehicles—a big SUV could mean more food to prepare, a run-of-the-mill sedan likely would mean less." How do you evaluate this description? In your view is there anything unsettling, problematic, or even troubling about the role performed by "Bob"? Does it differ in any appreciable way from the way this job might

be performed by an actual person? And if so, do these differences, in your view, matter?

- Take a moment to compare this article's description of "Hyperactive Bob" with McWilliams' description of Frankenfoods. In your view, do they present similar or contrasting examples of technology run amok? In each case, does this innovation strike you as positive and beneficial? Or troubling and dangerous? How?

Tying It All Together: Assignments for Writing and Research

1. RHETORICAL ANALYSIS: "SELLING CONVENIENCE"

From commercials extolling the newest cell phone "app." to the latest science fiction blockbuster movie, our pop culture is awash with images and stories that showcase different forms of technology. And more often than not, these innovations are promoted to the general public on the basis of their convenience. Choose an example of a new technology that, in your view, bears some connection to how or what we eat. Then conduct some primary research into the ways this particular innovation gets presented and promoted within our broader pop culture on the basis of its convenience. Next write a two- to three-page essay which summarizes and assesses your findings. What particular claims do proponents, promoters, and/or advertisers make about this technology? What aspects of our lives does it claim to make more convenient? As you present your findings, make sure you also offer some assessment or evaluation as well. How convincing do you find these claims to be? How credible? How compelling? And why?

2. PERSONAL REFLECTION: "THE TASTE OF TECHNOLOGY"

A number of the selections above examine the role that modern science and industry have played in changing the nature of what we eat. But what is our own experience in this regard? To what extent could we be said to live out the consequences of these changes in our own daily lives? First, choose a food you enjoy and which you find yourself eating on a fairly regular basis. Create a quick checklist of all the things about this food that make eating it one of your personal favorites. Then write a two- to three-page essay in which you reflect upon the role that science and/or technology has played in shaping your feelings. How many of this food's pleasures and payoffs derive from or depend upon a specific technological or scientific advance?

3. COMPARE AND CONTRAST: "THE REAL AND THE FAKE"

Whether overtly or implicitly, a number of the selections above invite their readers to consider the question of authenticity. In a world where food has become so thoroughly remade by scientific innovations, technological advancements, and industrial processes, how do we decide anymore what is and is not the "real thing"? Choose two readings from this chapter that, in your view, answer this question in different ways. Then write a three- to five-page essay in which you outline the key differences between them. On what basis does each essay define its model of authenticity? For each writer, what ways of eating, what forms of food, live up to the ideal of the "real thing"? Once you've presented this comparison, offer a quick assessment of which definition you find more compelling or convincing, and explain why.

4. VISUAL ANALYSIS: "HIDDEN COSTS"

Our media landscape is overrun with image technology. And yet rarely does such material invite us to consider the downside of all this innovation and invention. Choose an image from our current media that showcases and attempts to market a specific technology. Then write a two- to three-page essay in which you assess this example for what it *doesn't* show us: that is, those aspects that might complicate or undermine its intended promotional message. What potential problems does this image leave unaddressed? And in your view, would raising these concerns be a good or bad thing to do? Why?

5. ARGUMENT-BASED/PERSUASIVE WRITING: "THE IDEA(L) OF PROGRESS"

Taken together, the selections assembled above could be viewed as an extended attempt to question, or at least complicate, the cultural myth of "progress." Have all of the technological, industrial, and scientific changes we've witnessed over the last 50 years truly altered our eating practices for the better? Does change always, automatically mean improvement? Choose an example of a specific technological advancement that, in your view, has significantly altered the way Americans eat. Then write a three- to five-page essay in which you make the argument about the ways this particular change has altered our modern food system for the better or the worse. First, describe as specifically as you can what this particular change involves. What kind of technology does it concern? What aspect of our eating lives has it served to remake? Then, make the case about how this change should best be understood and evaluated. If it is indeed a change for the better, what particular benefits does it bring? If not, what harm has it caused?

CHAPTER 7

Race/Ethnicity

CONSUMING OTHERNESS: FOOD AND RACIAL/ETHNIC IDENTITY

What's the first thing that comes to mind when you hear the term "ethnic food"? Is it something like pickled pigs feet or dried plantains? Perhaps it's curry powder or canned coconut milk. However we choose to round out our own personal rosters, one thing is clear: ethnic food is a category that encompasses an extremely wide array of eating options. Given this, we might ask: what is it exactly that makes a given food ethnic? Is this designation primarily a matter of taste? A way of highlighting the novelty or newness of what we're eating? Or does this phrase have more to do with the way food can serve as a marker or symbol for cultural difference? Indeed despite how capacious a category it is, there does seem to be a basic rule of thumb that always holds true: a food qualifies as "ethnic" only when it is deemed in one way or another to stand for the broader culture of a particular group. According to this formula, ethnic food earns its moniker by offering itself as a kind of cultural guide, a culinary map to the mores, values, and traditions of a community different from our own—be it ethnic or racial, regional or national. This is the thinking, for example, that turns olive oil into a symbol of Italian culture; or that sees Brie cheese as an essential expression of French identity; or that casts chicken curry as a window on to Indian life. Whether we find such equivalences fascinating or facile, the assumption underlying them has become so deeply ingrained as to feel almost like second nature: when it comes to ethnic food, cuisine equals culture.

But is this logic truly sound? To be sure, food has long operated within different communities as a powerful locus of identification

175

and belonging, uniting collections of people into a coherent, self-identified group. For centuries, in fact, what food historians call the "traditions of the table" have served to cement the bonds that link members of a community both to a shared past and to each other. And this power has only been enhanced in recent years with the emergence of the mass marketplace, a development that has transformed food into a vehicle for connecting people not just *within* a given community, but *across* communities as well. These days foods from across the globe, representing hundreds of different culinary traditions, are so widely and abundantly available that the prospect for cross-cultural contact now seems to be, quite literally, at our fingertips. And yet the same changes which have placed such gustatory diversity so close at hand have also given rise to significant questions. In an age where such cross-culinary contact frequently comes in the form of a mass-marketed brand, is it always valid to treat "ethnic food" as a measure of genuine cultural difference? In a world where food—like virtually everything else in our modern economy—has been made into a marketable commodity, is it really fair to look upon the "ethnic" food we prepare or consume as a reliable barometer of racial, ethnic, or cultural identity? In the face of such rampant and pervasive commercialization, the notion of ethnic food as both a cultural touchstone and cultural passport may simply no longer stand up.

To test out this proposition, let's turn our attention once again to the local grocery store. As many of us know firsthand, it's hardly unusual for supermarkets to devote entire aisles to specialty food-stuffs labeled "ethnic." Nor is it unusual for stores to promote such items by presenting them as emissaries or representatives of a specific culture. A jar of salsa that includes a recipe for preparing a "traditional Cinco de Mayo dinner" is doing a good deal more than simply marketing the flavors or nutritional content of its product. It is also selling consumers a vision of cross-cultural access: a belief that such products offer a way to truly sample the experiences and traditions of people different from themselves. And yet in many ways this claim is at odds with the commercial nature of the product itself. They may proffer themselves as the custodians of an indigenous culinary tradition, but the truth is that the foods lining these shelves are more often than not mass-produced in the factories of corporate food conglomerates. By and large, to roam the ethnic food aisle is to find oneself face to face with such well-known brand names as Ramen noodles, Ortega taco seasoning, and Chef Boyardee spaghetti sauce. When we heat up a box of these noodles or dip a chip into a bowl of this salsa, are we treating ourselves to a slice of genuine cultural diversity? Or merely a mass-produced, simulated substitute—the image of diversity without the substance?

This is not to say that the rise of the modern food industry doesn't represent a significant milestone. Without a doubt, the exponential increase in the amount and types of food available—an increase, which the market has made possible—is proof of how much more complex and diverse American eating habits have become over the last 50 years. The American food consumer nowadays enjoys a range of eating options that would have been unthinkable several generations ago. But as our hypothetical grocery store example makes clear, this fact is more than simply a testament to the polyglot character of modern American society. It is also a reminder of how readily such diversity can be co-opted and transformed into an objectified something it is not. If nothing else, acknowledging this reality might lead us to think more mindfully about our own relationship to ethnic food. Do such products truly afford us greater contact with, enhanced understanding of, cuisines and cultures different from our own? When we buy one, what definition of cultural difference are we simultaneously "buying" into?

It is precisely this kind of self-scrutiny which this chapter invites us to undertake. Bringing together the work of writers from a range of different backgrounds, it asks us to think more critically about the ways food—cooking or consuming it, making or marketing it—can shape our attitudes toward and assumptions about racial, ethnic, and national difference. To what extent can food serve as a viable or reliable marker for racial or ethnic identity? In what ways are our assumptions and anxieties about racial or ethnic differences embedded in how we eat?

"Between Meals: Who Determines If Food Is Authentic?," *San Francisco Chronicle* (Nov. 7, 2006), www.sfgate.com

Michael Bauer

When it comes to the countless ethnic cuisines available these days, how do you know when you're getting the "real thing"? And more to the point, why should we even care? Casting a critical eye on our current food culture, Bauer invites us to take a second look at what he considers our unhealthy and ultimately fruitless obsession with authenticity. Despite what we've been led to believe, he cautions, we really can't draw definitive conclusions about other people and other cultures based on what they eat—nor should we.

◆

"Authenticity is to food what racism is to the human race. Deeming food authentic or inauthentic becomes a device, much like racism, to keep people in their places."

I was talking to Floyd Cardoz the other day, the pioneering Indian chef from Tabla in New York and author of the just-published "One Spice, Two Spice" cookbook. We got into a very interesting conversation about Indian food and its growth potential in the United States, which led to an even more fascinating discussion on authenticity.

One customer recently complained about a thin coconut milk curry she was eating at his restaurant.

"This isn't authentic," she asserted. "I'm from London, and I know good curry; it should be thicker."

He told her it was a recipe his mother made in Bombay and it was an exact replication. She remained unconvinced.

Her response is typical of the email I receive every time I review a restaurant that isn't Western. People have preconceived notions about various cuisines, and many of these notions are out of date.

According to some, if Indian food is served in upscale surroundings, for example, it can't be authentic. If the food is different than what they remember, then it's not the real thing. Other pioneering chefs—whether it's Charles Phan at Slanted Door or Richard Sandavol at Maya—could easily share similar stories.

Authenticity is to food what racism is to the human race. Deeming food authentic or inauthentic becomes a device, much like racism, to keep people in their places. In many cases, there's a little reverse discrimination at play.

I heard similar grumblings when I reviewed Dosa, a Southern Indian restaurant in the Mission. Many people cited restaurants in the South Bay that were much better, and part of the criteria mentioned was the lower prices. I maintain that Dosa celebrates the cuisine and does it with style and panache.

If you go to India (or Vietnam, Mexico or Morocco), you'll find that the traditional cuisine is evolving. In the end, it's a knowledge and respect for the flavors that determines whether a chef is being true to a culture.

Discussion/Writing Prompts

- When it comes to ethnic food, how do you understand our widespread pre-occupation with authenticity? Why, in your estimation, are so many of us so concerned with finding and eating meals that live up to the standard of the "real thing"? What makes achieving this goal so meaningful? So important? Do you share this feeling? How or how not?

- For Bauer, the search for the authentic ethnic meal is one destined to end in disappointment. What do you think? Is it, as Bauer contends, truly impossible to identify and define the real thing? In a one-page essay, make an argument in support of this search for authenticity. Fruitless or not, why is it nonetheless useful or positive to maintain the real thing as a culinary goal?

- Finn's essay could easily be read as both a description of and testimonial to an "authentic" ethnic cuisine. In a one-page essay, outline the particular ways her discussion of "soul food" challenges, or at least contrasts with, Bauer's argument concerning food and authenticity. Which aspects of this cuisine seem to fit the definition of the real thing? And how effectively does this depiction refute the claims Bauer makes in his own piece?

"Soul Food: A New Place at the Table," *the Root* (May 22, 2008)

Rachel Finn

While countless food anthologies and cookbooks include descriptions of "soul food," very few extend this focus to examine the story of American race relations that this cuisine also tells. Addressing this lacuna, Finn takes a closer look at this quintessentially African American form of cooking, and in the process, raises important questions about how we have learned to talk (and not talk) about race.

✦

> *"Why has so little attention been given to the food of*
> *African Americans, and the African Diaspora never been*
> *fully explored?"*

My own interest in the study of black food culture field began innocently enough as a child at the tables of my mother and grandmother where I savored hot water bread, oxtails and chess pie all the while pondering the logic of pig feet, stewed okra and banana pudding. My interest in the Diaspora grew stronger after living in France for a short time, as an *affaire d'amour* led me on a journey of discovery deep into the North African neighborhoods of Paris in search of the best Algerian pastries I could find. The affair ended, but the experience led to an article in *Gastronomica*, an obsession with Algerian food and culture I still can't shake, and an even deeper interest in the cultural and culinary connections among people of African descent outside of the continent.

I know that there are others who share my passion for our food culture, so I was thrilled to learn that Dillard University is creating an Institute for the Study of Culinary Cultures. To be housed within the university's department of African-American material culture, the institute will examine the foodways (i.e., the gathering, preparation and consumption of food of a cultural group) of the people of the African Diaspora.

After I read about the institute in *Saveur* magazine, I was so excited that I called its director, Jessica Harris. As I heard about all her expansive plans which include the creation of an online clearinghouse for the general public and an international conference on the food of the Diapsora, I couldn't help but wonder: Why had something like this not been created before now? Why has so little attention been given to the food of African Americans and the African Diaspora never been fully explored? Cookbook authors have provided scores of recipes for greens, cornbread and barbecue sauce but that seems to be where interest and research ends for most. Certainly there has never been an academic entity created with the singular focus of expanding the body of information on black foodways. There are organizations like the Southern Foodways Alliance that looks at the food of African Americans under the umbrella of Southern food and the Oxford Symposium on Food and Cookery, a self-described educational charity that focuses on the examination of the foodways and the food history of people around the world. While my own response to the dearth of material on black foodways—racism—was admittedly somewhat

parochial, Harris had a far more nuanced take on the situation:
She suggested that this lack of attention is a result of the conflict
that people feel in the Americas regarding enslavement and their
roles within it.

Upon reflection I realized that during slavery and until very recently in the Americas, blacks and whites have had very specific
roles in relationship to food, with whites in the role of consumers
almost exclusively and blacks in roles that included preparing,
cooking and disposing of the waste generated by whites. The sordid history of servitude has generated profound feelings of guilt,
shame and anger on both sides of the fence. For black people in
particular, that history continues to shape our food choices and
our lives in the kitchen and at the table.

In the United States, the body of work on African-American
foodways that has been compiled by black people has often been
in the context of our social condition, which has led us to exoticize
our own food under the guise of consciousness-raising or pride
(see the chapter entitled "Soul Food" in Eldridge Cleaver's *Soul On
Ice*). Ultimately, this has led outsiders to do the same. To be sure,
there are plenty of examples to the contrary, Harris herself, Bryant
Terry, the late Edna Lewis and others but it seems that there is a
disproportionate focus on the extremes of the cuisine—high fat,
sugar and salt contents, and of course offerings like chitlins, which
served very specific purposes for the ancestors that are no longer
beneficial to our health or dietary needs today. This is the norm
that has helped to marginalize black foodways: presenting a very
limited view of the diversity and richness of the food.

Within academia, the study of the foodways of people of
African descent, particularly in the United States, has been approached not as a legitimate, singular field of study, but as an area
of interest from scholars across the disciplines. The same can be
said of interest in the food of the Diaspora in the non-academic
culinary world of chefs, restaurants and foodies. The gravitas that
has characterized the study and emulation of European and Asian
cuisines seems thus far to have eluded the cuisine of people of
African descent (save Morocco) around the world. Thus, the idea
of an institute created by blacks devoted to the study of the foodways of black people outside of Africa is quite simply, a seminal
moment in the food history of African Americans and of the
African Diaspora in general.

The idea that the legacy of enslavement shapes our attitudes
about something as quotidian as our food is a poignant one. Going

beyond scholarship, this means that everything we choose to put into our mouths (or not), particularly as black people in the United States, is shaped by that legacy. This may be true in other parts of the Diaspora in the Americas, but it is undeniable in the United States, where even our food choices are somehow politicized and weighed down heavily with the complexity of our origins in the New World. From sitting down to a Sunday dinner that might include greens and cornbread, or heading to the local soul vegetarian restaurant for a meal, or firing up the grill in the park for a family gathering, or even preparing mushrooms and shallots for a tasty thyme-infused mushroom ragout to accompany a juicy steak or pork loin, most people, I am convinced, rarely connect choices that they make to the legacy that anchors our existence in the United States.

So many of us who have not thought about our food do not consider or perhaps take for granted that African-American cuisine is so much more than the social construct that is soul food. Flipping through Edna Lewis' classic work *The Taste of Country Cooking* substantiates this claim. First published in 1976, the book is filled with anecdotes of Lewis' childhood in the Virginia Piedmont during the early part of the 20th century. Most significantly it holds dynamic seasonal menus for every meal, with recipes for things like spiced Seckel pears, braised leg of mutton, and lentil and scallion salad alongside recipes for biscuits, sweet potato pie and fried chicken.

As I have begun to discover the wonders of the foodways of the African Diaspora in my own kitchen, incorporating what I have learned from Algerian, Dominican, Puerto Rican and Brazilian friends thus far, I have made room for orange flower water, coconut milk, sofrito and plantains, in my own larder. My hope is that the creation of the Institute of Culinary Cultures can help to spark a movement that helps African Americans see our food with new eyes, carefully considering it and embracing not only the regional elements of African-American foodways that make the cuisine so diverse, but also the techniques and ingredients that tie us to our brethren in the African Diaspora of the Americas and ultimately to Africa. I agree with a sentiment Harris shared: It will be "nice to have people who have the taste in their mouth, in their blood, if you will, writing about it." Nothing gives more credence to a cultural movement than having people within that culture accept and advance it.

Fur more information, check out the following resources:
Jessica Harris has stocked a full pantry with culinary litera-
ture. The Southern Foodways Alliance stores information on organization and programming. The Museum of the African
Diaspora in San Francisco has a permanent exhibition on culinary
traditions in the Diaspora.

Rachel Finn is a Chicago-based food writer.

Discussion/Writing Prompts

- How do you understand the term "soul food"? What are some of the images
  or ideas you associate with this phrase? To what extent does Finn's discussion invite you to rethink these associations?

- Finn takes a look at what she calls the "sordid history of servitude," a history
  that, in her view, has long structured the attitudes of whites and blacks toward food. "Upon reflection," she writes, "I realized that during slavery and
  until very recently in the Americas, blacks and whites have had very specific
  roles in relationship to food, with whites in the role of consumers almost exclusively and blacks in roles that included preparing, cooking, and disposing
  of the waste generated by whites." How do you respond to this claim? Do
  you agree that this kind of history has the potential to shape attitudes toward food along racial lines?

- Like Furiya, Finn is interested in exploring the relationship between food and
  racial/ethnic heritage. How do these two discussions compare? What similarities or differences do you see?

"Swallowing Fishbones," in *Bento Box in the Heartland: My Japanese Girlhood in Whitebread America* (2006)

LINDA FURIYA

*We're all familiar with the saying: "you are what you eat." When con-
sidered in relation to the immigrant experience in America, however,
this cliché takes on an entirely new meaning. To what extent, Furiya
asks, can one's traditional or inherited eating practices serve to define you outside the American mainstream? Chronicling her own
childhood efforts to make a home in what she terms "Whitebread
America," Furiya's memoir poses pointed questions about the role*

food can play in alternately enabling or undermining cultural assimilation.

———————— ✦ ————————

"I unlocked my lunch box and casually peeked under the lid. My stomach lurched. I expected a classic elementary school lunch of a bologna, cheese and Miracle Whip sandwich and a bag of Durkee's potato sticks, but all I saw were three round rice balls wrapped in wax paper."

My mother first told me this story when I was six years old, before I knew that the language she spoke was Japanese.

Her personal tale takes place in Tokyo during the 1930s, when she was a young girl. Her neighborhood, she explained, was a jigsaw puzzle of low-story, fragile houses constructed of wood and paper. The homes survived the many earthquakes that shook Japan, yet most burned away like dried leaves when Tokyo was bombed during World War II.

Every day a community of mothers in the neighborhood gathered together to feed their babies a midday meal and to rest from endless household duties and the tongues and ears of nosy in-laws.

While the older women gossiped and watched over the little ones, the younger women made lunch for the babies, who ate softer versions of what their mothers served at their tables—rice, fish, soup, and vegetables.

Often the fishmonger's wife brought a whole fish to broil until the skin charred and cracked on a small outside grill. The mothers slid the flaky, sweet, white meat off the bone with the tap of a chopstick.

Using their fingers to feel for any stray fish bones, they thoroughly mashed, pinched, and poked the tender fish meat before mixing it with rice and moistening it with *dashi* (fish stock). Despite all the care, sometimes a transparent bone, pliable and sharp as a shark's tooth, slipped past scrutiny.

I picture her wearing braids and standing in the distance, quietly observing yet part of the gathering. Now her short hair frames her face like the black slashes of an ink brush. In this story my mother explains how before modern medicine, the mortality rate was high not only for newborns, but even for healthy men, who were struck dead from illnesses that would start as a common cold.

"One day you are in good health, the next . . ." Mom's eyes flicker at this point, like two flints sparking. She snaps her fingers at the swiftness of it all. Back then, mothers needed reassurance that their babies were strong, and eating was an infant's first test of survival. If the baby didn't know how to eat, suck from its mother's nipple, or push out a fish bone, the child wouldn't know how to survive when she grew older.

One day during a feeding, my mothers story goes, the *wagashi*- (Japanese pastry) maker's baby sat still and silent, holding his mouthful of fish and rice.

"Eh?" grunted Obasan, the old matriarch of the group, as she peered at the baby through thick spectacles.

The *wagashi*-maker's wife nervously parted the baby on the back as all the other mothers talked quietly trying not to stare. Strings of saliva and bits of fish dribbled out of his mouth. His tiny bud of a tongue moved in and out before finally pushing out a small fish bone, the size of a pine needle.

The *wagashi*-maker's wife gushed with pride at her baby's grit for life. Obasan cackled loudly, proclaiming he would live a strong, healthy life, as the other women sighed and laughed with relief. Years later, Mom says, he became a doctor and people credited his success to overcoming the fish bone.

Another time the soba noodle–maker's baby swallowed a small bone. Reminiscent of the first infant, he sat still and silent, but no spittle and bone came out. Instead, he swallowed. Not long after, the baby developed a fever and refused to take his mother's milk. A doctor removed a small bone that had been lodged in his throat, and the soba–maker's wife began worrying about her baby's future. No one was surprised when he died of tuberculosis at the age often.

Unlike stories with resolution that I would become accustomed to hearing from teachers and other adults throughout my youth, Mom left the tale at that, leaving me baffled as to its lesson or moral. Growing up, whenever I complained about mistreatment by a friend or the unfairness of some school interaction, my mother repeated her story of the infants and the fish bones. Growing up in the only Japanese family in Versailles, Indiana, I quickly learned that I would have to overcome many fish bones. My very first notion of how different we really were struck me among the pastel-colored molded trays and long bleached wood tables of the school cafeteria.

My elementary school lunchroom was a sweaty, brightly lit place that reeked of hot cooking oil, Pine-Sol, and the yeast from rising bread dough. It was dead quiet when empty, and otherwise it echoed with the sound of children's high-pitched talk and laughter and heavy wood and metal chairs scraping against the tile floor.

I had never eaten a lunch before then without my parents. My two older brothers, Keven and Alvin, ate lunch at school. Mom was a stay-at-home mother. She churned out three meals a day as efficiently as a military mess hall. My father worked second shift at a factory in Columbus, Indiana, where he assembled truck engines. Because he started his shift midafternoon, he ate a hot, filling lunch at home to compensate for his dinner, a cold *bento* box of rice, meat, and vegetables, with a cup of green tea from his thermos.

These lunches with my parents were magnificent feasts made in our tiny kitchen. The size of a hall closet, the small room became alive during lunchtime, like a living, breathing creature, with steam puffing from the electric rice cooker, ratding from the simmering pots, and short clipping notes of Mom chopping with her steady hand guiding her *nakiri bocho* (Japanese vegetable knife).

At the dining room table, Dad and I grazed on cold Japanese appetizers—spicy wilted cabbage pickled in brine with lemon peel, garlic, smashed whole red chili peppers, and kombu (seaweed). Meanwhile, Mom prepared hot dishes—cubes of tofu garnished with ginger and bonito flakes (dried fish shavings). There was salmon fillet, if we could get it, grilled to the color of Turkish apricots on a Japanese wire stove-top contraption; or sirloin, sliced tissue-thin, sautéed with onions, soy sauce, and a dash of rice wine. And there was always a bowl of clear fish broth or cloudy miso soup and steamed white rice.

As I was used to such sumptuous lunches, it wasn't long before the novelty of my school's cafeteria fare wore off and my eyes wandered toward the lunch boxes other children brought from home. From inside the metal containers, they pulled out sandwiches with the crusts cut off, followed by tins of chocolate pudding and homemade cookies.

My best friend, Tracy Martin, was part of the lunch box brigade. Her mother packed the same lunch items everyday—a cold hot dog and applesauce. We also ate with Mary, a Copper-toned, baby-faced girl with a Clara Bow haircut, whose mother precut all the food in her lunch box, even her cookies, into bite-size pieces.

I wanted to be a part of this exclusive group, and after much pestering, I was thrilled when my mother relented and agreed to pack my lunches.

When I joined Tracy and Mary at lunchtime, carrying my own lunch box, I studied the girls, who carefully unpacked their containers as if they were unveiling family heirloom jewelry, observing the packed-lunch protocol. I unlocked my lunch box and casually peeked under the lid. My stomach lurched. I expected a classic elementary school lunch of a bologna, cheese, and Miracle Whip sandwich and a bag of Durkee's potato sticks, but all I saw were three round rice balls wrapped in waxed paper. Mom had made me an *obento*, a Japanese-style boxed meal.

I snapped the lunch box lid shut before the other girls caught a glimpse of what was inside. How could this have happened?

"Sandwich?" Mom asked in a genuinely astonished voice when I came home from school that afternoon protesting. "Why go to trouble to make lunch for just plain old sandwich?"

"That's what everyone else brings. That's what I want," I demanded. My desire to emulate my classmates was palpable. My *obento* lunches were a glaring reminder of the ethnic differences between my peers and me.

The agony of being different from my classmates was intensified the day Scott Leach pointed out the slanted shape of my eyes. Scott had snow-white hair and constantly dug his pinkie finger deep in his ear. One morning as we stood in the milk line, he turned to me and furrowed his eyebrows, pointing at my eyes as if they were insect specimens.

"Why do they look like lines?" he asked with a smirk far more adult than his age.

When the other kids laughed, I knew this wasn't a normal question. My throat tightened as if a fish bone were on the verge of lodging itself in my windpipe. I took a step back, bringing my index finger up to my mouth to shush him, only to witness him pull his own eyes back at the corners to more laughter from the classmates in line. Encouraged by the other children's reactions, Scott pulled his eyes back and tilted his head from side to side.

I stood there like a mannequin. I was filled with helpless, choking anxiety. The spell was broken only when the recess bell rang to go back to class. The incident initiated what became open season for teasing me.

A couple of days later at recess, after I won a round at hop-scotch, Susie Sillerhorn, a pinch-nosed blond and known sore loser, announced that she had heard my parents talking "sing-songy" in the grocery store. Susie's pal Donna Underwood joined in by pulling back her eyes until they appeared closed and made pinging nonsense noises. The other girls laughed.

Defiantly, I asked why she was doing that. "You should know what I'm saying. This is how your folks talk," she replied haugh-tily. I didn't know the name of it then, but the feeling this early in-teraction left me with was my first feeling of injustice.

Still, I wanted their friendship and to be accepted, so silently, but with deep resentment, I put up with friends who called me Chink and Jap. Some innate self-control wouldn't allow me to give my prosecutors the lesson they probably needed to learn, of know-ing they were hurting me. Eventually, though, the resentment, anger, and developing drive for self-preservation gave me the gumption to fight back.

My first stand, albeit lame, was against Tracy, who instantly resorted to calling me Jap when we got into an argument about whose tree swings were better. She watched my reaction with calm, steady eyes. Tracy knew the power behind the word.

Unable to think of anything to say, I spurted out the first thing that came to mind. I called her "pizzahead" because of her Italian ancestry. It was weak, like throwing confetti at an opponent, but it was my first stab at fighting back.

At night, I'd lie awake and fantasize about how to get re-venge. I imagined that Dad was an undercover agent on a special assignment, a foreign dignitary from Japan. His cover was a fac-tory job in a small Midwest town. I saw the surprised looks on my friends' faces when they realized we weren't who they thought we were. The meanest ones, including Susie and Donna, begged me to be their best friends. I smiled smugly and shook my head. My family was leaving Versailles and I wouldn't be go-ing to school there anymore, I explained. Then I enjoyed their looks of dismay and confusion, just as they had enjoyed them-selves when they teased me. A cavalcade of shiny black Cadillac sedans appeared and whisked us away. I waved at my classmates from the rearview window until they disappeared. I hugged my pillow and twisted my bedsheets so hard, wishing my fantasy would come true.

When I believed it couldn't get any worse, a turning point came one afternoon as I waited to use the playground swings.

Raymond Neilley, a chubby boy in JCPenney Huskies jeans, pulled his eyes back in the overused imitation my peers favored. "Chinky, chinky, Chinese," he sang, doing a little dance. For the first time, blinding fury replaced fear. First of all, I wasn't Chinese. I heard the other kids around me snickering as they encircled us and moved in closer. Dread prickled me like a scratchy blanket on a hot day. My mouth was cottony and my palms were slick. I could feel my heart beat quickly, rushing color to my face. Mom's fish bone story came to mind. It wasn't about swallowing or spitting, I realized, but about fight or flight.

"Shut up, fatso," I said, louder than a whisper. I recognized a flash of fear pass over Raymond's plump face, yet he continued to taunt me.

I raised my voice, making it commanding and deep. "I said shut up, you big ball of . . . lard!" I plucked this word out of a conversation I had overheard at the grocery store. It wasn't the choicest of names, but it had a nice menacing ring to it with high potential to damage, like the kind of mud balls my brothers threw when they fought with the neighborhood kids. Inside each firm handful of wet earth was a surprise, a skin-breaking chunk of gravel.

Raymond's darting eyes confirmed I had hit a raw nerve, filling me with giddy power.

Like a bombardier honing in on a target, I unleashed all the anger that I had pent up during the past weeks, screaming "fatso" and "lard" until the other children, like summer cicadas, joined in on my name-calling. Raymond didn't say anything. He stared and tried to figure out how the tables had turned.

After that the other kids thought twice before they teased me. If they tried, I fought back with everything I could get on them. Crossed eyes, crooked bangs, rotten teeth, dirty fingernails, moles, eyeglasses, and freckles were all fair game.

With the gift of victory, I began to shake the overwhelming need to be like my friends. So what if I played by myself, got the cold-shoulder treatment, or had to deal with whispering behind my back? Nothing, I decided, could be as bad as putting up with the name-calling and the dread of waiting for it to come. I understood now why some boys took a beating instead of accepting daily torment: It was pride. I lost a sense of innocence that first year of school, but from it grew a defined measure of self that would stay with me and emerge during difficult times in my life.

Discussion/Writing Prompts

- Take a moment to consider the book title from which this piece is excerpted. What point do you think Furiya is trying to make by juxtaposing her "Japanese Girlhood" against "Whitebread America"? What vision of American cuisine, and by extension American culture, does the term "whitebread" convey? And to what extent does this vision resonate with your own view? In your estimation, is mainstream America truly "whitebread"? How or how not?

- The central problem this piece explores concerns the fraught relationship between food and identity. From Furiya's childhood perspective, the eating traditions of her Japanese heritage pose a serious obstacle, imposing a distance between herself and peers by defining her as "other." For Furiya, the prospect of becoming truly American depends upon her family's willingness to prepare typical American meals. In a one-page essay, offer an analysis and an assessment of this particular logic. Is it valid to view food as a marker of one's identity? A reflection or statement of who and what we are?

- In many ways, Furiya's story raises the same questions that Bauer explores in his discussion of authenticity. Write a one-page essay in which you speculate about the particular ways Bauer might respond to and evaluate Furiya's story. Do you think he would view Furiya's search for a "true" American self as related or parallel to his own discussion of authenticity? How or how not?

"Through the Ages," AdAge.com

BETTY CROCKER

It's easy to create a list of dishes and cuisines that fall under the heading of "ethnic food." But what about the flip side? What can we point to as the most representative examples, the most faithful symbols, of what we might call "nonethnic food"? Reviewing the storied history of the Betty Crocker brand, this set of visual images would seem to offer us the ideal candidate. Highlighting this icon's long career as a cultural touchstone for countless white, middle class households, this profile gives us a glimpse of the role food plays in creating and reinforcing definitions of the American mainstream.

◆

"Long Before Martha Stewart, There Was Betty Crocker"

PRODUCT: Food products including cake mixes, frostings, microwave popcorn and biscuit mixes
DATE INTRODUCED: 1921
CREATOR: Washburn Crosby Co., a forerunner of General Mills

Long before Martha Stewart, there was Betty Crocker.

Betty was created in 1921 after a promotion for Gold Medal flour flooded Washburn Crosby Co. with questions about baking. To answer customers in a more personal manner, the company created a fictitious kitchen expert, pulling the name "Crocker" from a recently retired director of the company and adding the first name "Betty" because it sounded friendly.

Washburn Crosby's female employees were asked to submit handwriting samples for Betty's signature and the one selected as "most distinctive" is still Betty's signature today.

From these humble home-ec beginnings, Betty went on to become one of the first multimedia superstars. Beginning in 1924, she hosted the country's first radio cooking show, "Betty Crocker School of the Air," first on a local Minneapolis station and later on the NBC radio network.

During the 1930s she helped advise a cash-strapped nation on how to cook tasty budget meals. She was voted the second-most-famous woman in America after Eleanor Roosevelt, according to Fortune in 1945. It was only a matter of time before she wooed consumers on television.

After numerous guest appearances on CBS and NBC, where she taught stars such as George Burns and Gracie Allen to cook, Betty got her own show, "The Betty Crocker Search for the All-American Homemaker of Tomorrow." The series, featuring a variety of actresses playing Betty, ran from 1954 to 1976.

Meantime, behind-the-scenes Bettys were authoring cookbooks. Since the 1950s, more than 200 Betty Crocker cookbooks have been published. Betty also developed her own line of food products, starting with the famous Betty Crocker cake mixes.

Along the way, Betty's image was refined to reflect the changing image of women. Over the years she has had eight different "looks," from the first stern gray-haired, older woman in 1936 to today's olive-skinned, dark-haired Betty, a product of computer morphing.

Discussion/Writing Prompts

- What are your own impressions of the Betty Crocker logo? What images does it conjure? What ideas, qualities, or values do you associate with it?
- As a number of the selections in this chapter attest, it is not difficult to identify the pleasures and rewards of ethnic food. Based on this Web site's portrayal of Betty Crocker, what would you say are the pleasures and rewards of nonethnic food? How do these respective pay-offs compare? Which, in your view, seems more appealing? Why?
- Furiya and Finn both contrast the food traditions within their families with a style of eating they associate with mainstream American culture. First choose one of these two essays. Then write a one-page essay in which you discuss how the example of Betty Crocker seems to fit the definition of the American mainstream this essay advances. What aspects of the Betty Crocker promotional campaign, what elements of the "typical" household targeted by this campaign, identify this product as an emblem of mainstream America? How do these details differ from the food portrait sketched by Furiya or Finn?

Tying It All Together: Assignments for Research and Writing

1. RHETORICAL ANALYSIS: "THE REAL THING?"

One of the key questions underlying this chapter concerns the contested and complicated issue of authenticity. When it comes to the traditions and values that define a particular ethnic food, how do we know what is and is not the real thing? Choose a food product that, in your estimation, promotes itself as an authentic example or expression of a given (racial, ethnic, or national) community. In a two- to three-page essay, analyze the particular ways this product goes about selling its particular vision of authenticity. On what basis does it claim to reveal the truth about the community of which it is a part? And how convincing do you find these claims?

2. PERSONAL REFLECTION: "CONSUMING OTHERNESS"

The overarching focus of this chapter is on the role food can play in shaping or reinforcing our assumptions about racial/ethnic difference. From cookbook recipes to restaurant entrées, we have learned to approach different types of food as evidence of our cultural diversity. Choose a food product that, in your view, performs precisely this role: that represents a racial, ethnic, or national group of which you are not a part. In a two- to three-page essay, reflect upon the ways that this product influences the ways you think about and view this particular group. What vision, what understanding of this community does this food present? And how accurate or helpful do you find this depiction to be?

3. COMPARE AND CONTRAST: "CULTURAL DIFFERENCE/CULTURAL MIRROR"

In the same way that it shapes our notions of ethnic/racial difference, food can also serve as a powerful instrument for how we define ourselves. Indeed to contemplate traditions, practices, and backgrounds different from our own is always on some level to think more deeply about who and what we are. Choose an example of an ethnic food that, in your view, symbolizes a culture or community different from your own. Then write a two- to three-page essay in which you assess how such symbolism provides the foundation for thinking about and defining the culture or community to which you belong. How does the vision of community evoked by this food compare to your own? And more specifically, how does vision work as a counterpoint or contrast to the way you define yourself?

4. VISUAL ANALYSIS: "ETHNIC FOOD AND/AS CULTURAL STATUS"

When viewed through the prism of our commercial or popular culture, ethnic food not only stands as a cultural symbol but as a status symbol as well. To prepare or sample foods from a different cultural/culinary tradition, so goes the prevailing thinking, is to engage in an activity that enhances our public image or reputation. Choose an image from popular culture that, in your view, exemplifies the ways ethnic food can function as a status symbol. In a three- to five-page essay, analyze the particular ways this example goes about connecting this food to the issue of status. What payoffs or rewards supposedly go along with consuming this particular food? And how convincing do you find this message?

5. ARGUMENT-BASED/PERSUASIVE WRITING: "FOOD AND MEMORY"

Several of the selections above focus on the role food plays in stimulating and organizing memory—whether it be personal and familial or more broadly cultural. Left unspoken, however, is the larger question of why this role is so important. Why does it matter that food can serve as such a powerful spur to memory? Write a two- to three-page essay in which you argue either for or against the value of this particular role. In your view, is it important to note the ways food can function as an aid to memory? Does this role carry meaningful or beneficial consequences? If so, what? To whom? And if not, what other aspects of our relationship to food matter more? And why?

CREDITS

CHAPTER 1—NUTRITION

1. Michael Pollan, "Nutritionism," found in "From Food to Nutrients," from *In Defense of Food* by Michael Pollan, copyright © 2008 by Michael Pollan. Used by permission of The Penguin Press, a division of Penguin Group (USA) Inc.

2. Steve Ettlinger, "Where Does Polysorbate 60 Come From, Daddy?" from *Twinkie, Deconstructed* by Steve Ettlinger, copyright © 2007 by Steve Ettlinger. Used by permission of Hudson Street Press, an imprint of Penguin Group (USA) Inc.

3. Laura Fraser, "The French Paradox." *Salon* (Feb. 4, 2000). This piece was first published in Salon.com.

4. Ruth Reichl, "The Queen of Mold," from *Tender at the Bone* by Ruth Reichl, copyright © 1998 by Ruth Reichl. Used by permission of Random House, Inc.

CHAPTER 2—CONSUMERISM

1. Morgan Spurlock, "Do You Want Lies With That?" from *Don't Eat This Book* by Morgan Spurlock, copyright © 2005 by Morgan Spurlock. Used by permission of G.P. Putnam's Sons, a division of Penguin Group (USA) Inc.

2. Sara Dickerman, "Escalated Dining: Is Mall Food Becoming Classy?" from *Slate*, Food Section, 5/21/2004 issue.

3. Corby Kummer, "Open for Business: Eating Out as Group Therapy in Post-Katrina New Orleans" by Corby Krummer from *The Atlantic*, March 2006.

4. Patty Odell, "The Deadly Little Secret: Candy Cigarettes," from *The Big Fat Marketing Blog.*

CHAPTER 3—BODY IMAGE

1. Courtney E. Martin, "How to Address Obesity in a Fat-Phobic Society," *AlterNet.org* (Oct. 17, 2007).

2. Marya Hornbacher, "Childhood," pp. 9–17 from *Wasted: A Memoir of Anorexia and Bulimia* by Marya Hornbacher (New York: Harper Perennial, 1999).

3. "Oprah Celebrates 20,000th Pound Lost." Reprinted with permission of *The Onion*. Copyright © 2010, by Onion, Inc. www.theonion.com.

4. Leora Fulvio, "Food and Feelings," www.foodandfeelings.org, Leora Fulvio, MFT.

CHAPTER 4—ETHICS

1. Laurie Snyder, "Whence the Beef?: The Gruesome Trip From Pasture to Platter," from *Slate*, 2/26/2004 Issue.

2. Taylor Clark, "Meatless Like Me: I may be a vegetarian, but I still love the smell of bacon." From *Slate*, Food Section, 5/7/2008 Issue.

3. Anup Shah, "Causes of Hunger Are Related to Poverty," in *"Global Issues: Social, Political, Economic and Environmental Issues That Affect Us All"* http://www.globalissues.org/article/7/causes-of-hunger-are-related-to-poverty.

4. Eric Haas, "The Ethics of Eating: Consider the Farmworkers," *Civil Eats* (May 22, 2009).

CHAPTER 5—WORK

1. Frank Bruni, "My Week as a Waiter," *"A Critic at Every Table"* from *The New York Times*, Dining In/Dining Out Section, 1/25/2006 Issue. Page(s) Section F, Page 1, Column 1.

2. Francis Lam, "America's Dirty Food Jobs," *Salon* (Feb. 11, 2010)." This article first appeared in Salon.com, at *http://www.Salon.com.*

An online version remains in the Salon archives. Reprinted with permission.

3. Sarah Jaffe, "Rethinking Work: Cooking as Labor," *AlterNet.org* (March 10, 2010).

4. Thomas Rogers, "Competitive Eating: The Most American Sport?" *Salon*, (March 25, 2010). This article first appeared in Salon.com, at *http://www.Salon.com*. An online version remains in the Salon archives. Reprinted with permission.

CHAPTER 6—TECHNOLOGY

1. Hannah Wallace, "The Udder Truth" *Salon* (January 19, 2007). This article first appeared in Salon.com, at *http://www.Salon.com*. An online version remains in the Salon archives. Reprinted with permission.

2. Jamey Lionette, "Mass Production of Food Is Ruining Our Health," *The National Expositor* (Dec. 10, 2007).

3. Mary Dixon Lebeau, "At 50, TV Dinner Is Still Cookin'," *Christian Science Monitor* (Nov. 10, 2004).

4. James E. McWilliams, *"The Green Monster: Could Frankenfoods Be Good for the Environment?"* from *Slate*, 1/28/2009 Issue.

5. Corilyn Shropshire, "Fast-Food Assistant 'Hyperactive Bob' Example of Robots' Growing Role" *Pittsburgh Post-Gazette* (June 16, 2006). Copyright ©, *Pittsburgh Post-Gazette*, 2010, all rights reserved. Reprinted with permission.

CHAPTER 7—RACE/ETHNICITY

1. Michael Bauer, "Between Meals: Who Determines If Food Is Authentic?" San Francisco Chronicle (Nov. 7, 2006). (1865–) [Only Staff-Produced Materials May Be Used] by Michael Bauer. Copyright 2006 by San Francisco Chronicle. Reproduced with permission of San Francisco Chronicle in the format Textbook via Copyright Clearance Center.

2. Rachel Finn, "Soul Food: A New Place at the Table," *the Root* (May 22, 2008).